Avis O. Gacket

The Critical Writings of James Joyce

THE
CRITICAL WRITINGS
OF
JAMES JOYCE

Edited by

ELLSWORTH MASON

and

RICHARD ELLMANN

NEW YORK: THE VIKING PRESS

MCMLIX

Library of Congress catalog card number: 59-6868

Lithographed in the U.S.A. by The Murray Printing Company

Contents

Introduction

That Joyce wrote a good deal of criticism may come at first as a surprise. Criticism as an act of commingling with the works of another writer was in fact only rarely congenial to him. But there are other forms of criticism — the creation of new theories of art and artistic personality, the repudiation of contemporaries, the singling out of the few men present or past who have achieved artistic heroism, the justification of oneself — which were not at all alien to Joyce's talent. He did not depreciate the critical faculty; on the contrary, he widened the borders of his novels to make them include criticism. *A Portrait of the Artist as a Young Man* contains an aesthetic system; *Ulysses* contains a new and elaborate theory of Shakespeare's life and works in one chapter, and in another a group of parodies — themselves a form of criticism — of English prose styles; *Finnegans Wake* continues the parodies, and brings them up to date with examples from Yeats, Synge, Eliot, Wyndham Lewis, and others. While some of this material was written expressly for use in the novels, the aesthetic system and Shakespearian theory at least had a prior, independent existence. If Joyce did not call himself a critic, it was by choice, not incapacity.

This book includes fifty-seven essays, lectures, book reviews, programme notes, newspaper articles, letters to editors, and poems; they are critical in the general sense that they are evaluative. Not all of them are first-rate, but some of them are, and all of them help to make Joyce's development less elusive. The first was written when he was about fourteen, the last when he was fifty-five. The early pieces show some facility and an interest in style; but they do not persuade us that their author will write anything of consequence. They may give heart to adolescents who are searching their own writings for proof of artistic immortality, and not finding much. Then suddenly, in 1899, the tone begins to change; the young man finds a subject, and the subject is drama. He is so full of his discovery that he can talk of little else. He finds drama in a painting of the Crucifixion, he writes an article on Ibsen's *When We Dead Awaken*, and he brings together his ideas and enthusiasm in a culminating pronouncement, his paper on 'Drama and Life'.

This vehement paper, which appears here for the first time, is not to be confused with the paper of the same title that is described in *Stephen Hero*, which is actually a reworking of a subsequent essay on Mangan. This one is perhaps Joyce's most overt statement of an artistic credo; he dismisses Greek drama as 'played out', Shakespearian drama as 'dialogue in verse', and insists upon the greatness of modern drama alone. The past is done for, consigned by its conventions to the museum. Modern drama is greater because it is closer to the eternal laws of human behaviour, which do not change whatever the place or time, a postulate on which *Finnegans Wake* and *Ulysses* are written. It is nonsense to bewail the lack of heroism in modern times. 'Life we must accept as we see it before our eyes, men and women as we meet them in the real world.' The sentence sounds like a truism, but his novels were to make it alive.

In this essay, and in those that follow from 1900 to 1904, Joyce was fiercely assembling his arsenal of weapons. He tells his compatriots that they must cease to be provincial and folklorist and mere Irish, that they must accept Europe; he demands that Attic form be imposed on Irish passion; he composes a secular aesthetic to override the limits of Christian art; he declares that literature is the joyful affirmation of the human spirit, but that it can be so only if the writer breaks through hypocrisy, recognizes the brute body, maintains an 'indifferent sympathy' (instead of a didactic partisanship) towards the play of passions he describes, and moves about the lowlanders like a gallant stag. Many of the reviews of books which he wrote to order during this period touch upon these matters only fleetingly, yet phrases in them, such as his repudiation of 'those big words that make us so unhappy,' evoke aspects of the young man who is called Stephen Dedalus. The best pieces are the most worked. This group of condemnations and aspirations reaches its climax in the broadside, 'The Holy Office'. In it Joyce finds a point of attack, gathers in greater irony than ever before, and writes a poem in which the scatology only enhances the splendid pride. He saw correctly that an epoch was at an end, that the movement towards ethereal, yet somehow national, essences which George Russell and the early Yeats had heralded was done for; and he broke off with them and their followers as violently as he could.

Soon after he wrote 'The Holy Office' Joyce left Dublin for the continent with Nora Barnacle. During the next ten years he pub-

lished almost nothing in English except *Chamber Music*, which he
had written before his departure. He expressed himself directly
and publicly only in the nine articles he wrote for the Triestine
newspaper, *Il Piccolo della Sera*, and in the lectures he gave to a
popular audience in Trieste. In them his irony has become more
subdued and deliberate, still keen but more ingratiating. The
figures of Defoe and Blake are treated in the lectures with the
unexpected esteem which he gave later to his ancestral portraits.
The newspaper articles seem to compose themselves into a single
complex unit in which he voices now distrust, now nostalgia, for
Ireland. Never more Irish than when he attacks his country, after
parading Irish history as a succession of betrayals, he cannot help
invoking its special beauty and worth in the face of English
oppression. The Citizen in *Ulysses*, who is so windy about Irish
past glories and English injustices, turns out to be an aspect of
Joyce's mind as well as the butt of his satire. Joyce never becomes
an expatriate; he holds tenaciously to the character of the exile,
punishing himself and his country. In 1912 he issues another
declaration of mental war against Ireland in 'Gas from a Burner'.
He sees in his own mistreatment at the hands of a Dublin publisher
a symbol of the indignities which Ireland heaps upon the human
spirit.

After 1912 Joyce resisted Ezra Pound's efforts to persuade him
to turn a quick penny by writing literary articles. He excused himself on the ground that he had no subjects, but he had probably
discovered that his criticism was effective only when it had some
powerful instigation from his experience. He wrote no more
articles, but he occasionally expressed his critical opinions. The
most important statement of these during the First World War
was 'Dooleysprudence'. Joyce had left Trieste for Zurich in 1915,
and Switzerland, he found, was not only a refuge for him but an
appropriate one. Swiss neutrality was a perfect analogue for
artistic indifference. 'Dooleysprudence' adds Mr. Dooley as a
homely comrade to the heroic stag of 'The Holy Office', and it
suggests how completely the private, domestic life of Leopold
Bloom in *Ulysses* had supplanted in Joyce's mind the public,
Luciferian gestures of Stephen Dedalus in *A Portrait of the Artist
as a Young Man*.

In Paris, in the last two decades of his life, Joyce became adept
at refusing formal comment on his contemporaries, though in

private he would sometimes discuss them sharply enough. He drew further away now from the role of the man of letters, which he had always regarded with suspicion and distaste. Yet two fine pieces dealing with other artists date from this time. The first is 'From a Banned Writer to a Banned Singer', written in the style of *Finnegans Wake*. Here Joyce discriminates with obvious delight and friendliness the singing skills of John Sullivan, the tenor; in Sullivan's vocal strength and variety, as well as his failure to secure the public he deserved, he found a parallel to his own situation. Finally, he wrote an 'Epilogue to Ibsen's *Ghosts*', in which he returns to the dramatist who was the subject of his first published writing. The tone of the article on Ibsen he had written when he was eighteen was properly adulatory, as of disciple to master, but now he treats Ibsen jocularly as a comrade in arts. He re-writes *Ghosts* to suggest that Captain Alving is not so bad after all, and it is not hard to find a vindication of his own life as a Parisian *bon vivant* in the concluding lines:

> *Nay, more, were I not all I was,*
> *Weak, wanton, waster out and out,*
> *There would have been no world's applause*
> *And damn all to write home about.*

The attitude is the same as that of 'The Holy Office', but now befittingly made boisterous and successful.

The criticism of writers like Henry James or Thomas Mann attracts us mainly because of what they reveal about other writers. Joyce's criticism is important because of what it reveals about Joyce. All writers are egocentric by necessity, but Joyce is more so than most. These writings are best understood as part of that dramatized autobiography which he spent his life in piecing perfectly together.

* * * *

Of the writings included here, Nos. 1, 2, 3, 4, 5, 20, 35, 36, 43, and part of 49 have not been published before. No. 45 has been published only in Italian in *Il Piccolo della Sera* (Trieste). Nos. 6, 7, 8, 33, 47, most of 49, 50, 51, 52, 53, 54, 55, 56, and 57, have not been collected (though a few are available in Gorman's biography). Nos. 9, 10, 11, 12, 13, 14, 15, 16, 17, 18, 19, 21, 22, 23, 24, 25, 26, 27, 28, 29, 30, 31, and 32 (the book reviews) have previously been available only in a small edition, edited by Stanislaus Joyce and

Ellsworth Mason, and privately printed by the Mamalujo Press in Colorado Springs.

For expert assistance we are grateful to Dr. R. J. Hayes, Director, and to Patrick Henchy, Keeper. of Books, of the National Library of Ireland; Professors Walter B. Scott, Jr., Bentley Gilbert, Karl Kiralis, and John Thompson; and to Jens Nyholm, Director of the Northwestern University Library and his able staff, Miss Marjorie Wynne of the Yale University Library, John J. Slocum, and Dr. H. K. Croessmann. We are indebted to James F. Spoerri for lending us books from his collection. Our thanks are due to Mrs. Mary Bolton and Mrs. Lois Lentz for their diligence in typing the manuscript. We are grateful to Dr. Stephen J. McCarthy, Director of the Cornell University Library, and to the Yale University Library for permission to publish items in their collection, to Dr. C. G. Jung for permission to publish part of his letter to Joyce, and to Rinehart and Co. for permission to publish items included in Herbert Gorman's *James Joyce*. The publication of this material has been authorized by the Joyce Estate, and Miss Harriet Weaver, Joyce's literary executor, has obliged us by many kindnesses.

Joyce's writings have been cited in our notes as follows: *Book Reviews* (*The Early Joyce: the Book Reviews, 1902–1903*. Colorado Springs, The Mamalujo Press, 1955), *Epiphanies* (introd. and notes by O. A. Silverman, Buffalo, N.Y., Lockwood Memorial Library, 1956), *Finnegans Wake* (New York, Viking Press, and London, Faber and Faber, 1939), *Letters* (ed. by Stuart Gilbert. New York, Viking Press, and London, Faber and Faber, 1957), *Portrait* (*A Portrait of the Artist as a Young Man* in *The Portable James Joyce*, New York, Viking Press, 1947, and London, Jonathan Cape, 1924), *Stephen Hero* (New York, New Directions, and London, Jonathan Cape, 1944); *Ulysses* (New York, Random House, 1934, pagination identical with the Modern Library edition, and London, John Lane, 1936). When American and English editions are not identical, page references are given first to the American edition, then in parenthesis to the English edition.

E. M.
R. E.

The Critical Writings of James Joyce

1

Trust Not Appearances[1]

1896?

Joyce's skill in writing the weekly essay at Belvedere College[2] was recognized by his classmates and masters there. He received national recognition by winning, in 1897 and 1898, the prize for the best English composition in his grade in the Intermediate Examinations. 'Trust Not Appearances' is the only example that has survived of his weekly themes, and dates from about 1896, when he was fourteen. It is therefore the earliest example of his writing known.

AMDG[3]

TRUST NOT APPEARANCES

There is nothing so deceptive and for all that so alluring as a good surface. The sea, when beheld in the warm sunlight of a summer's day; the sky, blue in the faint and amber glimmer of an autumn sun, are pleasing to the eye: but, how different the scene, when the wild anger of the elements has waked again the discord of confusion, how different the ocean, choking with froth and foam, to the calm, placid sea, that glanced and rippled merrily in the sun. But the best examples of the fickleness of appearances are — Man and Fortune. The cringing, servile look; the high and haughty mien alike conceal the worthlessness of the character. Fortune that glittering bauble, whose brilliant shimmer has allured and trifled

---

[1] This essay is in a holograph manuscript in the Joyce papers at the Cornell University Library.

[2] See the passage on the weekly essay at Belvedere in the *Portrait*, p. 327 (87).

[3] Ad Majorem Dei Gloriam (For the Greater Glory of God), the motto of the Society of Jesus. See the description of Stephen writing a poem in the *Portrait*, p. 317 (77): 'From force of habit he had written at the top of the first page the initial letters of the jesuit motto: A.M.D.G.'

with both proud and poor, is as wavering as the wind. Still however, there is a 'something' that tells us the character of man. It is the eye. The only traitor that even the sternest will of a fiendish villian [*sic*] cannot overcome. It is the eye that reveals to man the guilt or innocence, the vices or the virtues of the soul. This is the only exception to the proverb 'Trust not appearance'. In every other case the real worth has to be searched for. The garb of royalty or of democracy are but the shadow that a 'man' leaves behind him. 'Oh! how unhappy is that poor man that hangs on princes' favours.'[1] The fickle tide of ever-changing fortune brings with it — good and evil. How beautiful it seems as the harbinger of good and how cruel as the messenger of ill! The man who waits on the temper of a King is but a tiny craft in that great ocean. Thus we see the hollowness of appearances. The hypocrite is the worst kind of villain yet under the appearance of virtue he conceals the worst of vices. The friend, who is but the fane of fortune, fawns and grovels at the feet of wealth. But, the man, who has no ambition, no wealth no luxury save contentment cannot hide the joy of happiness that flows from a clear conscience and an easy mind.

LDS[2]

JAMES A. JOYCE

[1] Joyce misquotes slightly from *Henry VIII*, III, ii, 366–7.
[2] Laus Deo Semper (Praise to God Forever). 'After this the letters L.D.S. were written at the foot of the page.' *Portrait*, p. 318 (78).

2

[Force]¹

1898

In Ulysses *Leopold Bloom tells the Cyclopian Citizen, 'But it's no use. Force, hatred, history, all that.' He goes on to defend love, 'the opposite of hatred', which he says is 'really life'. On September 27, 1898, Joyce, then beginning his matriculation course at University College, Dublin, took the same stand in a youthfully long-winded way. The first page of the essay, and several other pages, have been lost, but his subject was clearly force, and his theme the paradoxical one that force should be used to bring about the rule of kindness.*

Although the attitude is consistent with his later work, and the rhythms are remarkable for a boy of sixteen, the phrasing is not yet mature. Joyce had already felt the liberating influence of Ibsen and other writers; but he had not yet liberated his language, and could still use conventional rhetoric in a classroom exercise.

[The first half-page of the manuscript is missing.]

—both questions of moment and difficult to answer. And although it is, in the main, evident that the conquest gained in a righteous war, is itself righteous, yet it will not be necessary to digress into the regions of political economy, etc, but it will be as well to bear in mind, that all subjugation by force, if carried out and prosecuted by force is only so far successful in breaking men's spirits and aspirations. Also that it is, in the extreme, productive of ill-will and rebellion, that it is, again, from its beginning in unholy war, stamped with the stamp of ultimate conflict. But

¹ This essay is in a holograph manuscript of twenty-four half-pages in the Joyce papers at the Cornell University Library. Stanislaus Joyce used the back of the sheets for his diary, and so preserved 'Force' and the three essays that follow it.

17

indeed it seems barbaric to only consider subjugation, in the light of an oppressing force, since we shall see that more often is it an influence rather than a positive power, and find it better used than for the vain shedding of blood.

In the various grades of life there are many homely illustrations of its practice — none the truer, that they are without blaze or notoriety, and in the humblest places. The tiller who guides the plough through the ground, and breaks the 'stubborn glebe' is one. The gardener who prunes the wayward vine or compels the wild hedge into decent level, subjugating the savage element in 'trim gardens', is another. Both of these represent subjugation by force; but the sailor's method is more diplomatic. He has no plough to furrow the resisting wind, nor no[1] knife to check the rude violence of storm. He cannot, with his partial skill, get the better of its unruliness. When Aeolus has pronounced his fiat, there is no direct countermanding his order. That way the sailor cannot overcome him; but by veering, and patient trial, sometimes using the strength of the Wind, sometimes avoiding it, now advancing and now retreating, at last the shifting sails are set for a straight course, and amid the succeeding calm the vessel steers for port. The miller's wheel which although it restrains the stream yet allows it to proceed on its own way, when it has performed the required service, is an useful example. The water rushing in swift stream, is on the higher mountains a fierce power both to excite emotion and to flood the fields. But the magic miller changes its humour, and it proceeds on its course, with all its tangled locks in orderly crease, and laps its waves, in placid resignation, on the banks that slope soberly down from suburban villas. And more, its strength has been utilised for commercial ends, and it helps to feed, with fine flour and bread, no longer the poetical but the hungry.

After these subjugations of the elements, we come to the subjugation of animals. Long ago in Eden responsible Adam had a good time. The birds of the air and the beasts of the field, ministered to his comfort. At his feet slept the docile lion, and every animal was his willing servant. But when sin arose in Adam — before only a latent evil — and his great nature was corrupted

---

[1] Joyce's instructor had underlined these words and marked a stroke in the margin. There are a number of such corrections in the manuscript. All of Joyce's errors have been preserved in transcribing this manuscript.

and broken, there were stirred up also among beasts the unknown dregs of ferocity. A similar revolt took place among them against man, and they were no longer to be friendly servants but bitter foes to him. From that hour, in greater or less degree, more in one land than another, they have struggled against him and refused him service. Aided often by great strength they fought successfully. But at length by superior power, and because he was man and they were but brutes, they, at least to a great extent, were overcome. Some of them, as the dog, he made the guardians of his house; others, as the horses and oxen, the helpmates of his toils. Others again he could not conquer but merely guard against, but one race in particular threatened by its number and power, to conquer him; and here it may be as well to follow the fate of it and see how a superior power intervened to preserve for man his title, not in derision, of lord of the creation and to keep him safe from the fear of mammoth and of mastodon. The Zoo elephants are sorry descendants of those mighty monsters who once traversed the sites of smoky cities; who roamed in hordes, tameless and fearless, proud in their power, through fruitful regions and forests, where now are the signs of busy men and the monuments of their skill and toil; who spread themselves over whole continents and carried their terror to the north and south, bidding defiance to man that he could not subjugate them; and finally in the wane of their day, though they knew it not, trooped up to the higher regions of the Pole, to the doom that was decreed for them. There what man could not subdue, was subdued, for they could not withstand the awful changes that came upon the earth. Lands of bright bloom, by degrees, lost all beauty and promise. Luxuriance of trees and fullness of fruit gradually departed, and were not, and stunted growth of shrub and shrivelled berries that no suns would ripen, were found in their room. The tribes of the Mammoth were huddled together, in strange wonder, and this devastation huddled them still closer. From oases, yet left them, they peered at the advancing waves, that locked them in their barren homes. Amid the gradual ice and waters, they eked out the days of the life of their vanity and when nothing remained for them but death, the wretched animals died in the unkind cold of enduring winter, and to-day their colossal tusks and ivory bones, are piled in memorial mounds, on the New Siberian Islands. This is all of them that is left, that man may have good by their death, whom he was not

able to make his slaves when they lived, to tempt his greed across
the perilous, Polar seas, to those feasts of the wealth of bygone
times, that are strewn and bleaching beneath the desolate sky,
white and silent through the song of the changeless waves, and on
the verge of the eternal fathoms. What a subjugation has this
been — how awful and how complete! Scarce the remembrance of
the mammoth remains and no more is there the fear of the great
woolly elephant but contempt of his bulk and advantage of his
unwieldiness.

It is generally by intercourse with man, that animals have been
tamed and it is noticeable that the domestic tabby and the
despised pig rage in distant lands, with all their inbred fierceness
and strength. These with others are subjugated by constant war,
or driven from familiar haunts, and then their race dies out as the
bison of America is dying. Gradually all common animals are
subdued to man's rule, becoming once again his servants and
regaining something of former willingness, in the patient horse
and faithful dog. In some instances the vain-glory and conscious
victory of the three spears is observed. Thus, in the swampy
marshes of South America, the venomous snakes are lulled into
deadness, and lie useless and harmless, at the crooning of the
charmer and in shows and circuses before large crowds, broken-
spirited lions and in the streets the ungraceful bears are witnesses
to the power of man.

It may be that the desire to overcome and get the mastery of
things, which is expressed in man's history of progress, is in a
great measure responsible for his supremacy. Had it been that he
possessed no such desire, the trees and vegetation would have
choked the sunlight from him, barring all passage; the hills and
seas would have been the bounds of his dwellings; the unstemmed
mountain-stream would always snatch away his rude huts and the
ravaging hungry beasts stamp on the ashes of his fire. But his
superior mind overcame all obstacles, not however universally, for
in those places where seldom, the lower creation has usurped his
Kingdom, and his labour must be anew expended in hunting the
savage tiger through the jungles and forests of India, and in felling
the tree in Canadian woods.

The next important subjugation is that of race over race.
Among human families the white man is the predestined conqueror. The negro has given way before him, and the red men have

been driven by him out of their lands and homes. In far New
Zealand the sluggish Maoris in conceded sloth, permit him to
portion out and possess the land of their fathers. Everywhere that
region and sky allow, he has gone. Nor any longer does he or may
he practise the abuse of subjugation — slavery, at least in its
most degrading forms or at all so generally. Yet slavery only seems
to have appealed to the conscience of men when most utterly base
and inhuman and minor offences never troubled them. Happily
this could not continue and now any encroachment on the liberties
of others whether by troublesome Turk or not, is met with resolute
opposition and just anger. Rights when violated, institutions set
at nought, privileges disregarded, all these, not as shibboleths and
war-cries, but as deep-seated thorough realities, will happily
always call forth, not in foolish romantic madness nor for passionate
destruction, but with unyielding firmness of resistance, the energies
and sympathies of men to protect them and to defend them.

Hitherto we have only treated of man's subjugation

[*one-half page missing*]

often when a person gets embarked on a topic which in its vastness
almost completely swallows up his efforts, the subject dwarfs the
writer; or when a logician has to treat of great subjects, with a
view to deriving a fixed theory, he abandons the primal idea and
digresses into elaborate disquisitions, on the more inviting portions
of his argument. Again in works of fancy, a too prolific imagination
literally flys away with the author, and lands him in regions of
loveliness unutterable, which his faculties scarcely grasp, which
dazzles his senses, and defies speech, and thus his compositions
are beautiful indeed, but beautiful with the cloudiness and dream-
beauty of a visionary. Such a thing as this often affects poets of
high, fanciful temper, as Shelley, rendering their poetry vague and
misty. When however the gift — great and wonderful — of a
poetic sense, in sight and speech and feeling, has been subdued by
vigilance and care and has been prevented from running to extremes, the true and superior spirit, penetrates more watchfully
into sublime and noble places, treading them with greater fear and
greater wonder and greater reverence, and in humbleness looks up
into the dim regions, now full of light, and interprets, without
mysticism, for men the great things that are hidden from their
eyes, in the leaves of the trees and in the flowers, to console them,

to add to their worship, and to elevate their awe. This result proceeds from the subjugation of a great gift, and indeed it is so in all our possessions. We improve in strength when we husband it, in health when we are careful of it, in power of mental endurance when we do not over-tax it. Otherwise in the arts, in sculpture and painting, the great incidents that engross the artist's attention would find their expression, in huge shapelessness or wild daubs; and in the ear of the rapt musician, the loveliest melodies outpour themselves, madly, without time or movement, in chaotic mazes, 'like sweet bells jangled, out of tune and harsh.'

It has been pointed out what an influence this desire of man to overcome has exerted over the kingdom of animals and vegetation, and how it not merely destroys and conquers the worse features but betters and improves what is good. There are spots on this earth, where licence of growth holds absolute sway, where leaves choke the light and rankness holds the soil, where there are dangerous reptiles and fierce beasts, all untamed, amid surroundings of great beauty, in colour and fertility, but overshadowed by the horror of savage unrule. But the coming of man in his onward way, shall alter the face of things, good himself rendering good his own dominions. As has been written — 'when true servants of Heaven shall enter these Edens and the Spirit of God enter with them, another spirit will also be breathed into the physical air; and the stinging insect and venomous snake and poisonous tree, pass away before the power of the regenerate human soul' — This is the wished subjugation that must come in good time. And meanwhile we have considered the power of overcoming man, against the lower races of the world, and his influence in the subjugation of his own mental faculties, and there remains for us to consider the manifold influence of his desire to conquer, over his human instincts, over his work and business and over his reason.

In the sagas of Norway, in ancient epics in the tales of 'knights and barons bold' and to-day in the stories of Hall Caine,[1] we have abundant examples of the havoc that men's passions make, when they are allowed to spend their force in Bersirk freedom. Of course in conventional life there are fewer instances of such characters as Thor, Ospakar,[2] Jason, and Mylrea[3] as in those savage places

[1] For a more mature estimate of Hall Caine, see p. 89 below.
[2] Ospakar's story is told in the Norse Saga of the Banded Men.
[3] Daniel Mylrea in Hall Caine's novel *The Deemster*.

which were once their homes. Modern civilization will not permit such wholesale licence, as the then state of affairs gave occasion to. The brood of men now, in towns and cities, is not of fierce passion, at least not to such an extent as to make men subserve their rages. The ordinary man has not so often to guard against fits of demon's anger, though the Vendetta is is still common in Southern Europe but mankind has quite as many opportunities of subjugating himself or herself as before. The fretful temper, the base interpretation, the fool's conceitedness, the *fin-de-siècle* sneer, the gossiping, the refusal of aid, the hurting word and worthless taunt, together with ingratitude and the forgetting of friends — all these are daily waiting for us to subjugate. Above all, the much-maligned, greatest charity, so distinct from animal profusion and reckless liberality, that charitable deeds do not wholly constitute; but which springs from inner wells of gentleness and goodness; which is shy of attributing motives; 'which interprets everything for the best'; which dictates, from emotions of Heaven's giving, the sacrifice of all that is dear, in urgent need, which has its being and beauty from above; which lives and thrives in the atmosphere of thoughts, so upraised and so serene that they will not suffer themselves to be let down on earth among men, but in their own delicate air 'intimate their presence and commune with themselves' — this utter unselfishness in all things, how does it on the contrary, call for constant practice and worthy fulfilling!

Again in the case of man's mission, marked out for him from the gate of Eden, labour and toil, has not subjugation a direct influence, with advantage both to the world and to the man himself. 'Foul jungles' says Carlyle 'are cleared away, fair seedfields rise instead and stately cities, and withal the man

[one-half page missing]

greater difficulty for some to subjugate their reason, than their passions. For they pit the intellect and reason of men, with their vain theorisings, against the superhuman logic of belief. Indeed to a rightly constituted mind the bugbears of infidelity have no terrors and excite no feeling save contempt. Men have passions and reason, and the doctrine of licence is an exact counterpart of the doctrine of freethinking. Human reason has no part in wisdom, if it fulfils not the whole three attributes given by the inspired writer, if it is not 'pudica, pacifica et desursum' — chaste, peaceful

23

and from above. How can it thrive if it comes not from the seat of Wisdom but has its source elsewhere? And how can earthly intellects, if they blind their eyes to wisdom's epithets 'pudica, pacifica et desursum' hope to escape that which was the stumbling-block with Abelard and the cause of his fall.

The essence of subjugation lies in the conquest of the higher. Whatever is nobler and better, or reared upon foundations more solid, than the rest, in the appointed hour, comes to the appointed triumph. When right is perverted into might, or more properly speaking, when justice is changed to sheer strength, a subjugation ensues — but transient not lasting. When it is unlawful, as too frequently in the past it has been, the punishment invariably follows in strife through ages. Some things there are no subjugation can repress and if these preserve, as they do and will the germs of nobility, in good men and saintly lives, they preserve also for those who follow and obey, the promise of after victory and the solace and comfort of active expectation. Subjugation is 'almost of the essence of an empire and when it ceases to conquer, it ceases to be'. It is an innate part of human nature, responsible, in a great way, for man's place. Politically it is a dominant factor and a potent power in the issues of nations. Among the faculties of men it is a great influence, and forms part of the world's laws, unalterable and for ever — subjugation with the existence also of freedom, and even, within its sight, that there may be constant manifestation of powers over all, bringing all things under sway, with fixed limits and laws and in equal regulation, permitting the prowl

[one-half page missing]

power for force and of persuasion for red conquest, has brought about the enduring rule foretold, of kindness over all the good, for ever, in a new subjugation.

The End

written by
JAS. A. JOYCE
27/9/98

Note — the insertions in pencil are chiefly omissions in writing out.

3

The Study of Languages[1]

1898/9?

'The Study of Languages' must also have been written during Joyce's matriculation course, 1898-9, at University College. His style has become more energetic and less pretty. The allusion to Memmi's frescoes is more elaborate than anything in the essay on force, and the comment about Matthew Arnold (which the instructor has red-pencilled) more wilful. Although the study of languages enlisted Joyce's lifelong devotion, his arguments for it here do not muster up his full literary powers.

In the church of San' Maria Novella there are seven figures by Memmi, named the seven earthly Sciences. Reading from right to left, the first is the 'Art of Letters' and the seventh 'Arithmetic'. The first is oftener called Grammar, because it refers more directly to that branch of 'Letters'. Now the artist's idea in this arrangement was to shew the gradual progress from Science to Science, from Grammar to Rhetoric, from Rhetoric to Music and so on to Arithmetic. In selecting his subjects he assumes two things. First he assumes that the primary science is Grammar, that is, that science which is the first and most natural one to man, and also that Arithmetic is the last, not exactly as the culmination of the other six, but rather as the final, numbered expression of man's life. Secondly, or perhaps first, he assumes that Grammar, or Letters, is a science. His first assumption classes, if it does nothing more, Grammar and Arithmetic together as the first and last things in human knowledge. His second assumption, as we have

---

[1] This essay is in a holograph manuscript of ten half-pages in Stanislaus Joyce's diary, now in the Joyce papers at the Cornell University Library.

said, makes Grammar a science. Both of these assumptions are directly opposed to the opinions of many illustrious followers of Arithmetic, who deny that Letters is a science, and seem or affect to regard it as a totally different thing from Arithmetic. Literature is only at the root a science, that is in its Grammar and Characters, but such conduct is most senseless on the part of the Arithmeticians.

We hope that they will grant that it is essential for a man, who wishes to communicate in the ordinary way with his fellow-man, that he should know how to speak. We, on our part, will admit that, for the building of an intellectual man, his most important study is that of Mathematics. It is the study which most developes his mental precision and accuracy, which gives him a zest for careful and orderly method, which equips him, in the first place, for an intellectual career. We, the pluralized essayist,[1] say this, who were never an ardent votary of the subject, rather from disinclination to task work than because of a rooted aversion to it. In this we are supported by the great lights of the age, though Matthew Arnold has his own little opinion about the matter, as he had about other matters. Now while the advocates of more imaginative pursuits fully recognize the paramount importance of a mathematical education, it is deplorable that so many followers of the more rigid course, having assimilated unto themselves, a portion of the rigidity of that course, and a share of its uncompromising theorems, affect to regard the study of languages as altogether beneath them, and merely a random, occasional sort of study. Linguists must be allowed to make protest against such treatment and surely their defence is worthy of consideration.

For that which ennobles the study of Mathematics in the eyes of the wise, is the fact that it proceeds with regular course, that it is a science, a knowledge of facts, in contradistinction to literature, which is in the more elegant aspect of it, imaginary and notional. This draws a line of stern demarcation between the two; and yet as Mathematics and the Sciences of Numbers partake of the nature of that beauty which is omnipresent, which is expressed, almost noiselessly, in the order and symmetry of Mathematics, as in the charms of literature; so does Literature in turn share in the neatness and regularity of Mathematics. Moreover we do not, by any means, suffer such a premiss to pass unchallenged, but before

[1] Joyce's instructor expunged this phrase.

taking up the cudgels in behalf of Language and Literature, we wish it to be understood that we admit that the most important study for the mind is Mathematics, and our vindication of Literature will never venture to put it before Mathematics in that respect.

The statement the study of Languages is to be despised since it is imaginary and does not deal with facts nor deals in a precise way with ideas, is absurd. First, because the study of any language must begin at the beginning and must advance slowly and carefully, over ascertained ground. The Grammar of a language, its orthography and etymology are admitted as known. They are studies in the same manner as tables in Arithmetic, surely and accurately. Some will admit this but go on to say that thus far a language is to be approved of, but that the higher parts of syntax and style and history, are fanciful and imaginative. Now the study of languages is based on a mathematical foundation, and sure of its footing, and in consequence both in style and syntax there is always present a carefulness, a carefulness bred of the first implantings of precision. So they are no mere flourishings of unkempt, beautiful ideas but methods of correct expression ruled and directed by clear regulations, sometimes of facts, sometimes of ideas. And when of ideas their expression elevated from the hardness, which is sufficient for 'flat unraised' statements, by an over-added influence of what is beautiful in pathetic phrases, swelling of words, or torrents of invective, in tropes and varieties and figures, yet preserving even in moments of the greatest emotion, an innate symmetry.

Secondly even if we were disposed to admit, which we are far from doing, that unwarrantable 'since' of the mathematicians we should not admit that poetry and imagination, though not so deeply intellectual, are to be despised and their names to be cast out, totally. Are our libraries to contain only works of Science? Are Bacon and Newton to monopolize our shelves? and no place be found for Shakespeare and Milton? Theology is a Science, yet will either Catholic or Anglican, however profound and learned, taboo poetry from their studies, and the one banish a living, constant element of his Church and the other forbid the 'Christian Year'? The higher grades of language, style, syntax, poetry, oratory, rhetoric, are again the champions and exponents, in what way soever, of Truth. So in the figure of Rhetoric in Santa Maria's

27

church Truth is seen reflected in a Mirror. The notion of Aristotle and his school, that in a bad cause there can be true oratory, is utterly false. Finally, if they claim, Science advances more the civilization of the world, there must be some restriction imposed. Science may improve yet demoralize. Witness Dr. Benjulia.[1] Did the great Science of Vivisection improve him? 'Heart and Science'! yes, there is great danger in heartless science, very great danger indeed, leading only to inhumanity. Let it not be our case to stand like him, crushed and broken, aloof from sympathy at the door of his laboratory, while the maimed animals flee away terrified between his legs, into the darkness.[2] Do not think that science, human or divine, will effect on the one hand a great substantial change for good in men and things, if it merely consults the interests of men in its own interests, and does good to them it may do good to itself, and in everything pass over that first, most natural aspect of man, namely, as a living being, and regard him as an infinitely small actor, playing a most uninteresting part in the drama of worlds. Or on the other hand, if it proceeds, when directed towards divine objects, as a contrivance useful for extracting hard, rational inferences, ever induce in man an uplifting of trust and worship.

Having thus got rid of the obnoxious mathematicians, something is to be said about the study of languages and there chiefly in the study of our own. First, in the history of words there is much that indicates the history of men, and in comparing the speech of to-day with that of years ago, we have a useful illustration of the effect of external influences on the very words of a race. Sometimes they have changed greatly in meaning, as the word 'villain' because of customs now extinct, and sometimes the advent of an overcoming power may be attested by the crippled diction, or by the complete disuse of the original tongue, save in solitary, dear phrases, spontaneous in grief or gladness. Secondly, this knowledge tends to make our language purer and more lucid, and therefore tends also to improve style and composition. Thirdly, the names we meet in the literature of our language are handed down to us, as venerable names, not to be treated lightly but entitled beforehand to our respect. They are landmarks in the

---

[1] A heartless vivisectionist, the central figure in Wilkie Collins' novel *Heart and Science*.

[2] This incident is in chapter sixty-two of Collins' novel.

transition of a language, keeping it inviolate, directing its course straight on like an advancing way, widening and improving as it advances but staying always on the high road, though many byways branch off it at all parts and seem smooth to follow. Thus these names, as those of the masters of English, are standards for imitation and reference, and are valuable because their use of the language was also based on their study of it, and is for that reason deserving of great and serious attention. Fourthly, and this is the greatest of all, the careful study of the language, used by these men, is almost the only way to gain a thorough knowledge of the power and dignity, that are in the elements of a language and further to understand, as far as nature allows, the feelings of great writers, to enter into their hearts and spirits, to be admitted, by privilege, into the privacy of their proper thoughts. The study of their language is useful as well, not merely to add to our reading and store of thought, but to add to our vocabulary and imperceptibly to make us sharers in their delicateness or strength. How frequently it happens that when persons become excited, all sense of language seems to forsake them, and they splutter incoherently and repeat themselves, that their phrases may have more sound and meaning. Look, how great the difficulty that many have in expressing their most ordinary ideas in correct English. If it were only to rectify these errors which exist amongst us, the study of our language should recommend itself to us. How much more so, then, when it not alone cures these defects, but works such wonderful changes in our speech by the mere contact with good diction and introduces us to beauties, which cannot here be enlarged on but obtain only passing mention, to which our former ignorance or negligence denied us access.

Lest we should seem to dwell over long on our own language let us consider the case of the classics. In Latin — for the writer acknowledges humbly his ignorance of Greek — a careful and well-directed study must be very advantageous. For it acquaints us with a language, which has a strong element in English, and thus makes us know the derivations of many words, which we then apply more correctly and which have therefore a truer meaning for us. Again Latin is the recognised language of scholars and philosophers, and the weapon of the learned; whose books and thoughts are only open, through the medium of translation. Further, it is astonishing that Latin is like Shakespeare in everyone's mouth, without his seeming, in the least, to recognize the fact. Quotations are constantly employed, even by those who are not Latin scholars and common convenience would prompt us to study it. Then also it is the uniform language of the ritual of the Church. Moreover it is for those who study it a great help intellectually, for it has some terse expressions, that are more forcible than many of our similar expressions. For instance a single Latin phrase or word is so complex in meaning, and enters into the nature of so many words, and has yet a delicate shade of its own, that no single word in English will properly represent. Thus Vergil's Latin is said to be so idiomatic as to defy translation. Evidently careful rendering of such language into suitable English must be a great exercise in judgment and expression, if we were to count nothing else. But Latin besides being in its degraded form the language of schoolmen, is in a better form the language of Lucretius, Vergil, Horace, Cicero, Pliny and Tacitus, all of whom are great names and who have withstood dislodgment from their high seats for thousands of years — a fact which is sufficient in itself to gain them a reading. They are moreover interesting as the writers in a vast Republic, the greatest and vastest the world has seen, a Republic which during five hundred years was the home of nearly all the great men of action in that time, which made its name heard from Gibraltar to Arabia, and to the stranger-hating Briton, everywhere a name of power, and everywhere with conquest in its army's van. [*The manuscript ends here.*]

4

Royal Hibernian Academy
'Ecce Homo'[1]

1899

Joyce completed his matriculation course in June 1899, and enrolled as a regular student at University College, Dublin, the following September. The essay on 'Ecce Homo' was written in that month, a year after the essay on 'Force'. Its tone is quite different from the essays that precede it; Joyce does not want to impress or persuade but rather to state his own position. This he does with a new precision and assurance.

While his remarks on painting and sculpture sound naïve, his conception of drama does not. It liberates him and enables him to approach the subject of a religious painting from a purely aesthetic point of view. The separation anticipates his irreverent later development of Thomistic ideas to suit his literary purposes. Munkacsy has succeeded as a dramatist because he has treated Christ as a human being. Whether Christ was only that Joyce blandly does not say, but he makes clear that Munkacsy has chosen the best way to treat his material.

Munkacsy's[2] picture which has been exhibited in the principal cities of Europe, is now on view at the Royal Hibernian Academy. With the other two pictures 'Christ before Pilate' and 'Christ on Calvary' it forms almost a complete trilogy of the later portion of the Passion. Perhaps what strikes one most in the picture under

[1] This essay is in a holograph manuscript of fourteen half-pages in Stanislaus Joyce's diary at the Cornell University Library.
[2] Michael Munkacsy (1844–1900), a Hungarian painter who was attracting considerable attention in England at this time.

31

consideration is the sense of life, the realistic illusion. One could well fancy that the men and women were of flesh and blood, struck into silent trance, by the warlock's hand. Hence the picture is primarily dramatic, not an execution of faultless forms, or a canvas reproduction of psychology. By drama I understand the interplay of passions; drama is strife, evolution, movement, in whatever way unfolded. Drama exists as an independent thing, conditioned but not controlled by its scene. An idyllic portrait or an environment of haystacks do not constitute a pastoral drama, no more than rhodomontade and a monotonous trick of 'tutoyer' build up a tragedy. If there be only quiescence in one, or vulgarity in the second, as is generally the case, then in neither one nor the other is the note of true drama sounded for a moment. However subdued the tone of passions may be, however ordered the action or commonplace the diction, if a play, or a work of music, or a picture concerns itself with the everlasting hopes, desires and hates of humanity, or deals with a symbolic presentment of our widely related nature, albeit a phase of that nature, then it is drama. Maeterlinck's characters may be, when subjected to the searchlight of that estimable torch, common sense, unaccountable, drifting, fate-impelled creatures — in fact, as our civilization dubs them, uncanny. But in whatever dwarfed and marionette-like a manner, their passions are human, and so the exposition of them is drama. This is fairly obvious when applied to a stage subject but when the word drama is in an identical way, applied to Munkacsy, it may need perhaps an additional word of explanation.

In the statuary art the first step towards drama was the separation of the feet. Before that sculpture was a copy of the body, actuated by only a nascent impulse, and executed by routine. The infusion of life, or its semblance, at once brought soul into the work of the artist, vivified his forms and elucidated his theme. It follows naturally from the fact that the sculptor aims at producing a bronze or stone model of man, that his impulse should lead him to the portrayal of an instantaneous passion. Consequently although he has the advantage of the painter, in at the first glance deceiving the eye, his capability to be a dramatist is less broad than the painter's. His power of moulding can be equalized by the painter's backgrounds and skilful disposition of shades, and while in such a manner naturalism is produced on an areal canvas, the colours, which add another life, help his theme to its expression in a very much completer and clearer whole. Moreover, and this applies markedly in the present case, as the theme becomes loftier or more extended, it can manifestly obtain more adequate treatment in a large picture than in the crowding of colourless, perfectly-modelled statues in a tableau. Notably then does the difference hold in the instance of 'Ecce Homo' where some seventy figures are limned on one canvas. It is a mistake to limit drama to the stage; a drama can be painted as well as sung or acted, and 'Ecce Homo' is a drama.

In addition, it is much more deserving of the comment of a dramatic critic than the majority of the pieces which are directly under his notice in the theatre. To speak of the technical point of an artwork such as this is, to my thinking, somewhat superfluous. Of course the draping, and the upraised hands, and outstretched fingers reveal a technique and a skill, beyond criticism. The narrow yard is a scene of crowded figures, all drawn with a master's faithfulness. The one blemish is the odd, strained position of the governor's left hand. It gives one the impression of being maimed or crippled from the manner in which the cloak conceals it. The background is a corridor, opened on the spectator, with pillars upholding a verandah, on which the eastern shrubs show out against a sapphire sky. At the right hand and in the extreme corner, as you face the picture, a stairway of two flights, say some twenty steps in all leads to a platform which is thus almost at right angles to the line of the pillars. The garish sunlight falls directly over this platform leaving the rest of the court partly in the shade. The walls are decorated and at the back of the piazza is a narrow doorway crowded with Roman soldiery. The first half of the mob, that is, those next underneath the platform, is enclosed between the pillars and a swinging chain in the foreground, which is parallel to them. A decrepit street cur, the only animal in the picture, is crouching by it. On the platform in front of the soldiers, stand two figures. One has his hands bound in front and is standing facing the rabble, his fingers just touching the balustrade. A red mantle is so placed about the shoulders as to cover the entire back and a little of the foreshoulders and arms. The whole front of the figure is thus exposed to the waist. A crown of irregular, yellowish thorns is on the temples and head and a light, long reed barely supported between the clasped hands. It is Christ. The other figure is somewhat nearer the populace and leans a little towards them over the balustrade. The figure is pointing at Christ, the right arm in the most natural position of demonstration, and the left arm extended in the peculiar, crippled way I have already noticed. It is Pilate. Right underneath these two main figures, on the paved yard, is the tossing, tumbling Jewish rabble. The expressions conveyed in the varying faces, gestures, hands and opened mouths are marvellous. There is the palsied, shattered frame of a lewd wretch; his face is bruted animalism, feebly stirred to a grin. There is the broad back and brawny arm and tight clenched fist, but the face of the muscular 'protestant' is hidden. At his feet, in the angle where the stairway bends a woman is kneeling. Her face is dragged in an unwholesome pallor but quivering with emotion. Her beautifully rounded arms are displayed as a contrast of writhing pity against the brutality of the throng. Some stray locks of her copious hair are blown over them and cling to them as tendrils. Her expression is reverential, her eyes are straining up through her tears. She is the emblem of the contrite, she is the new figure of lamentation as against the severe, familiar types, she is of those, the sorrowstricken, who weep and mourn but yet are comforted. Presumably, from her shrinking pose, she is a magdalen. Near her is the street dog, and near him a street urchin. His back is turned but both arms are flung up high and apart in youthful exultation, the fingers pointing outwards, stiff and separate.

In the heart of the crowd is the figure of a man, furious at being jostled by a well clad Jew. The eyes are squinting with rage, and an execration foams on his lips. The object of his rage is a rich man, with that horrible cast of countenance, so common among the sweaters of modern Israël. I mean, the face whose line runs out over the full forehead to the crest of the nose and then recedes in a similar curve back to the chin, which, in this instance, is covered with a wispish, tapering beard. The upper lip is raised out of position, disclosing two long, white teeth, while the whole lower lip is trapped. This is the creature's snarl of malice. An arm is stretched forth in derision, the fine, snowy linen falling back upon the forearm. Immediately behind is a huge face, with features sprawled upon it, the jaws torn asunder with a coarse howl. Then there is the half profile and figure of the triumphant fanatic. The long gaberdine falls to the naked feet, the head is erect, the arms perpendicular, raised in conquest. In the extreme end is the bleared face of a silly beggar. Everywhere is a new face. In the dark hoods, under the conical headdresses, here hatred, there the mouth gaping open at its fullest stretch, the head thrown back on the nape. Here an old woman is hastening away, horrorstruck, and there is a woman of comely appearance but evidently a proletarian. She has fine, languid eyes, full features and figure, but marred with cross stupidity and perfect, if less revolting bestiality. Her child is clambering about her knees, her infant hoisted on her shoulder. Not even these are free from the all pervading aversion and in their small beady eyes twinkles the fire of rejection, the bitter unwisdom of their race. Close by are the two figures of John and Mary. Mary has fainted. Her face is of a grey hue, like a sunless dawn, her features rigid but not drawn. Her hair is jet black, her hood white. She is almost dead, but her force of anguish keeps her alive. John's arms are wound about her, holding her up, his face is half feminine in its drawing, but set in purpose. His rust coloured hair falls over his shoulders, his features express solicitude and pity. On the stairs is a rabbi, enthralled with amazement, incredulous yet attracted by the extraordinary central figure. Round about are the soldiers. Their mien is self-possessed contempt. They look on Christ as an exhibition and the rabble as a pack of unkennelled animals. Pilate is saved from the dignity his post would have given him, by the evidence that he is not Roman enough to spurn them. His face is round, his skull compact, the hair cropped short on it. He is shifting, uncertain of his next move, his eyes wide open in mental fever. He wears the white and red Roman toga.

It will be clear from all this that the whole forms a wonderful picture, intensely, silently dramatic, waiting but the touch of the wizard wand to break out into reality, life and conflict. As such too much tribute cannot be paid to it, for it is a frightfully real presentment of all the baser passions of humanity, in both sexes, in every gradation, raised and lashed into a demoniac carnival. So far praise must be given, but it is plain through all this, that the aspect of the artist is human, intensely, powerfully human. To paint such a crowd one must probe humanity with no scrupulous knife. Pilate is self-seeking, Mary is maternal, the weeping woman is penitent, John is a strong man, rent inside with great grief, the soldiers bear the impress of the stubborn unideality of conquest; their pride is uncompromising for are they not the over-

comers? It would have been easy to have made Mary a Madonna
and John an evangelist but the artist has chosen to make Mary a
mother and John a man. I believe this treatment to be the finer
and the subtler. In a moment such as when Pilate said to the Jews,
Behold the man, it would be a pious error but indubitably, an
error to show Mary as the ancestress of the devout rapt madonnas
of our churches. The depicting of these two figures in such a way
in a sacred picture, is in itself a token of the highest genius. If
there is to be anything superhuman in the picture, anything above
and beyond the heart of man, it will appear in Christ. But no
matter how you view Christ, there is no trace of that in his aspect.
There is nothing divine in his look, there is nothing superhuman.
This is no defect of hand on the part of the artist, his skill would
have accomplished anything. It was his voluntary position. Van
Ruith[1] painted a picture some years ago of Christ and the traders
in the temple. His intention was to produce elevated reprimand
and divine chastisement, his hand failed him and the result was
a weak flogger and a mixture of lovingkindness and repose, wholly
incompatible with the incident. Munkacsy on the contrary would
never be under the power of his brush, but his view of the event is
humanistic. Consequently his work is drama. Had he chosen to
paint Christ as the Incarnate Son of God, redeeming his creatures
of his own admirable will, through insult and hate, it would not
have been drama, it would have been Divine Law, for drama deals
with man. As it is from the artist's conception, it is powerful
drama, the drama of the thrice told revolt of humanity against a
great teacher.

The face of Christ is a superb study of endurance, passion, I
use the word in its proper sense, and dauntless will. It is plain that
no thought of the crowd obtrudes itself on his mind. He seems to
have nothing in common with them, save his features which are
racial. The mouth is concealed by a brown moustache, the chin
and up to the ears overgrown with an untrimmed but moderate
beard of the same colour. The forehead is low and projects somewhat on the eyebrows. The nose is slightly Jewish but almost
aquiline, the nostrils thin and sensitive, the eyes are of a pale blue
colour, if of any, and as the face is turned to the light, they are
lifted half under the brows, the only true position for intense

[1] Horace Van Ruith, a painter of the English school, exhibited his work at the
Royal Academy, London, from 1888 to 1909.

agony. They are keen, but not large, and seem to pierce the air, half in inspiration, half in suffering. The whole face is of an ascetic, inspired, wholesouled, wonderfully passionate man. It is Christ, as the Man of Sorrows, his raiment red as of them that tread in the winepress. It is literally Behold the Man.

It is this treatment of the theme that has led me to appraise it as a drama. It is grand, noble, tragic but it makes the founder of Christianity, no more than a great social and religious reformer, a personality, of mingled majesty and power, a protagonist of a world-drama. No objections will be lodged against it on that score by the public, whose general attitude when they advert to the subject at all, is that of the painter, only less grand and less interested.

Munkacsy's conception is as much greater than theirs, as an average artist is greater than an average greengrocer, but it is of the same kind, it is to pervert Wagner, the attitude of the town. Belief in the divinity of Christ is not a salient feature of secular Christendom. But occasional sympathy with the eternal conflict of truth and error, of right and wrong, as exemplified in the drama at Golgotha is not beyond its approval.

J.A.J.

Sept. 1899

5

Drama and Life[1]

1900

While he was a student at University College, Dublin, Joyce read two papers before the college's Literary and Historical Society. The first, 'Drama and Life', one of his most important artistic pronouncements, he delivered on January 20, 1900. It appears that the president of the college, Father William Delany, read the paper in advance and objected to its indifference to ethical content in drama. He proposed that some passages be modified, but Joyce refused with so much firmness that Delany at last gave way. The interview with the president is described, no doubt with many changes, in Stephen Hero.[2]

Joyce read his paper, as his brother Stanislaus declares, 'without emphasis', or, as he himself puts it in Stephen Hero, *'He read it quietly and distinctly, involving every hardihood of thought or expression in an envelope of low innocuous melody,' and delivered the final sentences 'in a tone of metallic clearness'. Several students objected vigorously to his argument, and the chairman also disagreed with it in his summing-up. In* Stephen Hero *Stephen does not deign to reply. But in actual life, as Judge Eugene Sheehy recalls, 'Joyce rose to reply at about ten o'clock when the bell was ringing in the landing outside to signal that it was time to wind up the proceedings. He spoke without a note for at least thirty minutes and dealt with each of his critics in turn. It was a masterly performance and delivered to the accompaniment of rounds of applause from the back benches.' After the debate one student clapped Joyce on the back and exclaimed, 'Joyce, that was magnificent but you're raving mad!'[3]*

---

[1] This essay is in a holograph manuscript of sixteen half-pages in Stanislaus Joyce's diary at the Cornell University Library.

[2] Pages 90–98 (77–85).

[3] *May It Please the Court* (Dublin, 1951), pp. 12–13. See also his essay in *Centenary History of the Literary and Historical Society* (Dublin, 1955) pp. 84–5.

Although the relations between drama and life are, and must be, of the most vital character, in the history of drama itself these do not seem to have been at all times, consistently in view. The earliest and best known drama, this side of the Caucasus, is that of Greece. I do not propose to attempt anything in the nature of a historical survey but cannot pass it by. Greek drama arose out of the cult of Dionysos, who, god of fruitage, joyfulness and earliest art, offered in his life-story a practical groundplan for the erection of a tragic and a comic theatre. In speaking of Greek drama it must be borne in mind that its rise dominated its form. The conditions of the Attic stage suggested a syllabus of greenroom proprieties and cautions to authors, which in after ages were foolishly set up as the canons of dramatic art, in all lands. Thus the Greeks handed down a code of laws which their descendants with purblind wisdom forthwith advanced to the dignity of inspired pronouncements. Beyond this, I say nothing. It may be a vulgarism, but it is literal truth to say that Greek drama is played out.[1] For good or for bad it has done its work, which, if wrought in gold, was not upon lasting pillars. Its revival is not of dramatic but of pedagogic significance. Even in its own camp it has been superseded. When it had thriven over long in hieratic custody and in ceremonial form, it began to pall on the Aryan genius. A reaction ensued, as was inevitable; and as the classical drama had been born of religion, its follower arose out of a movement in literature. In this reaction England played an important part, for it was the power of the Shakespearean clique that dealt the deathblow to the already dying drama. Shakespeare was before all else a literary artist; humour, eloquence, a gift of seraphic music, theatrical instincts — he had a rich dower of these. The work, to which he gave such splendid impulse, was of a higher nature than that which it followed. It was far from mere drama, it was literature in dialogue. Here I must draw a line of demarcation between literature and drama.[2]

[1] In *Stephen Hero*, p. 101 (88), a student objects 'that Mr Daedalus did not understand the beauty of the Attic theatre. He pointed out that Eschylus was an imperishable name and he predicted that the drama of the Greeks would outlive many civilizations'.

[2] Joyce was impressed by Verlaine's line in 'Art Poétique', 'Et tout le reste est littérature'. His dismissal of 'literature' here as an inferior form of verbal expression is repeated in 'James Clarence Mangan' (p. 75 below) and in the review of Rooney's *Poems and Ballads* (p. 86 below), then in *Stephen Hero*, p. 78 (65);

Human society is the embodiment of changeless laws which the whimsicalities and circumstances of men and women involve and overwrap. The realm of literature is the realm of these accidental manners and humours — a spacious realm; and the true literary artist concerns himself mainly with them. Drama has to do with the underlying laws first, in all their nakedness and divine severity, and only secondarily with the motley agents who bear them out. When so much is recognized an advance has been made to a more rational and true appreciation of dramatic art. Unless some such distinction be made the result is chaos. Lyricism parades as poetic drama, psychological conversation as literary drama, and traditional farce moves over the boards with the label of comedy affixed to it.

Both of these dramas having done their work as prologues to the swelling act, they may be relegated to the department of literary curios. It is futile to say that there is no new drama or to contend that its proclamation is a huge boom. Space is valuable and I cannot combat these assertions. However it is to me day-clear that dramatic drama must outlive its elders, whose life is only eked by the most dexterous management and the carefullest husbanding. Over this New School some hard hits have been given and taken. The public is slow to seize truth, and its leaders quick to miscall it. Many, whose palates have grown accustomed to the old food, cry out peevishly against a change of diet. To these use and want is the seventh heaven. Loud are their praises of the bland blatancy of Corneille, the starchglaze of Trapassi's[1] godliness, the Pumblechookian[2] woodenness of Calderon. Their infantile plot juggling sets them agape, so superfine it is. Such critics are not to be taken seriously but they are droll figures! It is of course patently true that the 'new' school masters them on their own ground. Compare the skill of Haddon Chambers and Douglas Jerrold, of Sudermann and Lessing. The 'new' school in this branch of its art is superior. This superiority is only natural, as it accompanies work of immeasurably higher calibre. Even the least part of Wagner — his music — is beyond Bellini. Spite of the outcry of these lovers of the past, the masons are building for Drama, an

---

in the *Portrait*, however, he gives up this distinction, and has Stephen refer to literature as 'the highest and most spiritual art'.

[1] Pietro Metastasio (1698–1782), born Trapassi.

[2] From Pumblechook, a servile character in Dickens' *Great Expectations*.

ampler and loftier home, where there shall be light for gloom, and wide porches for drawbridge and keep.

Let me explain a little as to this great visitant. By drama I understand the interplay of passions to portray truth; drama is strife, evolution, movement in whatever way unfolded; it exists, before it takes form, independently; it is conditioned but not controlled by its scene. It might be said fantastically that as soon as men and women began life in the world there was above them and about them, a spirit, of which they were dimly conscious, which they would have had sojourn in their midst in deeper intimacy and for whose truth they became seekers in after times, longing to lay hands upon it. For this spirit is as the roaming air, little susceptible of change, and never left their vision, shall never leave it, till the firmament is as a scroll rolled away. At times it would seem that the spirit had taken up his abode in this or that form — but on a sudden he is misused, he is gone and the abode is left idle. He is, one might guess, somewhat of an elfish nature, a nixie, a very Ariel. So we must distinguish him and his house. An idyllic portrait, or an environment of haystacks does not constitute a pastoral play, no more than rhodomontade and sermonizing build up a tragedy.[1] Neither quiescence nor vulgarity shadow forth drama. However subdued the tone of passions may be, however ordered the action or commonplace the diction, if a play or a work of music or a picture presents the everlasting hopes, desires and hates of us, or deals with a symbolic presentment of our widely related nature, albeit a phase of that nature, then it is drama. I shall not speak here of its many forms. In every form that was not fit for it, it made an outburst, as when the first sculptor separated the feet. Morality, mystery, ballet, pantomine, opera, all these it speedily ran through and discarded. Its proper form 'the drama' is yet intact. 'There are many candles on the high altar, though one fall.'

Whatever form it takes must not be superimposed or conventional. In literature we allow conventions, for literature is a comparatively low form of art. Literature is kept alive by tonics, it flourishes through conventions in all human relations, in all actuality. Drama will be for the future at war with convention, if it is to realize itself truly. If you have a clear thought of the body

[1] From here to the end of this paragraph, Joyce paraphrases a passage in 'Royal Hibernian Academy "Ecce Homo" ', p. 32 above.

of drama, it will be manifest what raiment befits it. Drama of so wholehearted and admirable a nature cannot but draw all hearts from the spectacular and the theatrical, its note being truth and freedom in every aspect of it. It may be asked what are we to do, in the words of Tolstoi.[1] First, clear our minds of cant and alter the falsehoods to which we have lent our support. Let us criticize in the manner of free people, as a free race, recking little of ferula and formula. The Folk is, I believe, able to do so much. Securus judicat orbis terrarum,[2] is not too high a motto for all human artwork. Let us not overbear the weak, let us treat with a tolerant smile the stale pronouncements of those matchless serio-comics — the 'litterateurs'. If a sanity rules the mind of the dramatic world there will be accepted what is now the faith of the few, there will be past dispute written up the respective grades of Macbeth and The Master Builder.[3] The sententious critic of the thirtieth century may well say of them — Between him and these there is a great gulf fixed.

There are some weighty truths which we cannot overpass, in the relations between drama and the artist. Drama is essentially a communal art and of widespread domain. The drama — its fittest vehicle almost presupposes an audience, drawn from all classes. In an artloving and art-producing society the drama would naturally take up its position at the head of all artistic institutions. Drama is moreover of so unswayed, so unchallengeable a nature that in its highest forms it all but transcends criticism. It is hardly possible to criticize The Wild Duck, for instance; one can only brood upon it as upon a personal woe. Indeed in the case of all Ibsen's later work dramatic criticism, properly so called, verges on impertinence. In every other art personality, mannerism of touch, local sense, are held as adorments, as additional charms. But here the artist forgoes his very self and stands a mediator in awful truth before the veiled face of God.

If you ask me what occasions drama or what is the necessity for it at all, I answer Necessity. It is mere animal instinct applied to

---

[1] *What Are We to Do?* is the title of a book by Tolstoy.

[2] 'Untroubled, the world judges', St. Augustine, *Contra Epistolam Parmeniani*, III, 24.

[3] A speaker objects, in *Stephen Hero*, p. 78 (65), 'Everyone knew that *Macbeth* would be famous when the unknown authors of whom Mr Daedalus was so fond were dead and forgotten.'

the mind. Apart from his world-old desire to get beyond the flaming ramparts, man has a further longing to become a maker and a moulder. That is the necessity of all art. Drama is again the least dependent of all arts on its material. If the supply of mouldable earth or stone gives out, sculpture becomes a memory, if the yield of vegetable pigments ceases, the pictorial art ceases. But whether there be marble or paints, there is always the artstuff for drama. I believe further that drama arises spontaneously out of life and is coeval with it. Every race has made its own myths and it is in these that early drama often finds an outlet. The author of Parsifal has recognized this and hence his work is solid as a rock. When the mythus passes over the borderline and invades the temple of worship, the possibilities of its drama have lessened considerably. Even then it struggles back to its rightful place, much to the discomfort of the stodgy congregation.

As men differ as to the rise, so do they as to the aims of drama. It is in most cases claimed by the votaries of the antique school that the drama should have special ethical claims, to use their stock phrase, that it should instruct, elevate, and amuse. Here is yet another gyve that the jailers have bestowed. I do not say that drama may not fulfil any or all of these functions, but I deny that it is essential that it should fulfil them. Art, elevated into the overhigh sphere of religion, generally loses its true soul in stagnant quietism. As to the lower form of this dogma it is surely funny. This polite request to the dramatist to please point a moral, to rival Cyrano, in iterating through each act 'A la fin de l'envoi je touche' is amazing. Bred as it is of an amiable-parochial disposition we can but waive it. Mr Beoerly sacked with strychnine, or M. Coupeau in the horrors are nothing short of piteous in a surplice and dalmatic apiece. However this absurdity is eating itself fast, like the tiger of story, tail first.

A yet more insidious claim is the claim for beauty. As conceived by the claimants beauty is as often anaemic spirituality as hardy animalism. Then, chiefly because beauty is to men an arbitrary quality and often lies no deeper than form, to pin drama to dealing with it, would be hazardous. Beauty is the swerga[1] of the aesthete; but truth has a more ascertainable and more real dominion.[2] Art

---

[1] The heaven of the Gods in Hindu literature.
[2] Compare the treatment of truth and beauty in the Pola Notebook (pp. 146–8 below).

is true to itself when it deals with truth. Should such an untoward event as a universal reformation take place on earth, truth would be the very threshold of the house beautiful.

I have just one other claim to discuss, even at the risk of exhausting your patience. I quote from Mr Beerbohm Tree. 'In these days when faith is tinged with philosophic doubt, I believe it is the function of art to give us light rather than darkness. It should not point to our relationship with monkeys but rather remind us of our affinity with the angels.' In this statement there is a fair element of truth which however requires qualification. Mr Tree contends that men and women will always look to art as the glass wherein they may see themselves idealized. Rather I should think that men and women seldom think gravely on their own impulses towards art. The fetters of convention bind them too strongly. But after all art cannot be governed by the insincerity of the compact majority but rather by those eternal conditions, says Mr Tree, which have governed it from the first. I admit this as irrefutable truth. But it were well we had in mind that those eternal conditions are not the conditions of modern communities. Art is marred by such mistaken insistence on its religious, its moral, its beautiful, its idealizing tendencies. A single Rembrandt is worth a gallery full of Van Dycks. And it is this doctrine of idealism in art which has in notable instances disfigured manful endeavour, and has also fostered a babyish instinct to dive under blankets at the mention of the bogey of realism. Hence the public disowns Tragedy, unless she rattles her dagger and goblet, abhors Romance which is not amenable to the laws of prosody, and deems it a sad effect in art if, from the outpoured blood of hapless heroism, there does not at once spring up a growth of sorrowful blossoms. As in the very madness and frenzy of this attitude, people want the drama to befool them, Purveyor supplies plutocrat with a parody of life which the latter digests medicinally in a darkened theatre, the stage literally battening on the mental offal of its patrons.

Now if these views are effete what will serve the purpose? Shall we put life — real life — on the stage? No, says the Philistine chorus, for it will not draw. What a blend of thwarted sight and smug commercialism. Parnassus and the city Bank divide the souls of the pedlars. Life indeed nowadays is often a sad bore. Many feel like the Frenchman that they have been born too late in a

world too old, and their wanhope and nerveless unheroism point
on ever sternly to a last nothing, a vast futility and meanwhile —
a bearing of fardels. Epic savagery is rendered impossible by
vigilant policing, chivalry has been killed by the fashion oracles
of the boulevards. There is no clank of mail, no halo about
gallantry, no hat-sweeping, no roystering! The traditions of
romance are upheld only in Bohemia. Still I think out of the
dreary sameness of existence, a measure of dramatic life may be
drawn. Even the most commonplace, the deadest among the living,
may play a part in a great drama. It is a sinful foolishness to sigh
back for the good old times, to feed the hunger of us with the cold
stones they afford. Life we must accept as we see it before our eyes,
men and women as we meet them in the real world, not as we
apprehend them in the world of faery. The great human comedy
in which each has share, gives limitless scope to the true artist,
to-day as yesterday and as in years gone. The forms of things, as
the earth's crust, are changed. The timbers of the ships of
Tarshish[1] are falling asunder or eaten by the wanton sea; time has
broken into the fastnesses of the mighty; the gardens of Armida[2]
are become as treeless wilds. But the deathless passions, the
human verities which so found expression then, are indeed deathless, in the heroic cycle, or in the scientific age, Lohengrin, the
drama of which unfolds itself in a scene of seclusion, amid half-
lights, is not an Antwerp legend but a world drama. Ghosts, the
action of which passes in a common parlour, is of universal import
— a deepset branch on the tree, Igdrasil, whose roots are struck
in earth, but through whose higher leafage the stars of heaven are
glowing and astir. It may be that many have nothing to do with
such fable, or think that their wonted fare is all that is of need to
them. But as we stand on the mountains today, looking before and
after, pining for what is not, scarcely discerning afar the patches
of open sky; when the spurs threaten, and the track is grown with
briers, what does it avail that into our hands we have given us a
clouded cane for an alpenstock, or that we have dainty silks to
shield us against the eager, upland wind? The sooner we understand our true position, the better; and the sooner then will we be
up and doing on our way. In the meantime, art, and chiefly drama,
may help us to make our resting places with a greater insight and

1 'Jehoshaphat made ships of Tarshish to go to Ophir for gold.' I Kings 22:48.
2 Gardens of sweet indolence in Tasso's *Gerusalemme Liberata*.

a greater foresight, that the stones of them may be bravely builded, and the windows goodly and fair. '. . . what will you do in our Society, Miss Hessel?' asked Rörlund — 'I will let in fresh air, Pastor.' — answered Lona.[1]

JAS. A. JOYCE
January 10, 1900

[1] The curtain speech of Act I, Ibsen's *Pillars of Society.*

6

Ibsen's New Drama[1]

1900

Joyce's first formal publication was an essay on Ibsen's valedictory play, When We Dead Awaken. *Before he was eighteen he brashly entered into correspondence with W. L. Courtney, the editor of the eminent* Fortnightly Review. *Courtney agreed to consider an article on the play, and Joyce wrote it with copious quotations from a French translation. Since William Archer's translation was about to be published, the article was held up so that the quotations might be put into English. 'Ibsen's New Drama' appeared in the April 1, 1900, issue of the* Fortnightly, *and Joyce, to the amazement of his professors and classmates, received twelve guineas for it. With the money he took his father to London in May or June of 1900. He called on Courtney, who was surprised to find his assertive critic to be so young.*

The article came to Ibsen's notice, and he asked Archer to thank his 'very benevolent' admirer. Archer did so, and a three-year correspondence between him and Joyce ensued. Joyce valued Archer's opinion enough to submit his early poems and a first play to him for criticism. He was also encouraged to pursue his study of Dano-Norwegian, and in March 1901, felt competent enough to write a letter in that language to Ibsen, regretting that his article had been 'immature and hasty' and implying that, while the master had done much, his disciple would do more.

There was no shortage of articles on Ibsen in the English press in the 1890's, although reviews like the Athenaeum *continued to frown on his work as radical. To Yeats, on the other hand, who was then engaged in starting an Irish theatre in Dublin, Ibsen was middle-class and already passé; but Joyce's enthusiasm was like that of*

[1] Published in the *Fortnightly Review*, n.s., v. 67 (April 1, 1900) 575–90.

Shaw, whose Quintessence of Ibsenism (1891) *he had read. The closeness of the bond between Ibsen and Joyce is suggested by the* Portrait, *where Stephen Dedalus, much like Rubek in* When We Dead Awaken, *throws off the cerements of his soul and is drawn by the young woman wading in the sea to seek life and freedom.*

———————

Twenty years have passed since Henrik Ibsen wrote *A Doll's House*, thereby almost marking an epoch in the history of drama. During those years his name has gone abroad through the length and breadth of two continents, and has provoked more discussion and criticism than that of any other living man. He has been upheld as a religious reformer, a social reformer, a Semitic lover of righteousness, and as a great dramatist. He has been rigorously denounced as a meddlesome intruder, a defective artist, an incomprehensible mystic, and, in the eloquent words of a certain English critic, 'a muck-ferreting dog'.[1] Through the perplexities of such diverse criticism, the great genius of the man is day by day coming out as a hero comes out amid the earthly trials. The dissonant cries are fainter and more distant, the random praises are rising in steadier and more choral chaunt. Even to the uninterested bystander it must seem significant that the interest attached to this Norwegian has never flagged for over a quarter of a century. It may be questioned whether any man has held so firm an empire over the thinking world in modern times. Not Rousseau; not Emerson; not Carlyle; not any of those giants of whom almost all have passed out of human ken. Ibsen's power over two generations has been enhanced by his own reticence. Seldom, if at all, has he condescended to join battle with his enemies. It would appear as if the storm of fierce debate rarely broke in upon his wonderful calm. The conflicting voices have not influenced his work in the very smallest degree. His output of dramas has been regulated by the utmost order, by a clockwork routine, seldom found in the case of genius. Only once he answered his assailants after their violent attack on *Ghosts*. But from *The Wild Duck* to *John Gabriel Borkman*, his dramas have appeared almost mechanically at intervals of two years. One is apt to overlook the sustained energy which such a plan of campaign demands; but even surprise at this

[1] The epithet had been applied not to Ibsen, but to Ibsen's admirers. Joyce caught up the phrase from Shaw's *Quintessence of Ibsenism* (1891).

must give way to admiration at the gradual, irresistible advance of this extraordinary man. Eleven plays, all dealing with modern life, have been published. Here is the list: *A Doll's House*, *Ghosts*, *An Enemy of the People*, *The Wild Duck*, *Rosmersholm*, *The Lady from the Sea*, *Hedda Gabler*, *The Master Builder*, *Little Eyolf*, *John Gabriel Borkman*, and lastly — his new drama, published at Copenhagen, December 19th, 1899 — *When We Dead Awaken*. This play is already in process of translation into almost a dozen different languages — a fact which speaks volumes for the power of its author. The drama is written in prose, and is in three acts.

To begin an account of a play of Ibsen's is surely no easy matter. The subject is, in one way, so confined, and, in another way, so vast. It is safe to predict that nine-tenths of the notices of this play will open in some such way as the following: 'Arnold Rubek and his wife, Maja, have been married for four years, at the beginning of the play. Their union is, however, unhappy. Each is discontented with the other.' So far as this goes, it is unimpeachable; but then it does not go very far. It does not convey even the most shadowy notion of the relations between Professor Rubek and his wife. It is a bald, clerkly version of countless, indefinable complexities. It is as though the history of a tragic life were to be written down rudely in two columns, one for the pros and the other for the cons. It is only saying what is literally true, to say that, in the three acts of the drama, there has been stated all that is essential to the drama. There is from first to last hardly a superfluous word or phrase. Therefore, the play itself expresses its own ideas as briefly and as concisely as they can be expressed in the dramatic form. It is manifest, then, that a notice cannot give an adequate notion of the drama. This is not the case with the common lot of plays, to which the fullest justice may be meted out in a very limited number of lines. They are for the most part reheated dishes — unoriginal compositions, cheerfully owlish as to heroic insight, living only in their own candid claptrap — in a word, stagey. The most perfunctory curtness is their fittest meed. But in dealing with the work of a man like Ibsen, the task set the reviewer is truly great enough to sink all his courage. All he can hope to do is to link some of the more salient points together in such a way as to suggest rather than to indicate, the intricacies of the plot. Ibsen has attained ere this to such mastery over his art that, with apparently easy dialogue, he presents his men and women passing through different soul-crises. His analytic method is thus made use of to the fullest extent, and into the comparatively short space of two days the life in life of all his characters is compressed. For instance, though we only see Solness during one night and up to the following evening, we have in reality watched with bated breath the whole course of his life up to the moment when Hilda Wangel enters his house. So in the play under consideration, when we see Professor Rubek first, he is sitting in a garden chair, reading his morning paper, but by degrees the whole scroll of his life is unrolled before us, and we have the pleasure not of hearing it read out to us, but of reading it for ourselves, piecing the various parts, and going closer to see wherever the writing on the parchment is fainter or less legible.

As I have said, when the play opens, Professor Rubek is sitting in the gardens of a hotel, eating, or rather having finished, his breakfast. In another chair, close beside him, is sitting Maja Rubek, the Professor's wife. The scene is in Norway, a popular health resort near the sea. Through the trees can be seen the town harbour, and the fjord, with steamers plying over it, as it stretches past headland and river-isle out to the sea. Rubek is a famous sculptor, of middle age, and Maja, a woman still young, whose bright eyes have just a shade of sadness in them. These two continue reading their respective papers quietly in the peace of the morning. All looks so idyllic to the careless eye. The lady breaks the silence in a weary, petulant manner by complaining of the deep peace that reigns about them. Arnold lays down his paper with mild expostulation. Then they begin to converse of this thing and that; first of the silence, then of the place and the people, of the railway stations through which they passed the previous night, with their sleepy porters and aimlessly shifting lanterns. From this they proceed to talk of the changes in the people, and of all that has grown up since they were married. Then it is but a little further to the main trouble. In speaking of their married life it speedily appears that the inner view of their relations is hardly as ideal as the outward view might lead one to expect. The depths of these two people are being slowly stirred up. The leaven of prospective drama is gradually discerned working amid the *fin-de-siècle* scene. The lady seems a difficult little person. She complains of the idle promises with which her husband had fed her aspirations.

MAJA. You said you would take me up to a high mountain and show me all the glory of the world.

RUBEK (*with a slight start*). Did I promise you that, too?

In short, there is something untrue lying at the root of their union. Meanwhile the guests of the hotel, who are taking the baths, pass out of the hotel porch on the right, chatting and laughing men and women. They are informally marshalled by the inspector of the baths. This person is an unmistakable type of the conventional official. He salutes Mr. and Mrs. Rubek, enquiring how they slept. Rubek asks him if any of the guests take their baths by night, as he has seen a white figure moving in the park during the night. Maja scouts the notion, but the inspector says that there is a strange lady, who has rented the pavilion which is to the left, and who is staying there, with one attendant — a Sister of Mercy. As they are talking, the strange lady and her companion pass slowly through the park and enter the pavilion. The incident appears to affect Rubek, and Maja's curiosity is aroused.

MAJA (*a little hurt and jarred*). Perhaps this lady has been one of your models, Rubek? Search your memory.

RUBEK (*looks cuttingly at her*). Model?

MAJA (*with a provoking smile*). In your younger days, I mean. You are said to have had such innumerable models — long ago, of course.

RUBEK (*in the same tone*). Oh, no, little Frau Maja. I have in reality had only one single model. One and one only for everything I have done.

While this misunderstanding is finding outlet in the foregoing conversation, the inspector, all at once, takes fright at some person who is approaching. He attempts to escape into the hotel, but the high-pitched voice of the person who is approaching arrests him.

ULFHEIM's voice (*heard outside*). Stop a moment, man. Devil take it all, can't you stop? Why do you always scuttle away from me?

With these words, uttered in strident tones, the second chief actor enters on the scene. He is described as a great bear-killer,

51

thin, tall, of uncertain age, and muscular. He is accompanied by his servant, Lars, and a couple of sporting dogs. Lars does not speak a single word in the play. Ulfheim at present dismisses him with a kick, and approaches Mr. and Mrs. Rubek. He falls into conversation with them, for Rubek is known to him as the celebrated sculptor. On sculpture this savage hunter offers some original remarks.

ULFHEIM . . . We both work in a hard material, madam — both your husband and I. He struggles with his marble blocks, I daresay; and I struggle with tense and quivering bear-sinews. And we both of us win the fight in the end — subdue and master our material. We don't give in until we have got the better of it, though it fight never so hard.

RUBEK (*deep in thought*). There's a great deal of truth in what you say.

This eccentric creature, perhaps by the force of his own eccentricity, has begun to weave a spell of enchantment about Maja. Each word that he utters tends to wrap the web of his personality still closer about her. The black dress of the Sister of Mercy causes him to grin sardonically. He speaks calmly of all his near friends, whom he has dispatched out of the world.

MAJA. And what did you do for your nearest friends?
ULFHEIM. Shot them, of course.
RUBEK (*looking at him*). Shot them?
MAJA (*moving her chair back*). Shot them dead?
ULFHEIM (*nods*). I never miss, madam.

However, it turns out that by his nearest friends he means his dogs, and the minds of his hearers are put somewhat more at ease. During their conversation the Sister of Mercy has prepared a slight repast for her mistress at one of the tables outside the pavilion. The unsustaining qualities of the food excite Ulfheim's merriment. He speaks with a lofty disparagement of such effeminate diet. He is a realist in his appetite.

ULFHEIM (*rising*). Spoken like a woman of spirit, madam. Come with me, then! They [his dogs] swallow whole, great, thumping meat-bones — gulp them up and then gulp them down again. Oh, it's a regular treat to see them!

On such half-gruesome, half-comic invitation Maja goes out with him, leaving her husband in the company of the strange lady who enters from the pavilion. Almost simultaneously the Professor and the lady recognize each other. The lady has served Rubek as model for the central figure in his famous masterpiece, 'The Resurrection Day'. Having done her work for him, she had fled in an unaccountable manner, leaving no traces behind her. Rubek and she drift into familiar conversation. She asks him who is the lady who has just gone out. He answers, with some hesitation, that she is his wife. Then he asks if she is married. She replies that she is married. He asks her where her husband is at present.

RUBEK. And where is he now?

IRENE. Oh, in a churchyard somewhere or other, with a fine, handsome monument over him; and with a bullet rattling in his skull.

RUBEK. Did he kill himself?

IRENE. Yes, he was good enough to take that off my hands.

RUBEK. Do you not lament his loss, Irene?

IRENE (*not understanding*). Lament? What loss?

RUBEK. Why, the loss of Herr von Satow, of course.

IRENE. His name was not Satow.

RUBEK. Was it not?

IRENE. My second husband is called Satow. He is a Russian.

RUBEK. And where is he?

IRENE. Far away in the Ural Mountains. Among all his gold-mines.

RUBEK. So he lives there?

IRENE (*shrugs her shoulders*). Lives? Lives? In reality I have killed him.

RUBEK (*starts*). Killed — !

IRENE. Killed him with a fine sharp dagger which I always have with me in bed ——

Rubek begins to understand that there is some meaning hidden beneath these strange words. He begins to think seriously on himself, his art, and on her, passing in review the course of his life since the creation of his masterpiece, 'The Resurrection Day'. He sees that he has not fulfilled the promise of that work, and comes to realize that there is something lacking in his life. He asks Irene how she has lived since they last saw each other. Irene's answer to his query is of great importance, for it strikes the key note of the entire play.

IRENE (*rises slowly from her chair and says quiveringly*). I was dead for many years. They came and bound me — lacing my arms together at my back. Then they lowered me into a grave-vault, with iron bars before the loophole. And with padded walls, so that no one on the earth above could hear the grave-shrieks.

In Irene's allusion to her position as model for the great picture, Ibsen gives further proof of his extraordinary knowledge of women. No other man could have so subtly expressed the nature of the relations between the sculptor and his model, had he even dreamt of them.

IRENE. I exposed myself wholly and unreservedly to your gaze [*more softly*] and never once did you touch me . . . .

* * * *

RUBEK (*looks impressively at her*). I was an artist, Irene.

IRENE (*darkly*). That is just it. That is just it.

Thinking deeper and deeper on himself and on his former attitude towards this woman, it strikes him yet more forcibly that there are great gulfs set between his art and his life, and that even in his art his skill and genius are far from perfect. Since Irene left him he has done nothing but paint portrait busts of townsfolk. Finally, some kind of resolution is enkindled in him, a resolution to repair his botching, for he does not altogether despair of that. There is just a reminder of the will-glorification of *Brand* in the lines that follow.

RUBEK (*struggling with himself, uncertainly*). If we could, oh, if only we could . . . .

IRENE. Why can we not do what we will?

In fine, the two agree in deeming their present state insufferable. It appears plain to her that Rubek lies under a heavy obligation to her, and with their recognition of this, and the entrance of Maja, fresh from the enchantment of Ulfheim, the first act closes.

RUBEK. When did you begin to seek for me, Irene?

IRENE (*with a touch of jesting bitterness*). From the time when

I realized that I had given away to you something rather indispensable. Something one ought never to part with.

RUBEK (*bowing his head*). Yes, that is bitterly true. You gave me three or four years of your youth.

IRENE. More, more than that I gave you — spendthrift as I then was.

RUBEK. Yes, you were prodigal, Irene. You gave me all your naked loveliness —

IRENE. To gaze upon —

RUBEK. And to glorify . . . .

* * * *

IRENE. But you have forgotten the most precious gift.

RUBEK. The most precious . . . what gift was that?

IRENE. I gave you my young living soul. And that gift left me empty within — soulless [*looks at him with a fixed stare*]. It was that I died of, Arnold.

It is evident, even from this mutilated account, that the first act is a masterly one. With no perceptible effort the drama rises, with a methodic natural ease it develops. The trim garden of the nineteenth-century hotel is slowly made the scene of a gradually growing dramatic struggle. Interest has been roused in each of the characters, sufficient to carry the mind into the succeeding act. The situation is not stupidly explained, but the action has set in, and at the close the play has reached a definite stage of progression.

The second act takes place close to a sanatorium on the mountains. A cascade leaps from a rock and flows in steady stream to the right. On the bank some children are playing, laughing and shouting. The time is evening. Rubek is discovered lying on a mound to the left. Maja enters shortly, equipped for hill-climbing. Helping herself with her stick across the stream, she calls out to Rubek and approaches him. He asks how she and her companion are amusing themselves, and questions her as to their hunting. An exquisitely humorous touch enlivens their talk. Rubek asks if they intend hunting the bear near the surrounding locality. She replies with a grand superiority.

MAJA. You don't suppose that bears are to be found in the naked mountains, do you?

The next topic is the uncouth Ulfheim. Maja admires him because he is so ugly — then turns abruptly to her husband saying, pensively, that he also is ugly. The accused pleads his age.

RUBEK (*shrugging his shoulders*). One grows old. One grows old, Frau Maja!

This semi-serious banter leads them on to graver matters. Maja lies at length in the soft heather, and rails gently at the Professor. For the mysteries and claims of art she has a somewhat comical disregard.

MAJA (*with a somewhat scornful laugh*). Yes, you are always, always an artist.

and again —

MAJA. . . . Your tendency is to keep yourself to yourself and — think your own thoughts. And, of course, I can't talk properly to you about your affairs. I know nothing about Art and that sort of thing. [*With an impatient gesture.*] And care very little either, for that matter.

She rallies him on the subject of the strange lady, and hints maliciously at the understanding between them. Rubek says that he was only an artist and that she was the source of his inspiration. He confesses that the five years of his married life have been years of intellectual famine for him. He has viewed in their true light his own feelings towards his art.

RUBEK (*smiling*). But that was not precisely what I had in my mind.

MAJA. What then?

RUBEK (*again serious*). It was this — that all the talk about the artist's vocation and the artist's mission, and so forth, began to strike me as being very empty and hollow and meaningless at bottom.

MAJA. Then what would you put in its place?

RUBEK. Life, Maja.

The all-important question of their mutual happiness is touched upon, and after a brisk discussion a tacit agreement to separate is effected. When matters are in this happy condition Irene is descried coming across the heath. She is surrounded by the sportive chil-

dren and stays awhile among them. Maja jumps up from the grass
and goes to her, saying, enigmatically, that her husband requires
assistance to 'open a precious casket'. Irene bows and goes towards Rubek, and Maja goes joyfully to seek her hunter. The
interview which follows is certainly remarkable, even from a
stagey point of view. It constitutes, practically, the substance of
the second act, and is of absorbing interest. At the same time it
must be added that such a scene would tax the powers of the
mimes producing it. Nothing short of a complete realization of the
two *rôles* would represent the complex ideas involved in the conversation. When we reflect how few stage artists would have
either the intelligence to attempt it or the powers to execute it,
we behold a pitiful revelation.

In the interview of these two people on the heath, the whole
tenors of their lives are outlined with bold steady strokes. From
the first exchange of introductory words each phrase tells a chapter of experiences. Irene alludes to the dark shadow of the Sister
of Mercy which follows her everywhere, as the shadow of Arnold's
unquiet conscience follows him. When he has half-involuntarily
confessed so much, one of the great barriers between them is
broken down. Their trust in each other is, to some extent, renewed,
and they revert to their past acquaintance. Irene speaks openly of
her feelings, of her hate for the sculptor.

IRENE (*again vehemently*). Yes, for you — for the artist who
had so lightly and carelessly taken a warm-blooded body, a young
human life, and worn the soul out of it — because you needed it
for a work of art.

Rubek's transgression has indeed been great. Not merely has
he possessed himself of her soul, but he has withheld from its
rightful throne the child of her soul. By her child Irene means the
statue. To her it seems that this statue is, in a very true and very
real sense, born of her. Each day as she saw it grow to its full
growth under the hand of the skilful moulder, her inner sense of
motherhood for it, of right over it, of love towards it, had become
stronger and more confirmed.

IRENE (*changing to a tone full of warmth and feeling*). But that
statue in the wet, living clay, that I loved — as it rose up, a vital
human creature out of these raw, shapeless masses — for that was
our creation, our child. Mine and yours.

It is, in reality, because of her strong feelings that she has kept aloof from Rubek for five years. But when she hears now of what he has done to the child — her child — all her powerful nature rises up against him in resentment. Rubek, in a mental agony, endeavours to explain, while she listens like a tigress whose cub has been wrested from her by a thief.

RUBEK. I was young then — with no experience of life. The Resurrection, I thought, would be most beautifully and exquisitely figured as a young unsullied woman — with none of a life's experience — awakening to light and glory without having to put away from her anything ugly and impure.

With larger experience of life he has found it necessary to alter his ideal somewhat, he has made her child no longer a principal, but an intermediary figure. Rubek, turning towards her, sees her just about to stab him. In a fever of terror and thought he rushes into his own defence, pleading madly for the errors he has done. It seems to Irene that he is endeavouring to render his sin poetical, that he is penitent but in a luxury of dolour. The thought that she has given up herself, her whole life, at the bidding of his false art, rankles in her heart with a terrible persistence. She cries out against herself, not loudly, but in deep sorrow.

IRENE (*with apparent self-control*). I should have borne children into the world — many children — real children — not such children as are hidden away in grave-vaults. That was my vocation. I ought never to have served you — poet.

Rubek, in poetic absorption, has no reply, he is musing on the old, happy days. Their dead joys solace him. But Irene is thinking of a certain phrase of his which he had spoken unwittingly. He had declared that he owed her thanks for her assistance in his work. This has been, he had said, a truly blessed *episode* in my life. Rubek's tortured mind cannot bear any more reproaches, too many are heaped upon it already. He begins throwing flowers on the stream, as they used in those bygone days on the lake of Taunitz. He recalls to her the time when they made a boat of leaves, and yoked a white swan to it, in imitation of the boat of Lohengrin. Even here in their sport there lies a hidden meaning.

IRENE. You said I was the swan that drew your boat.

RUBEK. Did I say so? Yes, I daresay I did [*absorbed in the game*]. Just see how the sea-gulls are swimming down the stream!

IRENE (*laughing*). And all your ships have run ashore.

RUBEK (*throwing more leaves into the brook*). I have ships enough in reserve.

While they are playing aimlessly, in a kind of childish despair, Ulfheim and Maja appear across the heath. These two are going to seek adventures on the high tablelands. Maja sings out to her husband a little song which she has composed in her joyful mood. With a sardonic laugh Ulfheim bids Rubek good-night and disappears with his companion up the mountain. All at once Irene and Rubek leap to the same thought. But at that moment the gloomy figure of the Sister of Mercy is seen in the twilight, with her leaden eyes looking at them both. Irene breaks from him, but promises to meet him that night on the heath.

RUBEK. And you will come, Irene?

IRENE. Yes, certainly I will come. Wait for me here.

RUBEK (*repeats dreamily*). Summer night on the upland. With you. With you. [*His eyes meet hers.*] Oh, Irene, that might have been our life. And that we have forfeited, we two.

IRENE. We see the irretrievable only when [*breaks short off*].

RUBEK (*looks inquiringly at her*). When? . . .

IRENE. When we dead awaken.

The third act takes place on a wide plateau, high up on the hills. The ground is rent with yawning clefts. Looking to the right, one sees the range of the summits half-hidden in the moving mists. On the left stands an old, dismantled hut. It is in the early morning, when the skies are the colour of pearl. The day is beginning to break. Maja and Ulfheim come down to the plateau. Their feelings are sufficiently explained by the opening words.

MAJA (*trying to tear herself loose*). Let me go! Let me go, I say!

ULFHEIM. Come, come! are you going to bite now? You're as snappish as a wolf.

When Ulfheim will not cease his annoyances, Maja threatens to run over the crest of the neighbouring ridge. Ulfheim points out that she will dash herself to pieces. He has wisely sent Lars away after the hounds, that he may be uninterrupted. Lars, he says, may be trusted not to find the dogs too soon.

MAJA (*looking angrily at him*). No, I daresay not.

ULFHEIM (*catching at her arm*). For Lars — he knows my — my methods of sport, you see.

Maja, with enforced self-possession, tells him frankly what she thinks of him. Her uncomplimentary observations please the bear-hunter very much. Maja requires all her tact to keep him in order. When she talks of going back to the hotel, he gallantly offers to carry her on his shoulders, for which suggestion he is promptly snubbed. The two are playing as a cat and a bird play. Out of their skirmish one speech of Ulfheim's rises suddenly to arrest attention, as it throws some light on his former life.

ULFHEIM (*with suppressed exasperation*). I once took a young girl — lifted her up from the mire of the streets, and carried her in my arms. Next my heart I carried her. So I would have borne her all through life, lest haply she should dash her foot against a stone . . . . [*With a growling laugh.*] And do you know what I got for my reward?

MAJA. No. What did you get?

ULFHEIM (*looks at her, smiles and nods*). I got the horns! The horns that you can see so plainly. Is not that a comical story, madam bear-murderess?

As an exchange of confidence, Maja tells him her life in summary — and chiefly her married life with Professor Rubek. As a result, these two uncertain souls feel attracted to each other, and Ulfheim states his case in the following characteristic manner:

ULFHEIM. Should not we two tack our poor shreds of life together?

Maja, satisfied that in their vows there will be no promise on his part to show her all the splendours of the earth, or to fill her dwelling-place with art, gives a half-consent by allowing him to carry her down the slope. As they are about to go, Rubek and Irene, who have also spent the night on the heath, approach the same plateau. When Ulfheim asks Rubek if he and madame have ascended by the same pathway, Rubek answers significantly.

RUBEK. Yes, of course [*With a glance at* MAJA]. Henceforth the strange lady and I do not intend our ways to part.

While the musketry of their wit is at work, the elements seem to feel that there is a mighty problem to be solved then and there, and that a great drama is swiftly drawing to a close. The smaller figures of Maja and Ulfheim are grown still smaller in the dawn of the tempest. Their lots are decided in comparative quiet, and we cease to take much interest in them. But the other two hold our gaze, as they stand up silently on the fjaell, engrossing central figures of boundless, human interest. On a sudden, Ulfheim raises his hand impressively towards the heights.

ULFHEIM. But don't you see that the storm is upon us? Don't you hear the blasts of wind?

RUBEK (*listening*). They sound like the prelude to the Resurrection Day.

* * * *

MAJA (*drawing* ULFHEIM *away*). Let us make haste and get down.

As he cannot take more than one person at a time, Ulfheim promises to send aid for Rubek and Irene, and, seizing Maja in his arms, clambers rapidly but warily down the path. On the desolate mountain plateau, in the growing light, the man and the woman are left together — no longer the artist and his model. And the shadow of a great change is stalking close in the morning silence. Then Irene tells Arnold that she will not go back among the men and women she has left; she will not be rescued. She tells him also, for now she may tell all, how she had been tempted to kill him in frenzy when he spoke of their connection as an episode of his life.

RUBEK (*darkly*). And why did you hold your hand?

IRENE. Because it flashed upon me with a sudden horror that you were dead already — long ago.

But, says Rubek, our love is not dead in us, it is active, fervent and strong.

IRENE. The love that belongs to the life of earth — the beautiful, miraculous life of earth — the inscrutable life of earth — that is dead in both of us.

There are, moreover, the difficulties of their former lives. Even here, at the sublimest part of his play, Ibsen is master of himself and his facts. His genius as an artist faces all, shirks nothing. At the close of *The Master Builder*, the greatest touch of all was the horrifying exclamation of one without, 'O! the head is all crushed in.' A lesser artist would have cast a spiritual glamour over the tragedy of Bygmester Solness. In like manner here Irene objects that she has exposed herself as a nude before the vulgar gaze, that Society has cast her out, that all is too late. But Rubek cares for such considerations no more. He flings them all to the wind and decides.

RUBEK (*throwing his arms violently around her*). Then let two of the dead — us two — for once live life to its uttermost, before we go down to our graves again.

IRENE (*with a shriek*). Arnold!

RUBEK. But not here in the half-darkness. Not here with this hideous dank shroud flapping around us!

IRENE (*carried away by passion*). No, no — up in the light and in all the glittering glory! Up to the Peak of Promise!

RUBEK. There we will hold our marriage-feast, Irene — oh! my beloved!

IRENE (*proudly*). The sun may freely look on us, Arnold.

RUBEK. All the powers of light may freely look on us — and all the powers of darkness too [*seizes her hand*] — will you then follow me, oh my grace-given bride!

IRENE (*as though transfigured*). I follow you, freely and gladly, my lord and master!

RUBEK (*drawing her along with him*). We must first pass through the mists, Irene, and then ——

IRENE. Yes, through all the mists, and then right up to the summit of the tower that shines in the sunrise.

> *The mist-clouds close in over the scene.* RUBEK *and* IRENE, *hand in hand, climb up over the snowfield to the right and soon disappear among the lower clouds. Keen storm-gusts hurtle and whistle through the air.*
>
> *The* SISTER OF MERCY *appears upon the rubble-slope to the left. She stops and looks around silently and searchingly.*
>
> MAJA *can be heard singing triumphantly far in the depths below.*

MAJA. I am free! I am free! I am free!
No more life in the prison for me!
I am free as a bird! I am free!

Suddenly a sound like thunder is heard from high up on the snowfield, which glides and whirls downwards with rushing speed. RUBEK *and* IRENE *can be dimly discerned as they are whirled along with the masses of snow and buried in them.*

THE SISTER OF MERCY (*gives a shriek, stretches out her arms towards them, and cries*), Irene! [*Stands silent a moment, then makes the sign of the cross before her in the air, and says*], Pax Vobiscum!

MAJA's *triumphant song sounds from still further down below.*

Such is the plot, in a crude and incoherent way, of this new drama. Ibsen's plays do not depend for their interest on the action, or on the incidents. Even the characters, faultlessly drawn though they be, are not the first thing in his plays. But the naked drama — either the perception of a great truth, or the opening up of a great question, or a great conflict which is almost independent of the conflicting actors, and has been and is of far-reaching importance — this is what primarily rivets our attention. Ibsen has chosen the average lives in their uncompromising truth for the groundwork of all his later plays. He has abandoned the verse form, and has never sought to embellish his work after the conventional fashion. Even when his dramatic theme reached its zenith he has not sought to trick it out in gawds or tawdriness. How easy it would have been to have written *An Enemy of the People* on a speciously loftier level — to have replaced the *bourgeois* by the legitimate hero! Critics might then have extolled as grand what they have so often condemned as banal. But the surroundings are nothing to Ibsen. The play is the thing. By the force of his genius, and the indisputable skill which he brings to all his efforts, Ibsen has, for many years, engrossed the attention of the civilized world. Many years more, however, must pass before he will enter his kingdom in jubilation, although, as he stands to-day, all has been done on his part to ensure his own worthiness to enter therein. I do not propose here to examine into every detail of dramaturgy connected with this play, but merely to outline the characterization.

In his characters Ibsen does not repeat himself. In this drama — the last of a long catalogue — he has drawn and differentiated with his customary skill. What a novel creation is Ulfheim! Surely

the hand which has drawn him has not yet lost her cunning.
Ulfheim is, I think, the newest character in the play. He is a kind
of surprise-packet. It is as a result of his novelty that he seems to
leap, at first mention, into bodily form. He is superbly wild,
primitively impressive. His fierce eyes roll and glare as those of
Yégof or Herne. As for Lars, we may dismiss him, for he never
opens his mouth. The Sister of Mercy speaks only once in
the play, but then with good effect. In silence she follows
Irene like a retribution, a voiceless shadow with her own symbolic
majesty.

Irene, too, is worthy of her place in the gallery of her compeers.
Ibsen's knowledge of humanity is nowhere more obvious than in
his portrayal of women. He amazes one by his painful introspec-
tion; he seems to know them better than they know themselves.[1]
Indeed, if one may say so of an eminently virile man, there is a
curious admixture of the woman in his nature. His marvellous
accuracy, his faint traces of femininity, his delicacy of swift touch,
are perhaps attributable to this admixture. But that he knows
women is an incontrovertible fact. He appears to have sounded
them to almost unfathomable depths. Beside his portraits the
psychological studies of Hardy and Turgénieff, or the exhaustive
elaborations of Meredith, seem no more than sciolism. With a
deft stroke, in a phrase, in a word, he does what costs them
chapters, and does it better. Irene, then, has to face great comparison; but it must be acknowledged that she comes forth of it
bravely. Although Ibsen's women are uniformly true, they, of
course, present themselves in various lights. Thus Gina Ekdal is,
before all else, a comic figure, and Hedda Gabler a tragic one — if
such old-world terms may be employed without incongruity. But
Irene cannot be so readily classified; the very aloofness from passion, which is not separable from her, forbids classification. She
interests us strangely — magnetically, because of her inner power
of character. However perfect Ibsen's former creations may be,
it is questionable whether any of his women reach to the depth
of soul of Irene. She holds our gaze for the sheer force of her
intellectual capacity. She is, moreover, an intensely spiritual

---

[1] Compare Jung's remark about Joyce in his letter to Joyce about *Ulysses*:
'The 40 pages of non stop run in the end is a string of veritable psychological
peaches. I suppose the devil's grandmother knows so much about the real psychology of a woman, I didn't.'

creation — in the truest and widest sense of that. At times she is liable to get beyond us, to soar above us, as she does with Rubek. It will be considered by some as a blemish that she — a woman of fine spirituality — is made an artist's model, and some may even regret that such an episode mars the harmony of the drama. I cannot altogether see the force of this contention; it seems pure irrelevancy. But whatever may be thought of the fact, there is small room for complaint as to the handling of it. Ibsen treats it, as indeed he treats all things, with large insight, artistic restraint, and sympathy. He sees it steadily and whole, as from a great height, with perfect vision and an angelic dispassionateness, with the sight of one who may look on the sun with open eyes.[1] Ibsen is different from the clever purveyor.

Maja fulfills a certain technical function in the play, apart from her individual character. Into the sustained tension she comes as a relief. Her airy freshness is as a breath of keen air. The sense of free, almost flamboyant, life, which is her chief note, counterbalances the austerity of Irene and the dullness of Rubek. Maja has practically the same effect on this play, as Hilda Wangel has on *The Master Builder*. But she does not capture our sympathy so much as Nora Helmer. She is not meant to capture it.

Rubek himself is the chief figure in this drama, and, strangely enough, the most conventional. Certainly, when contrasted with his Napoleonic predecessor, John Gabriel Borkman, he is a mere shadow. It must be borne in mind, however, that Borkman is alive, actively, energetically, restlessly alive, all through the play to the end, when he dies; whereas Arnold Rubek is dead, almost hopelessly dead, until the end, when he comes to life. Notwithstanding this, he is supremely interesting, not because of himself, but because of his dramatic significance. Ibsen's drama, as I have said, is wholly independent of his characters. They may be bores, but the drama in which they live and move is invariably powerful. Not that Rubek is a bore by any means! He is infinitely more interesting in himself than Torvald Helmer or Tesman, both of whom possess certain strongly-marked characteristics. Arnold Rubek is, on the other hand, not intended to be a genius, as

---

[1] This image of artistic detachment was to grow, with some assistance from Flaubert, into Stephen Dedalus' picture of the artist 'like the God of the creation, . . . within or behind or beyond or above his handiwork, invisible, refined out of existence, indifferent, paring his fingernails.'

perhaps Eljert Lövborg is. Had he been a genius like Eljert he would have understood in a truer way the value of his life.[1] But, as we are to suppose, the facts that he is devoted to his art and that he has attained to a degree of mastery in it — mastery of hand linked with limitation of thought — tell us that there may be lying dormant in him a capacity for greater life, which may be exercised when he, a dead man, shall have risen from among the dead.

The only character whom I have neglected is the inspector of the baths, and I hasten to do him tardy, but scant, justice. He is neither more nor less than the average inspector of baths. But he is that.

So much for the characterization, which is at all times profound and interesting. But apart from the characters in the play, there are some noteworthy points in the frequent and extensive side-issues of the line of thought. The most salient of these is what seems, at first sight, nothing more than an accidental scenic feature. I allude to the environment of the drama. One cannot but observe in Ibsen's later work a tendency to get out of closed rooms. Since *Hedda Gabler* this tendency is most marked. The last act of *The Master Builder* and the last act of *John Gabriel Borkman* take place in the open air. But in this play the three acts are *al fresco*. To give heed to such details as these in the drama may be deemed ultra-Boswellian fanaticism. As a matter of fact it is what is barely due to the work of a great artist. And this feature, which is so prominent, does not seem to me altogether without its significance.

Again, there has not been lacking in the last few social dramas a fine pity for men — a note nowhere audible in the uncompromising rigour of the early eighties. Thus in the conversion of Rubek's views as to the girl-figure in his masterpiece, 'The Resurrection Day', there is involved an all-embracing philosophy, a deep sympathy with the cross-purposes and contradictions of life, as they may be reconcilable with a hopeful awakening — when the manifold travail of our poor humanity may have a glorious issue. As to the drama itself, it is doubtful if any good purpose can be served by attempting to criticize it. Many things would tend to prove this. Henrik Ibsen is one of the world's great

---

[1] Joyce's interest in the character of Lövborg led him later to offer to play the part for the Irish Literary Theatre, if they would produce *Hedda Gabler*.

men before whom criticism can make but feeble show. Appreciation, hearkening is the only true criticism. Further, that species of criticism which calls itself dramatic criticism is a needless adjunct to his plays. When the art of a dramatist is perfect the critic is superfluous. Life is not to be criticized, but to be faced and lived. Again, if any plays demand a stage they are the plays of Ibsen. Not merely is this so because his plays have so much in common with the plays of other men that they were not written to cumber the shelves of a library, but because they are so packed with thought. At some chance expression the mind is tortured with some question, and in a flash long reaches of life are opened up in vista, yet the vision is momentary unless we stay to ponder on it. It is just to prevent excessive pondering that Ibsen requires to be acted. Finally, it is foolish to expect that a problem, which has occupied Ibsen for nearly three years, will unroll smoothly before our eyes on a first or second reading. So it is better to leave the drama to plead for itself. But this at least is clear, that in this play Ibsen has given us nearly the very best of himself. The action is neither hindered by many complexities, as in *The Pillars of Society*, nor harrowing in its simplicity, as in *Ghosts*. We have whimsicality, bordering on extravagance, in the wild Ulfheim, and subtle humour in the sly contempt which Rubek and Maja entertain for each other. But Ibsen has striven to let the drama have perfectly free action. So he has not bestowed his wonted pains on the minor characters. In many of his plays these minor characters are matchless creations. Witness Jacob Engstrand, Tönnesen, and the demonic Molvik! But in this play the minor characters are not allowed to divert our attention.

On the whole, *When We Dead Awaken* may rank with the greatest of the author's work — if, indeed, it be not the greatest. It is described as the last of the series, which began with *A Doll's House* — a grand epilogue to its ten predecessors. Than these dramas, excellent alike in dramaturgic skill, characterization, and supreme interest, the long roll of drama, ancient or modern, has few things better to show.

JAMES A. JOYCE

7

The Day of the Rabblement

1901

The Irish Literary Theatre, which was to become the Abbey Theatre, began its performances in May 1899, with Yeats's play, The Countess Cathleen. *Joyce was in the audience and applauded it vigorously; he refused to join his fellow-students in protesting its heresy. He also liked the company's second play, Edward Martyn's* The Heather Field.[1] *He attended, in February 1900, a performance of the new play by George Moore and Edward Martyn,* The Bending of the Bough, *and liked it well enough to write a play of his own,* A Brilliant Career, *probably with the intention of submitting it to the Irish Literary Theatre. But William Archer, who read the play in manuscript, pointed out serious flaws in it, and Joyce went no further.*

Meanwhile the theatre had become definitely, and to his mind, obnoxiously Irish. He was dismayed to learn in October 1901, that the next plays would be Douglas Hyde's Casad-an-Súgán, *written in Irish, and an unrealistic play,* Diarmuid and Grania, *which Yeats and Moore had taken from Irish heroic legend. On the morning of October 15, 1901, Joyce quickly wrote an indignant article condemning the theatre for its parochialism.*

He submitted the article to the editor of St. Stephen's, *a new magazine which some students of University College had just begun to publish. The article was rejected not by the editor but by the adviser, Father Henry Browne. Joyce appealed to the president of the college, but while he disavowed any responsibility for the rejection he did not overrule Father Browne. Meanwhile Joyce's friend, Francis Skeffington, met the same rebuff for an essay he had written on 'A Forgotten Aspect of the University Question', in which he advocated equal status for women. Joyce proposed that they join and publish the*

---

[1] See Joyce's programme note to this play, written in 1918 (pp. 251–2 below).

essays together at their own expense. Since neither agreed with the other's position, while both resented censorship, they added a preface which read: 'These two Essays were commissioned by the Editor of St. Stephen's for that paper, but were subsequently refused insertion by the Censor. The writers are now publishing them in their original form, and each writer is responsible only for what appears under his own name. F.J.C.S. J.A.J.' About eighty-five copies were printed for them by a stationery shop on Stephen's Green, Gerrard Brothers, probably in November 1901; *they were distributed by the two authors and by Stanislaus Joyce, who remembered delivering one to George Moore's maidservant. A review of the pamphlet was published in* St. Stephen's *in December; it disagreed violently with Joyce's position and even recalled bitterly his refusal, a year and a half before, to sign the* Countess Cathleen *petition.*[1]

———————

No man, said the Nolan,[2] can be a lover of the true or the good unless he abhors the multitude;[3] and the artist, though he may employ the crowd, is very careful to isolate himself. This radical principle of artistic economy applies specially to a time of crisis, and today when the highest form of art has been just preserved by desperate sacrifices, it is strange to see the artist making terms with the rabblement. The Irish Literary Theatre is the latest movement of protest against the sterility and falsehood of the

One of Joyce's epiphanies indicates that the students' banter amused him:

> Hanna Sheehy — O, there are sure to be great crowds.
> Skeffington — In fact, it'll be, as our friend Jocax
> would say, the day of the rabblement.
> Maggie Sheehy — (*declaims*) — Even now the rabblement
> may be standing by the door.
> *Epiphanies*, p. 11.

[2] Giordano Bruno of Nola (1548?–1600), a favourite philosopher of Joyce, whose name is mentioned constantly in *Finnegans Wake*. In *My Brother's Keeper*, p. 146 (153), Stanislaus Joyce writes: 'Jim had kept the reference to "the Nolan" advisedly, overriding objections from me, his doubting Thomas. He intended that the readers of his article should have at first a false impression that he was quoting some little-known Irish writer — the definite article before some old family names being a courtesy title in Ireland — so that when they discovered their error, the name of Giordano Bruno might perhaps awaken some interest in his life and work. Laymen, he repeated, should be encouraged to think.'

[3] Joyce probably borrowed the quotation from I. Frith, *Life of Giordano Bruno, the Nolan* (London, 1887), where on p. 165 Bruno is quoted: 'No man truly loves goodness and truth who is not incensed with the multitude.'

modern stage. Half a century ago the note of protest was uttered in Norway, and since then in several countries long and disheartening battles have been fought against the hosts of prejudice and misinterpretation and ridicule. What triumph there has been here and there is due to stubborn conviction, and every movement that has set out heroically has achieved a little. The Irish Literary Theatre gave out that it was the champion of progress, and proclaimed war against commercialism and vulgarity. It had partly made good its word and was expelling the old devil, when after the first encounter it surrendered to the popular will. Now, your popular devil is more dangerous than your vulgar devil. Bulk and lungs count for something, and he can gild his speech aptly. He has prevailed once more, and the Irish Literary Theatre must now be considered the property of the rabblement of the most belated race in Europe.

It will be interesting to examine here. The official organ of the movement spoke of producing European masterpieces, but the matter went no further. Such a project was absolutely necessary. The censorship is powerless in Dublin, and the directors could have produced *Ghosts* or *The Dominion of Darkness* if they chose. Nothing can be done until the forces that dictate public judgement are calmly confronted. But, of course, the directors are shy of presenting Ibsen, Tolstoy or Hauptmann, where even *Countess Cathleen* is pronounced vicious and damnable. Even for a technical reason this project was necessary. A nation which never advanced so far as a miracle-play affords no literary model to the artist, and he must look abroad. Earnest dramatists of the second rank, Sudermann, Björnson, and Giacosa, can write very much better plays than the Irish Literary Theatre has staged. But, of course, the directors would not like to present such improper writers to the uncultivated, much less to the cultivated, rabblement. Accordingly, the rabblement, placid and intensely moral, is enthroned in boxes and galleries amid a hum of approval — *la bestia Trionfante*[1] — and those who think that Echegaray[2] is 'morbid', and titter coyly when Mélisande[3] lets down her hair, are not sure but they are the trustees of every intellectual and poetic treasure.

[1] Bruno wrote *Spaccio della Bestia Trionfante*, in which, however, the beast is not the rabblement of men but of human vices.

[2] José Echegaray y Eizaguirre (1832–1916), Spanish dramatist.

[3] In Maeterlinck's *Pelléas et Mélisande*.

Meanwhile, what of the artists? It is equally unsafe at present to say of Mr. Yeats that he has or has not genius. In aim and form *The Wind among the Reeds* is poetry of the highest order, and *The Adoration of the Magi* (a story which one of the great Russians might have written)[1] shows what Mr. Yeats can do when he breaks with the half-gods. But an aesthete has a floating will, and Mr. Yeats's treacherous instinct of adaptability must be blamed for his recent association with a platform from which even self-respect should have urged him to refrain. Mr. Martyn and Mr. Moore are not writers of much originality. Mr. Martyn, disabled as he is by an incorrigible style, has none of the fierce, hysterical power of Strindberg, whom he suggests at times; and with him one is conscious of a lack of breadth and distinction which outweighs the nobility of certain passages. Mr. Moore, however, has wonderful mimetic ability, and some years ago his books might have entitled him to the place of honour among English novelists. But though *Vain Fortune* (perhaps one should add some of *Esther Waters*) is fine, original work, Mr. Moore is really struggling in the backwash of that tide which has advanced from Flaubert through Jakobsen to D'Annunzio: for two entire eras lie between *Madame Bovary* and *Il Fuoco*. It is plain from *Celibates* and the later novels that Mr. Moore is beginning to draw upon his literary account, and the quest of a new impulse may explain his recent startling conversion. Converts are in the movement now, and Mr. Moore and his island have been fitly admired. But however frankly Mr. Moore may misquote Pater and Turgenieff to defend himself, his new impulse has no kind of relation to the future of art.

In such circumstances it has become imperative to define the position. If an artist courts the favour of the multitude he cannot escape the contagion of its fetichism and deliberate self-deception, and if he joins in a popular movement he does so at his own risk. Therefore, the Irish Literary Theatre by its surrender to the trolls has cut itself adrift from the line of advancement. Until he has freed himself from the mean influences about him — sodden enthusiasm and clever insinuation and every flattering influence of

---

[1] At a later meeting with Yeats, Joyce praised this story and *The Tables of the Law* so highly that in republishing them Yeats added a prefatory note saying: 'I do not think I should have reprinted them had I not met a young man in Ireland the other day, who liked them very much and nothing else that I have written.'

vanity and low ambition — no man is an artist at all. But his true servitude is that he inherits a will broken by doubt and a soul that yields up all its hate to a caress; and the most seeming-independent are those who are the first to reassume their bonds. But Truth deals largely with us. Elsewhere there are men who are worthy to carry on the tradition of the old master who is dying in Christiania. He has already found his successor in the writer of *Michael Kramer*,[1] and the third minister[2] will not be wanting when his hour comes. Even now that hour may be standing by the door.[3]

JAMES A. JOYCE

October 15th, 1901

[1] Gerhart Hauptmann. Joyce had translated *Vor Sonnenaufgang* in the summer of 1901, and had also translated *Michael Kramer*, probably in the same year.

[2] No doubt a reference to James Joyce.

[3] 'I tell you the younger generation will one day come and thunder at my door!' Ibsen, *The Master Builder*, Act I.

8

James Clarence Mangan[1]

1902

Joyce's essay on Mangan, delivered first as an address to the Literary and Historical Society of University College, Dublin, on February 15, 1902, was published in the unofficial college magazine, St. Stephen's, *in May of that year. Its air of discovering Mangan is a little pretentious, for Yeats and Lionel Johnson had both preceded Joyce in looking closely and admiringly at Mangan's verse, and several editions of Mangan's works had appeared during the ten years before Joyce wrote. The difficulties of the essay stem in part from its highly adorned, rhythmical style, and in part from Joyce's interest in developing a theory of the imaginative and artistic needs of Ireland at the same time that he sympathetically describes Mangan's unhappy career. So with one hand he praises Mangan's imaginative power, and with the other regrets the poet's melancholy acceptance of Ireland's woe as eternal, and, like Yeats, rejects his arid joylessness. The fusing of a classical strength and serenity to the intense romantic imagination is apparently what Joyce is calling for in his introduction and conclusion.*

In Stephen Hero *Joyce closely paraphrases the aesthetic theory of the Mangan essay, omits all mention of Mangan, and calls the essay 'Drama and Life', thus deliberately confusing it with the paper he had read two years before to the same college society.*

'Memorial I would have . . . a constant presence with those that love me.'

It is many a day since the dispute of the classical and romantic schools began in the quiet city of the arts, so that criticism, which

[1] Published in *St. Stephen's*, v. 1, no. 6 (May 1902) 116–18.

73

has wrongly decided that the classical temper is the romantic temper grown older, has been driven to recognize these as constant states of mind.[1] Though the dispute has been often ungentle (to say no more) and has seemed to some a dispute about names and with time has become a confused battle, each school advancing to the borders of the other and busy with internal strife, the classical school fighting the materialism which attends it, and the romantic school to preserve coherence, yet as this unrest is the condition of all achievement,[2] it is so far good, and presses slowly towards a deeper insight which will make the schools at one. Meanwhile no criticism is just which avoids labour by setting up a standard of maturity by which to judge the schools. The romantic school is often and grievously misinterpreted, not more by others than by its own, for that impatient temper which, as it could see no fit abode here for its ideals, chose to behold them under insensible figures, comes to disregard certain limitations, and, because these figures are blown high and low by the mind that conceived them, comes at times to regard them as feeble shadows moving aimlessly about the light, obscuring it;[3] and the same temper, which assuredly has not grown more patient, exclaims that the light is changed to worse than shadow, to darkness even, by any method which bends upon these present things and so works upon them and fashions them that the quick intelligence may go beyond them to their meaning, which is still unuttered. Yet so long as this place in nature is given us, it is right that art should do no violence to that gift, though it may go far beyond the stars and the waters in the service of what it loves. Wherefore the highest praise must be withheld from the romantic school (though the most enlight-

[1] 'Classicism is not the manner of any fixed age or of any fixed country; it is a constant state of the artistic mind.' *Stephen Hero*, pp. 78 (65–6).

[2] 'To many spectators the dispute had seemed a dispute about names, a battle in which the position of the standards could never be foretold for a minute. Add to this internecine warfare — the classical school fighting the materialism that must attend it, the romantic school struggling to preserve coherence — and behold from what ungentle manners criticism is bound to recognize the emergence of all achievement.' *Stephen Hero*, p. 79 (66).

[3] 'The romantic temper, so often and so grievously misinterpreted and not more by others than by its own, is an insecure, unsatisfied, impatient temper which sees no fit abode here for its ideals and chooses therefore to behold them under insensible figures. As a result of this choice it comes to disregard certain limitations. Its figures are blown to wild adventures, lacking the gravity of solid bodies, and the mind that has conceived them ends by disowning them.' *Stephen Hero*, p. 78 (66).

ened of Western poets[1] be thereby passed over), and the cause of
the impatient temper must be sought in the artist and in his
theme. Nor must the laws of his art be forgotten in the judgment
of the artist, for no error is more general than the judgment of a
man of letters by the supreme laws of poetry. Verse, indeed, is not
the only expression of rhythm, but poetry in any art transcends
the mode of its expression; and to name what is less than poetry
in the arts, there is need of new terms, though in one art the term
'literature'[2] may be used. Literature is the wide domain which lies
between ephemeral writing and poetry[3] (with which is philosophy),
and just as the greater part of verse is not literature, so even
original writers and thinkers must often be jealously denied the
most honourable title; and much of Wordsworth, and almost all
of Baudelaire, is merely literature in verse and must be judged by
the laws of literature. Finally, it must be asked concerning every
artist how he is in relation to the highest knowledge and to those
laws which do not take holiday because men and times forget
them. This is not to look for a message but to approach the temper
which has made the work, an old woman praying, or a young man
fastening his shoe, and to see what is there well done and how
much it signifies. A song by Shakespeare or Verlaine, which seems
so free and living and as remote from any conscious purpose as
rain that falls in a garden or the lights of evening, is discovered to
be the rhythmic speech of an emotion otherwise incommunicable,
at least so fitly.[4] But to approach the temper which has made art
is an act of reverence and many conventions must be first put off,
for certainly the inmost region will never yield to one who is enmeshed with profanities.[5]

That was a strange question which the innocent Parsifal asked

[1] Stanislaus Joyce points out that by this cryptic phrase his brother meant
Blake.

[2] For Joyce, a derogatory term.

[3] See footnote 2, p. 39 above.

[4] Compare Joyce's definition of the lyrical form in the *Portrait*, p. 481 (243).

[5] 'The critic is he who is able, by means of the signs which the artist affords, to
approach the temper which has made the work and to see what is well done therein
and what it signifies. For him a song by Shakespeare which seems so free and
living, as remote from any conscious purpose as rain that falls in a garden or as
the lights of evening, discovers itself as the rhythmic speech of an emotion otherwise incommunicable, or at least not so fitly. But to approach the temper which
has made art is an act of reverence before the performance of which many conventions must be first put off for certainly that inmost region will never yield its secret
to one who is enmeshed with profanities.' *Stephen Hero*, p. 79 (66).

— 'Who is good?'[1] and it is recalled to mind when one reads certain criticisms and biographies, for which the influence of a modern writer,[2] misunderstood as the worship of broad-cloth, is answerable. When these criticisms are insincere they are humorous, but the case is worse when they are as sincere as such things can be. And so, when Mangan is remembered in his country (for he is sometimes spoken of in literary societies), his countrymen lament that such poetic faculty was mated with so little rectitude of conduct, surprised to find this faculty in a man whose vices were exotic and who was little of a patriot. Those who have written of him, have been scrupulous in holding the balance between the drunkard and the opium-eater, and have sought to discover whether learning or imposture lies behind such phrases as 'from the Ottoman' or 'from the Coptic': and save for this small remembrance, Mangan has been a stranger in his country, a rare and unsympathetic figure in the streets, where he is seen going forward alone like one who does penance for some ancient sin. Surely life, which Novalis has called a malady of the spirit,[3] is a heavy penance for him who has, perhaps, forgotten the sin that laid it upon him, a sorrowful portion, too, because of that fine artist in him which reads so truly the lines of brutality and of weakness in the faces of men that are thrust in upon his path. He bears it well for the most part, acquiescing in the justice which has made him a vessel of wrath, but in a moment of frenzy he breaks silence, and we read how his associates dishonoured his person with their slime and venom, and how he lived as a child amid coarseness and misery and that all whom he met were demons out of the pit and that his father was a human boa-constrictor.[4] Certainly he is wiser who accuses no man of acting unjustly towards him, seeing that what is called injustice is never so but is an aspect of justice, yet they who think that such a terrible tale is the figment of a disordered brain do not know how keenly a sensitive boy suffers from contact with a gross nature. Mangan, however, is not without some consolation, for his sufferings have cast him inwards, where for many

[1] In Wagner's *Parsifal*, Act I.
[2] Stanislaus Joyce points out that Browning is meant.
[3] Novalis, *Fragmente*, Vermischten Inhalts, p. 135.
[4] Joyce is quoting Mangan's 'Fragment of an Unpublished Autobiography', *Irish Monthly*, v. 10 (1882) 678: 'If anyone can imagine such an idea as a human boa-constrictor, without his alimentative propensities, he will be able to form some notion of the character of my father.' In *Finnegans Wake* Joyce has Shem say, 'Mynfadher was a boer constructor,' p. 180.

ages the sad and the wise have elected to be. When someone told him that the account which he had given of his early life, so full of things which were, indeed, the beginnings of sorrows, was wildly overstated, and partly false, he answered — 'Maybe I dreamed it.' The world, you see, has become somewhat unreal for him, and he has begun to contemn that which is, in fine, the occasion of much error. How will it be with those dreams which, for every young and simple heart, take such dear reality upon themselves? One whose nature is so sensitive cannot forget his dreams in a secure, strenuous life. He doubts them, and puts them from him for a time, but when he hears men denying them with an oath he would acknowledge them proudly, and where sensitiveness has induced weakness, or, as here, refined upon natural weakness, would even compromise with the world, and win from it in return the favour of silence, if no more, as for something too slight to bear a violent disdain, for that desire of the heart so loudly derided, that rudely entreated idea. His manner is such that none can say if it be pride or humility that looks out of that vague face, which seems to live only because of those light shining eyes and of the fair silken hair above it, of which he is a little vain. This purely defensive reserve is not without dangers for him, and in the end it is only his excesses that save him from indifference. Something has been written of an affair of the heart between him and a pupil of his, to whom he gave lessons in German, and, it seems, he was an actor afterwards in a love-comedy of three, but if he is reserved with men, he is shy with women, and he is too self-conscious, too critical, knows too little of the soft parts of conversation, for a gallant. And in his strange dress, in which some have seen eccentricity, and others affectation — the high, conical hat, the loose trousers many sizes too big for him, and the old umbrella, so like a bagpipes — one may see a half-conscious expression of this. The lore of many lands goes with him always, eastern tales and the memory of curiously printed medieval books which have rapt him out of his time — gathered together day by day and embroidered as in a web. He has acquaintance with a score of languages, of which, upon occasion, he makes a liberal parade, and has read recklessly in many literatures, crossing how many seas, and even penetrating into Peristan, to which no road leads that the feet travel. In Timbuctooese, he confesses with a charming modesty which should prevent detractors, he is slightly deficient, but this is no cause for regret. He is interested, too, in the life of the seeress of Prevorst,[1] and in all phenomena of the middle nature and here, where most of all the sweetness and resoluteness of the soul have power, he seems to seek in a world, how different from that in which Watteau may have sought, both with a certain graceful inconstancy, 'what is there in no satisfying measure or not at all.'[2]

His writings, which have never been collected and which are unknown, except for two American editions of selected poems and some pages of prose, published by Duffy, show no order and sometimes very little thought. Many of his essays are pretty fooling when read once, but one cannot but discern some fierce energy beneath the banter, which follows up the phrases with no good intent, and there is a likeness between the desperate writer, himself the victim of too dexterous torture, and the contorted writing. Mangan, it must be remembered, wrote with no native literary tradition to guide him, and for a public which cared for matters of the day, and for poetry only so far as it might illustrate these. He could not often revise what he wrote, and he has often striven with Moore and Walsh[3] on their own ground. But the best of what he has written makes its appeal surely, because it was conceived by the imagination which he called, I think, the mother of things, whose dream are we, who imageth us to herself, and to ourselves, and imageth herself in us — the power before whose breath the mind in creation is (to use Shelley's image) as a fading coal.[4] Though even in the best of Mangan the presence of alien emotions is sometimes felt the presence of an imaginative personality reflecting the light of imaginative beauty is more vividly felt. East and West meet in that personality (we know how); images interweave there like soft, luminous scarves and words ring like brilliant mail, and whether the song is of Ireland or of Istambol it has the same refrain, a prayer that peace may come again to her who has lost her peace, the moonwhite pearl of his soul, Ameen.[5] Music and odours and lights are spread about her,

[1] Frédérique Hauffe, an early nineteenth-century victim of psychosomatic hallucination.

[2] From Pater's 'A Prince of Court Poets', in *Imaginary Portraits*.

[3] Edward Walsh, the Irish poet.

[4] In *Defence of Poetry*. Joyce repeats Shelley's phrase in the Mangan lecture (p. 182 below), in the *Portrait*, p. 479 (272), and in *Ulysses*, p. 192 (183).

[5] Joyce takes the name from Mangan's poem 'The Last Words of Al-Hassan'.

and he would search the dews and the sands that he might set another glory near her face. A scenery and a world have grown up about her face, as they will about any face which the eyes have regarded with love. Vittoria Colonna[1] and Laura and Beatrice — even she upon whose face many lives have cast that shadowy delicacy, as of one who broods upon distant terrors and riotous dreams, and that strange stillness before which love is silent, Mona Lisa — embody one chivalrous idea, which is no mortal thing, bearing it bravely above the accidents of lust and faithlessness and weariness; and she whose white and holy hands have the virtue of enchanted hands, his virgin flower, and flower of flowers, is no less than these an embodiment of that idea. How the East is laid under tribute for her and must bring all its treasures to her feet! The sea that foams over saffron sands, the lonely cedar on the Balkans, the hall dama- scened with moons of gold and a breath of roses from the gulistan — all these shall be where she is in willing service: reverence and peace shall be the service of the heart, as in the verses 'To Mihri':

> *My starlight, my moonlight, my midnight, my noonlight,*
> *Unveil not, unveil not!*

And where the music shakes off its languor and is full of the ecstasy of combat, as in the 'Lament for Sir Maurice FitzGerald', and in 'Dark Rosaleen', it does not attain to the quality of Whit- man indeed, but is tremulous with all the changing harmonies of Shelley's verse. Now and then this note is hoarsened and a troop of unmannerly passions echoes it derisively, but two poems at least sustain the music unbroken, the 'Swabian Popular Song',[2]

---

[1] Michelangelo's inspiration.
[2] This poem, a useful example of Joyce's taste at the time, begins:

> *Where are they, the belovèd,*
> *The gladsome, all?*
> *Where are they, the belovèd,*
> *The gladsome all?*
> *They left the festal hearth and hall*
> *They pine afar from us in alien climes.*
> *O, who shall bring them back to us once more?*
> *Who shall restore*
> *Life's fairy floral times?*
> *Restore*
> *Life's fairy, floral times?*

and a translation of two quatrains by Wetzel.[1] To create a little flower, Blake said, is the labour of ages, and even one lyric has made Dowland immortal;[2] and the matchless passages which are found in other poems are so good that they could not have been written by anyone but Mangan. He might have written a treatise on the poetical art for he is more cunning in his use of the musical echo than is Poe, the high priest of most modern schools, and there is a mastery, which no school can teach, but which obeys an interior command, which we may trace in 'Kathaleen-Ny-Houlahan', where the refrain changes the trochaic scheme abruptly for a line of firm, marching iambs.[3]

All his poetry remembers wrong and suffering and the aspiration of one who has suffered and who is moved to great cries and gestures when that sorrowful hour rushes upon the heart. This is the theme of a hundred songs but of none so intense as these songs which are made in noble misery, as his favourite Swedenborg would say, out of the vastation of soul. Naomi would change her name to Mara, because it has gone bitterly with her, and is it not the deep sense of sorrow and bitterness which explains these names and titles and this fury of translation in which he has sought to lose himself? For he has not found in himself the faith of the solitary, or the faith, which in the middle age, sent the spires singing up to heaven, and he waits for the final scene to end the penance. Weaker than Leopardi, for he has not the courage of his own despair but forgets all ills and forgoes his scorn at the showing of some favour, he has, perhaps for this reason, the memorial he

---

[1] The poem, actually three quatrains, is Wetzel's 'Good Night':

> *Good Night, Good Night, my Lyre!*
> *A long, a last Good Night!*
> *In ashes lies the fire*
> *That lent me Warmth and Light.*
>
> *With Love, Life too is fled;*
> *My bosom's blood is cold;*
> *My mind is all but dead;*
> *My heart is growing old.*
>
> *Soon will my sad eyes close,*
> *O, Lyre, on Earth and Thee!*
> *I go to woo Repose*
> *In God's Eternity!*

[2] Joyce's favourite among Dowland's songs, according to Stanislaus Joyce, was 'Weep ye no more, sad fountains'.

[3] The line is:

> *May he show forth His might in saving Kathaleen Ny-Houlahan!*

would have had — a constant presence with those that love him — and bears witness, as the more heroic pessimist bears witness against his will to the calm fortitude of humanity, to a subtle sympathy with health and joyousness which is seldom found in one whose health is safe. And so he does not shrink from the grave and the busy workings of the earth so much as from the unfriendly eyes of women and the hard eyes of men. To tell the truth, he has been in love with death all his life, like another,[1] and with no woman, and he has the same gentle manner as of old to welcome him whose face is hidden with a cloud, who is named Azrael.[2] Those whom the flames of too fierce love have wasted on earth become after death pale phantoms among the winds of desire,[3] and, as he strove here towards peace with the ardour of the wretched, it may be that now the winds of peace visit him and he rests, and remembers no more this bitter vestment of the body.

Poetry, even when apparently most fantastic, is always a revolt against artifice, a revolt, in a sense, against actuality. It speaks of what seems fantastic and unreal to those who have lost the simple intuitions which are the tests of reality; and, as it is often found at war with its age, so it makes no account of history, which is fabled by the daughters of memory,[4] but sets store by every time less than the pulsation of an artery, the time in which its intuitions start forth, holding it equal in its period and value to six thousand years.[5] No doubt they are only men of letters who insist on the succession of the ages, and history or the denial of reality, for they are two names for one thing, may be said to be that which deceives the whole world. In this, as in much else, Mangan is the type of his race. History encloses him so straitly that even his fiery moments do not set him free from it. He, too, cries out, in his life and in his mournful verses, against the injustice of despoilers, but never laments a deeper loss than the loss of plaids and ornaments. He inherits the latest and worst part of a legend upon which the

[1] Presumably Keats.

[2] The angel of death in Mohammedan mythology. Mangan's poem is entitled 'The Angel of Death'.

[3] *Inferno*, Canto 5.

[4] 'Fabled by the daughters of memory.' *Ulysses*, p. 25 (21); the phrase is from Blake's notes on *A Vision of the Last Judgment* (London, Nonesuch Press, 1948) pp. 637–8.

[5] This phrasing, which Joyce took from Blake's *Milton* (Sections 30–1) is repeated in the Blake lecture, (p. 222 below).

line has never been drawn out and which divides against itself as
it moves down the cycles.[1] And because this tradition is so much
with him he has accepted it with all its griefs and failures, and has
not known how to change it, as the strong spirit knows, and so
would bequeath it: the poet who hurls his anger against tyrants
would establish upon the future an intimate and far more cruel
tyranny. In the final view the figure which he worships is seen to
be an abject queen upon whom, because of the bloody crimes that
she has done and of those as bloody that were done to her, madness is come and death is coming, but who will not believe that
she is near to die and remembers only the rumour of voices
challenging her sacred gardens and her fair, tall flowers that have
become the food of boars. Novalis said of love that it is the Amen
of the universe,[2] and Mangan can tell of the beauty of hate; and
pure hate is as excellent as pure love. An eager spirit would cast
down with violence the high traditions of Mangan's race — love
of sorrow for the sake of sorrow and despair and fearful menaces —
but where their voice is a supreme entreaty to be borne with
forbearance seems only a little grace; and what is so courteous
and so patient as a great faith?

Every age must look for its sanction to its poetry and philosophy, for in these the human mind, as it looks backward or
forward, attains to an eternal state. The philosophic mind inclines
always to an elaborate life — the life of Goethe or of Leonardo da
Vinci; but the life of the poet is intense — the life of Blake or of
Dante — taking into its centre the life that surrounds it and
flinging it abroad again amid planetary music.[3] With Mangan a
narrow and hysterical nationality receives a last justification, for
when this feeble-bodied figure departs dusk begins to veil the
train of the gods, and he who listens may hear their footsteps
leaving the world. But the ancient gods, who are visions of the
divine names, die and come to life many times, and, though there
is dusk about their feet and darkness in their indifferent eyes, the

---

[1] 'He stood towards the myth upon which no individual mind had ever drawn
out a line of beauty and to its unwieldy tales that divided themselves as they
moved down the cycles in the same attitude as towards the Roman catholic religion, the attitude of a dull witted loyal serf.' *Portrait*, p. 442 (205).

[2] *Fragmente*, Fortsetzung, p. 452.

[3] 'The poet is the intense centre of the life of his age to which he stands in a
relation than which none can be more vital. He alone is capable of absorbing in
himself the life that surrounds him **and of flinging it abroad again amid planetary**
music.' *Stephen Hero*, p. 80 (67).

miracle of light is renewed eternally in the imaginative soul.[1] When the sterile and treacherous order is broken up, a voice or a host of voices is heard singing, a little faintly at first, of a serene spirit which enters woods and cities and the hearts of men, and of the life of earth — det dejlige vidunderlige jordliv det gaadefulde jordliv[2] — beautiful, alluring, mysterious.

Beauty, the splendour of truth,[3] is a gracious presence when the imagination contemplates intensely the truth of its own being or the visible world, and the spirit which proceeds out of truth and beauty is the holy spirit of joy. These are realities and these alone give and sustain life. As often as human fear and cruelty, that wicked monster begotten by luxury, are in league to make life ignoble and sullen and to speak evil of death the time is come wherein a man of timid courage seizes the keys of hell and of death, and flings them far out into the abyss, proclaiming the praise of life, which the abiding splendour of truth may sanctify, and of death, the most beautiful form of life.[4] In those vast courses which enfold us and in that great memory[5] which is greater and more generous than our memory, no life, no moment of exaltation is ever lost; and all those who have written nobly have not written in vain, though the desperate and weary have never heard the silver laughter of wisdom. Nay, shall not such as these have part, because of that high, original purpose which remembering painfully or by way of prophecy they would make clear, in the continual affirmation of the spirit?[6]

JAMES A. JOYCE

[1] The cyclical theory here expressed is orthodox Theosophy, in which Joyce was much interested, and anticipates the death of Finnegan and his rebirth as Earwicker.

[2] 'This beautiful, miraculous earth-life, this inscrutable earth-life,' Ibsen's *When We Dead Awaken*, Act III.

[3] 'Beauty, the splendour of truth, has been born,' *Stephen Hero*, p. 80 (68); 'Plato, I believe, said that beauty is the splendour of truth,' *Portrait*, p. 473 (236). See also Flaubert's letter, footnote 1, p. 141 below, from which Joyce took this quotation.

[4] 'Death is the highest form of life.' *Ulysses*, p. 493 (479).

[5] Also a theosophical notion, but Joyce probably learned the phrase from Yeats, who sometimes calls it, following Henry More, 'anima mundi.'

[6] 'Thus the spirit of man makes a continual affirmation', *Stephen Hero*, p. 80 (68). 'Bloom dissented tacitly from Stephen's views on the eternal affirmation of man in literature', *Ulysses*, p. 650 (627).

9

An Irish Poet[1]

1902

The Irish literary revival was always in danger of becoming, as Joyce remarked in Ulysses, 'all too Irish,' and would probably have come to nothing if Yeats had not gained his point that literature should be national but not patriotic. Such a distinction was too subtle to be rigidly enforced, and William Rooney was one of the poetasters whose verse was distinguished by its patriotic fervour alone. Rooney had helped Arthur Griffith to found the Sinn Fein ('We Ourselves') movement and had been a principal contributor to its newspaper the United Irishman; *some time after Rooney died in 1901, at the age of twenty-eight, the newspaper published a collection of his verse. Though Joyce was sympathetic, as his brother makes clear, to the aims and methods of Sinn Fein, he did not hesitate to attack Rooney as a poet. Griffith responded sarcastically to Joyce's unsigned review in the* Daily Express *(which was notoriously pro-English) by publishing an advertisement for Rooney's book in the* United Irishman *on December 20, 1902. In it he quoted much of the hostile review and added as his only comment a single bracketed word to Joyce's sentence: 'And yet he might have written well if he had not suffered from one of those big words [Patriotism] which make us so unhappy.' In 'The Dead' Gabriel Conroy is similarly twitted by the patriotic Miss Ivors for his book reviews in the 'West Briton'* Daily Express.

These are the verses of a writer lately dead, whom many consider the Davis[2] of the latest national movement. They are issued from

[1] A review of William Rooney's *Poems and Ballads*, published in the *Daily Express*, Dublin, December 11, 1902.

[2] Thomas Davis (1814–45), the most prominent of the *Nation* poets and the literary hero of the nationalist faction even at this time.

headquarters, and are preceded by two introductions wherein there is much said concerning the working man, mutual improvement, the superior person, shady musical plays, etc. They are illustrative of the national temper, and because they are so the writers of the introductions do not hesitate to claim for them the highest honours. But this claim cannot be allowed, unless it is supported by certain evidences of literary sincerity. For a man who writes a book cannot be excused by his good intentions, or by his moral character; he enters into a region where there is question of the written word, and it is well that this should be borne in mind, now that the region of literature is assailed so fiercely by the enthusiast and the doctrinaire.

An examination of the poems and ballads of William Rooney does not warrant one in claiming for them any high honours. The theme is consistently national, so uncompromising, indeed, that the reader must lift an eyebrow and assure himself when he meets on page 114 the name of D'Arcy MacGee.[1] But the treatment of the theme does not show the same admirable consistency. In 'S. Patrick's Day' and in 'Dromceat' one cannot but see an uninteresting imitation of Denis Florence M'Carthy and of Ferguson;[2] even Mr. T. D. Sullivan[3] and Mr. Rolleston[4] have done something in the making of this book. But 'Roilig na Riogh' is utterly lacking in the high distinctive virtue of 'The Dead at Clonmacnoise', and Mr. Rolleston, who certainly is not driven along by any poetic impulse, has written a poem because the very failure of the poetic impulse pleases in an epitaph. So much can careful writing achieve, and there can be no doubt that little is achieved in these verses, because the writing is so careless, and is yet so studiously mean. For, if carelessness is carried very far, it is like to become a positive virtue,[5] but an ordinary carelessness is nothing but a false and mean expression of a false and mean idea.

[1] Thomas D'Arcy MacGee (1825–68), one of the *Nation* poets involved in the uprising of '48, fled to Canada with a price on his head but later became a Minister of the Crown. During the Fenian movement he revisited Ireland and denounced the movement with such fervour that Irish partisans assassinated him in Ottawa in 1868.

[2] Sir Samuel Ferguson (1810–86).

[3] Timothy Daniel Sullivan (1827–1914), who appears disguised in 'From a Banned Writer to a Banned Singer' (p. 260 below).

[4] Thomas William Rolleston (1857–1920).

[5] Stanislaus Joyce wrote his brother in Paris in 1902 that carelessness — by which perhaps Joyce meant recklessness — could scarcely be a literary virtue,

Mr. Rooney, indeed, is almost a master in that 'style', which is neither good nor bad. In the verses of Maedhbh he writes:

> 'Mid the sheltering hills, by the spreading waters,
> They laid her down and her cairn raised
> The fiercest-hearted of Erin's daughters —
> The bravest nature that ever blazed.

Here the writer has not devised, he has merely accepted, mean expressions, and even where he has accepted a fine expression, he cannot justify his use of it. Mangan's Homeric epithet of 'wine-dark' becomes in his paper a colourless and meaningless epithet, which may cover any or all of the colours of the spectrum. How differently did Mangan write when he wrote:

> Knowest thou the castle that beetles over
> The wine-dark sea![1]

Here a colour rises in the mind and is set firmly against the golden glow in the lines that follow.

But one must not look for these things when patriotism has laid hold of the writer. He has no care then to create anything according to the art of literature, not the greatest of the arts,[2] indeed, but at least an art with a definite tradition behind it, possessing definite forms. Instead we find in these pages a weary succession of verses, 'prize' poems — the worst of all. They were written, it seems, for papers and societies week after week, and they bear witness to some desperate and weary energy. But they have no spiritual and living energy, because they come from one in whom the spirit is in a manner dead, or at least in its own hell, a weary and foolish spirit, speaking of redemption and revenge, blaspheming against tyrants, and going forth, full of tears and curses, upon its infernal labours. Religion and all that is allied thereto can manifestly persuade men to great evil, and by writing these verses, even though they should, as the writers of the prefaces think, enkindle the young men of Ireland to hope and activity, Mr. Rooney has been persuaded to great evil.

---

but that 'studious meanness', on the other hand, might serve a writer well. In defending *Dubliners* in a letter to Grant Richards of May 5, 1906, Joyce remarked, 'I have written it for the most part in a style of scrupulous meanness.'

[1] Joyce's liking for Mangan's blend of Shakespeare and Homer is understandable, since both the wine-dark sea and the beetling castle are cited in *Ulysses*.

[2] See footnote 2, p. 39 above.

And yet he might have written well if he had not suffered from one of those big words which make us so unhappy.[1] There is no piece in the book which has even the first quality of beauty, the quality of integrity, the quality of being separate and whole, but there is one piece in the book which seems to have come out of a conscious personal life. It is a translation of some verses by Dr. Douglas Hyde, and is called 'A Request', and yet I cannot believe that it owes more than its subject to its original. It begins:

> In that last dark hour when my bed I lie on,
> My narrow bed of the deal board bare,
> My kin and neighbours around me standing,
> And Death's broad wings on the thickening air.

It proceeds to gather desolation about itself, and does so in lines of living verse, as in the lines that follow. The third line is feeble, perhaps, but the fourth line is so astonishingly good that it cannot be overpraised:

> When night shall fall and my day is over
> And Death's pale symbol shall chill my face,
> When heart and hand thrill no more responsive,
> Oh Lord and Saviour, regard my case!

And when it has gathered about itself all the imagery of desolation, it remembers the Divine temptation, and puts up its prayer to the Divine mercy. It seems to come out of a personal life which has begun to realize itself, but to which death and that realization have come together. And in this manner, with the gravity of one who remembers all the errors of his members and his sins of speech, it goes into silence.

[1] 'I fear those big words, Stephen said, that make us so unhappy.' *Ulysses*, p. 32 (28).

10

George Meredith[1]

1902

Joyce as a young man liked the novels of Meredith. In Stephen Hero *the insistent comment and slightly patronizing air of the author probably owe something to Meredith's model, and Stephen's ecstasy in the fourth chapter of the* Portrait *is very likely indebted to comparable ecstasies in* The Ordeal of Richard Feverel. *In* Ulysses *Stephen borrows Meredith's definition of the sentimentalist to confound Buck Mulligan, and Joyce adapts Meredith's most radical technical device — the repetition of theme words with increasing ramifications until they coalesce in a significant statement. And, as his review implies, Joyce was interested in Meredith's vigorous wrestle with the problems of secular affirmation in a shaken age.*

Joyce had reservations about Meredith, too. Some are mentioned in his review. He was annoyed, as his brother Stanislaus discloses in My Brother's Keeper, *by Meredith's royalist poem, 'The Voyage of the Ophir', which celebrates the voyage around the empire taken in 1901 by the Prince and Princess of Wales; he told Stanislaus he would like to dedicate the story, 'An Encounter', to the author of that poem, presumably as a counter to smugness. In general, Meredith's poetry seemed to him the 'not very meritorious verse by a prose writer',[2] and he was indignant when John Quinn, in 1924, sold the manuscript of* Ulysses *to A. S. W. Rosenbach for $1975 and then bought back two manuscript poems of Meredith for $1400.*

M r. George Meredith has been included in the English men of letters series,[3] where he may be seen in honourable nearness to

[1] A review of Walter Jerrold's *George Meredith*, published in the *Daily Express*, Dublin, December 11, 1902.

[2] *Letters*, p. 211.

[3] Joyce's error for *English Writers Today*.

Mr. Hall Caine and Mr. Pinero. An age which has too keen a scent for contemporary values will often judge amiss, and, therefore, one must not complain when a writer who is, even for those who do not admire him unreservedly, a true man of letters, comes by his own in such a strange fashion. Mr. Jerrold in the biographical part of his book has to record a more than usual enormity of public taste, and if his book had recorded only this, something good would have been done; for it is certain that the public taste should be reproved, while it is by no means certain that Mr. Meredith is a martyr.

Mr. Jerrold confesses his faith in novels and plays[1] alike, and he will have it that 'Modern Love' is on the same plane with the 'Vita Nuova'. No one can deny to Mr. Meredith an occasional power of direct compelling speech (in a picture of a famine he wrote 'starving lords were wasp and moth')[2] but he is plainly lacking in that fluid quality, the lyrical impulse, which, it seems, has been often taken from the wise and given unto the foolish. And it is plain to all who believe in the tradition of literature that this quality cannot be replaced.

Mr. Meredith's eager brain, which will not let him be a poet, has, however, helped him to write novels which are, perhaps, unique in our time. Mr. Jerrold subjects each novel to a superficial analysis, and by doing so he has, I think, seized a fallacy for his readers. For these novels have, for the most part, no value as epical art, and Mr. Meredith has not the instinct of the epical artist.[3] But they have a distinct value as philosophical essays, and they reveal a philosopher at work with much cheerfulness upon a very stubborn problem. Any book about the philosopher is worth reading, unless we have given ourselves over deliberately to the excellent foppery of the world, and though Mr. Jerrold's book is not remarkable, it is worth reading.

[1] A slip for 'poems'.

[2] 'The Appeasement of Demeter'.

[3] Joyce's use of the terms 'lyrical' and 'epical' in this review suggests that he was working out the distinctions of the lyrical, epical and dramatic which he was to set down in his journal three months later, on March 6, 1903, and to use in the *Portrait*. His concern with defining these categories may stem from Yeats' discussion of the dramatic, lyrical, epical and romantic temperaments in his introduction to Lady Gregory's *Cuchulain of Muirthemne*, published earlier in 1902.

11

Today and Tomorrow in Ireland[1]

1903

Stephen Gwynn was one of the prominent Anglo-Irish intellectuals who took up the cause of Irish nationalism. Joyce welcomed his interest in the new Irish writers and Irish industries, but took the occasion to reiterate his contention, expressed earlier in 'The Day of the Rabblement' and 'James Clarence Mangan', that among Irish writers only Mangan and Yeats were worthy of note. No doubt their incantatory misery fulfilled some need of his own.

In this book, the latest addition to the already formidable mass of modern Anglo-Irish literature, Mr. Gwynn has collected ten essays from various reviews and journals, essays differing widely in interest, but for all of which he would claim a unity of subject. All the essays deal directly or indirectly with Ireland, and they combine in formulating a distinct accusation of English civilization and English modes of thought. For Mr. Gwynn, too, is a convert to the prevailing national movement, and professes himself a Nationalist, though his nationalism, as he says, has nothing irreconcilable about it. Give Ireland the status of Canada and Mr. Gwynn becomes an Imperialist at once. It is hard to say into what political party Mr. Gwynn should go, for he is too consistently Gaelic for the Parliamentarians, and too mild for the true patriots, who are beginning to speak a little vaguely about their friends the French.

Mr. Gwynn, however, is at least a member of that party which

[1] A review of Stephen Gwynn's *Today and To-morrow in Ireland*, published in the *Daily Express*, Dublin, January 29, 1903.

seeks to establish an Irish literature and Irish industries. The first essays in his book are literary criticisms, and it may be said at once that they are the least interesting. Some are mere records of events and some seem written to give English readers a general notion of what is meant by the Gaelic revival. Mr. Gwynn has evidently a sympathy with modern Irish writers, but his criticism of their work is in no way remarkable. In the opening essay he has somehow the air of discovering Mangan,[1] and he transcribes with some astonishment a few verses from 'O'Hussey's Ode to the Maguire'. Few as the verses are, they are enough to show the real value of the work of the modern writers, whom Mr. Gwynn regards as the voice of Celticism proper. Their work varies in merit, never rising (except in Mr. Yeats's case) above a certain fluency and an occasional distinction, and often falling so low that it has a value only as documentary evidence. It is work which has an interest of the day, but collectively it has not a third part of the value of the work of a man like Mangan, that creature of lightning, who has been, and is, a stranger among the people he ennobled, but who may yet come by his own as one of the greatest romantic poets among those who use the lyrical form.

Mr. Gwynn, however, is more successful in those essays which are illustrative of the industrial work which has been set in movement at different points of Ireland. His account of the establishing of the fishing industry in the West of Ireland is extremely interesting, and so are his accounts of dairies, old-fashioned and new-fashioned, and of carpet-making. These essays are written in a practical manner, and though they are supplemented by many quotations of dates and figures, they are also full of anecdotes. Mr. Gwynn has evidently a sense of the humorous, and it is pleasing to find this in a revivalist. He tells how, fishing one day, it was his fortune to meet with an old peasant whose thoughts ran all upon the traditional tales of his country and on the histories of great families. Mr. Gwynn's instinct as a fisherman got the better of his patriotism, and he confesses to a slight disappointment when, after a good catch on an unfavourable day, he earned no word of praise from the peasant, who said, following his own train

[1] Mangan's name was well known in Ireland, and in 1903 and 1904 two volumes of his prose and poetry were published under the editorship of D. J. O'Donoghue. But Joyce probably has more particularly in mind that his own celebration of Mangan was published eight months before Gwynn's book.

of thought, 'The Clancartys was great men, too. Is there any of them living?' The volume, admirably bound and printed, is a credit to the Dublin firm to whose enterprise its publication is due.[1]

[1] The last line of this review, as a letter from Joyce to his brother makes clear, was added by the editor.

12

A Suave Philosophy[1]

1903

As a young man Joyce bought and read a number of books of eastern mysticism and theosophy, sharing for a moment the interest which agitated Europe and America at the end of the nineteenth century. His review of Hall's book indicates how sympathetically he regarded a philosophy like Buddhism which put war aside as irrelevant. His own hatred of force emerges in both Exiles *and* Ulysses, *and the weapons of Stephen Dedalus in the* Portrait — *silence, exile, and cunning — are appropriately non-violent.*

In this book one reads about a people whose life is ordered according to beliefs and sympathies which will seem strange to us. The writer has very properly begun his account of that life by a brief exposition of Buddhism, and he sets forth so much of its history as illustrates its main principles. He omits some incidents which are among the most beautiful of the Buddhist legend — the kindly devas strewing flowers under the horse, and the story of the meeting of Buddha and his wife. But he states at some length the philosophy (if that be the proper name for it) of Buddhism.[2] The Burmese people seem naturally adapted to follow such a wise passive philosophy. Five things are the five supreme evils for them — fire, water, storms, robbers, and rulers. All things that are inimical to human peace are evil. Though Buddhism is essentially a philosophy built against the evils of existence, a philosophy which places its end in the annihilation of the personal life and

[1] A review of H. Fielding-Hall's *The Soul of a People*, published in the *Daily Express*, Dublin, February 6, 1903.
[2] 'Nothing could be further from the truth than to call . . . Buddhism a philosophy', Fielding-Hall, p. 22.

the personal will, the Burmese people have known how to trans-
form it into a rule of life at once simple and wise.

Our civilization, bequeathed to us by fierce adventurers, eaters
of meat and hunters, is so full of hurry and combat, so busy about
many things which perhaps are of no importance, that it cannot
but see something feeble in a civilization which smiles as it refuses
to make the battlefield the test of excellence. There is a Burmese
saying — 'The thoughts of his heart, these are the wealth of a
man', and Mr. Hall, who has lived in Burma for many years, draws
a picture of Burmese life which shows that a happiness, founded
upon peace of mind in all circumstances, has a high place in the
Burmese table of values. And happiness abides among this people:
the yellow-robed monks begging alms, the believers coming to tell
their beads in the temple, tiny rafts drifting down the river on the
night of some festival, each one bearing upon it a tiny lamp, a girl
sitting at evening in the shadow of the eaves until the young men come
'courting' — all this is part of a suave philosophy which does not
know that there is anything to justify tears and lamentations.[1] The
courtesies of life are not neglected; anger and rudeness of manners
are condemned; the animals themselves are glad to be under masters
who treat them as living beings worthy of pity and toleration.

Mr. Hall is one of the conquerors of this people, and as he does
not think it a warrior people he cannot predict for it any great
political future. But he knows that peace lies before it, and, perhaps in literature, or in some art, a national temper so serene and
order-loving may achieve itself. He gives a version of the story of
Ma Pa Da, which he calls 'Death, the Deliverer', and this story
itself is so pitiful that one would wish to know more of the Burmese
popular tales. He gives elsewhere a rendering in prose of a Burmese
love-song, which has, as may be seen, kept some of its charm,
though it has lost, no doubt, much of its music:

'The moon wooed the lotus in the night, the lotus was wooed by
the moon, and my sweetheart is their child. The flower opened in
the night, and she came forth; the petals moved and she was born.

'She is more beautiful than any flower; her face is as delicate as
the dusk; her hair is as night falling over the hills; her skin is as
bright as the diamond. She is very full of health, no sickness can
come near her.

---

[1] ' "What is there that can justify tears and lamentations?" — *Saying of the
Buddha*', Fielding-Hall, p. 144.

'When the wind blows I am afraid, when the breezes move I fear. I fear lest the south wind take her, I tremble lest the breath of evening woo her from me — so light is she, so graceful.

'Her dress is of gold, of silk and gold, and her bracelets are of fine gold. She has precious stones in her ears, but her eyes, what jewels can compare unto them?

'She is proud, my mistress; she is very proud, and all men are afraid of her. She is so beautiful and so proud that all men fear her.

'In the whole world there is none anywhere that can compare unto her'.[1]

Mr. Hall has written a most pleasing book in an easy and temperate style, a book which is full of interesting manners and stories. One is glad to see that even in these days of novels, religious and sensational, this book has run to four editions.

[1] Joyce modernizes the language slightly by substituting 'flower' twice for 'blossom' and 'has' for 'hath'.

13

An Effort at Precision in Thinking[1]

1903

He must be a hardy man who contends that the disputants in this book are common people. They are, happily for the peace of human animals, very uncommon people. For common people will not argue for any considerable time as to whether succession of appearances is or is not anything more than the appearance of succession. But these uncommon people, whose colloquies are recorded here at somewhat distressing length by Mr. Anstie, argue about such subtleties with a precision which is more apparent than real. The speakers will seem more precise than they are, for at one time they dispute eagerly over certainty of thought, though certainty is not a habit of the mind at all, but a quality of propositions, and the speakers are really arguing about certitude, and more than once all the speakers are agreed that sense impressions mark the furthest limit of knowledge, and that 'reasonable belief' is an oxymoron — conclusions with which the man of the people, who is no philosopher, professes himself in loud accord. However, this book is an effort at precision in thinking, even if it does not always provoke that stimulated attention which one speaker calls a form of activity.

[1] A review of James Anstie's *Colloquies of Common People*, published in the *Daily Express*, Dublin, February 6, 1903.

14

Colonial Verses[1]

1903

These are colonial verses. The colonial Esau is asked on page 3 would he change his pottage for Jacob's birthright[2] — a question which evidently expects the answer, No. One piece is named 'Is Canada Loyal?' and Mr. Wolley proclaims that it is loyal. His verse is for the most part loyal, and where it is not, it describes Canadian scenery. Mr. Wolley says that he is a barbarian; he does not want the 'murmurous muddle' of the choir; he wants a 'clean-cut creed', 'plain laws for plain men'. There is a piece called 'Tableau', about a girl dreaming in a picture gallery. It begins: 'I wonder if it's really true that you are only paint.'

[1] A review of Clive Phillips-Wolley's *Songs of an English Esau*, published in the *Daily Express*, Dublin, February 6, 1903.

[2] Esau and Jacob, and the invader and the native, are among the brother-opposites who pursue their conflict in *Finnegans Wake*.

15

Catilina[1]

1903

Ibsen wrote his first play, Catilina, *when he was twenty-one, and Joyce was the same age when he wrote his review of a French translation of it. While recognizing the play's immaturity, he was more interested in the way it anticipated the flowering of Ibsen's early manner in* Peer Gynt. *He was taken with the reckless, extravagant Catiline, passionately involved with himself more than with his loves, part saviour and part destroyer, torn between ruthlessness and pity, and he must have remarked the passage in which Catiline declares,*

> I dreamed that, winged like Icarus of old,
> I flew aloft beneath the vault of heaven.

The early Ibsen, mirrored in Catilina, *helped to shape Joyce's conception of his own youth. That he called himself Dedalus instead of Icarus was due in part to his desire to represent his hero as the daring maker rather than the daring doer, but there are suggestions in the* Portrait, *which become explicit in* Ulysses, *that the proud, fallen Stephen is Icarus too.*

Joyce's review becomes more eloquent and more irrelevant as it proceeds. It demonstrates how ready he was, with slight pretext, to turn upon professional critics who did not admire Ibsen enough, and upon younger contemporaries who, putting off belief, threw out precision too. The image of Ibsen's ironic self-possession as the fortress of a turbulent spirit caught Joyce's imagination. Here, as in later books, he describes war, politics, and religion as making their hysterical demands while the artist moves calmly apart.

The French translators of this play have included in their preface some extracts from Ibsen's preface to the Dresden edition

[1] A review of a French translation of Ibsen's *Catilina*, published in the *Speaker*, London, n.s., v. 7 (March 21, 1903) 615.

of 1875, and these extracts tell somewhat humorously the history of Ibsen's early years. The play was written in 1848, when Ibsen was twenty, a poor student working all day in a druggist's shop, and studying during the night as best he could. Sallust and Cicero, it seems, awakened his interest in the character of Catiline, and he set to work to write a tragedy, in part historical, and in part political, a reflection of the Norway of his day. The play was politely refused by the directors of the Christiania Theatre and by all the publishers. One of Ibsen's friends, however, published it at his own expense, fully convinced that the play would at once make the writer's name famous in the world. A few copies were sold and, as Ibsen and his friend were in need of money, they were glad to sell the remainder to a pork-butcher. 'For some days', Ibsen writes, 'we did not lack the necessaries of life.' This is a sufficiently instructive history, and it is well to remember it when reading a play which Ibsen publishes simply that his work may be complete. For the writer of *Catilina* is not the Ibsen of the social dramas, but, as the French translators joyfully proclaim, an ardent romantic exulting in disturbance and escaping from all formal laws under cover of an abundant rhetoric. This will not appear so strange when it is remembered that the young Goethe was somewhat given to alchemical researches, and as, to quote Goethe himself, the form in which a man goes into the shadows is the form in which he moves among his posterity, posterity will probably forget Ibsen the romantic as completely as it forgets Goethe and his athanor.

Yet, in some ways, this earlier manner suggests the later manner. In *Catilina* three figures are projected against the background of a restless and moribund society — Catiline, Aurelia, his wife, and Fulvia,[1] a vestal virgin. Ibsen is known to the general public as a man who writes a play about three people[2] — usually one man and two women — and even critics, while they assert their admiration for Ibsen's 'unqualified objectivity', find that all his women are the same woman renamed successively Nora, Rebecca, Hilda, Irene — find, that is to say, that Ibsen has no power of objectivity at all. The critics, speaking in the name of the audience, whose idol is common sense, and whose torment is to be confronted with a clear

[1] A slip for Furia, the actual name of the character in Ibsen's play.

[2] Joyce found the formula of three almost as congenial as Ibsen did; it is used in 'The Dead', *Exiles*, *Ulysses*, and *Finnegans Wake*.

work of art that reflects every obscurity like a mirror, have sometimes had the courage to say that they did not understand the system
of three. They will be pleased to learn that some of the characters
in *Catilina* are in as sorry a plight as themselves. Here is a passage
in which Curius, a young relative of Catiline, professes his inability
to understand Catiline's relations with Fulvia and Aurelia:

> CURIUS: *Les aimerais-tu toutes deux à la fois?*
> *Vraiment je n'y comprends plus rien.*
> CATILINA: *En effet c'est singulier et je n'y comprends*
> *rien moi-même.*

But perhaps that he does not understand is part of the tragedy,
and the play is certainly the struggle between Aurelia, who is
happiness and the policy of non-interference, and Fulvia, who is
at first the policy of interference and who, when she has escaped
from the tomb to which her sin had brought her, becomes the
figure of Catiline's destiny. Very little use is made in this play of
alarms and battles, and one can see that the writer is not interested
in the usual property of romanticism. Already he is losing the
romantic temper when it should be at its fiercest in him, and, as
youth commonly brooks no prevention, he is content to hurl himself upon the world and establish himself there defiantly until his
true weapons are ready to his hand. One must not take too seriously the solution of the drama in favour of Aurelia, for by the
time the last act is reached the characters have begun to mean
nothing to themselves and in the acted play would be related to
life only by the bodies of the performers. And here is the most
striking difference between Ibsen's earlier manner and his later
manner, between romantic work and classical work. The romantic
temper, imperfect and impatient as it is, cannot express itself
adequately unless it employs the monstrous or heroic. In *Catilina*
the women are absolute types, and the end of such a play cannot
but savour of dogma — a most proper thing in a priest but a most
improper in a poet. Moreover, as the breaking-up of tradition,
which is the work of the modern era, discountenances the absolute
and as no writer can escape the spirit of his time, the writer of
dramas must remember now more than ever a principle of all
patient and perfect art which bids him express his fable in terms
of his characters.[1]

[1] Here again Joyce shows his devotion to Aristotle's aesthetic.

As a work of art *Catilina* has little merit, and yet one can see in it what the directors of the Christiania theatre and the publishers failed to see — an original and capable writer struggling with a form that is not his own. This manner continues, with occasional lapses into comedy, as far as *Peer Gynt*, in which, recognizing its own limitations and pushing lawlessness to its extreme limit, it achieves a masterpiece. After that it disappears and the second manner begins to take its place, advancing through play after play, uniting construction and speech and action more and more closely in a supple rhythm, until it achieves itself in *Hedda Gabler*. Very few recognize the astonishing courage of such work and it is characteristic of our age of transition to admire the later manner less than the earlier manner. For the imagination has the quality of a fluid, and it must be held firmly, lest it become vague, and delicately, that it may lose none of its magical powers.[1] And Ibsen has united with his strong, ample, imaginative faculty a pre-occupation with the things present to him. Perhaps in time even the professional critic, accepting the best of the social dramas for what they are — the most excellent examples of skill and intellectual self-possession — will make this union a truism of professional criticism. But meanwhile a young generation which has cast away belief and thrown precision after it, for which Balzac is a great intellect and every sampler who chooses to wander amid his own shapeless hells and heavens a Dante without the unfortunate prejudices of Dante,[2] will be troubled by this pre-occupation, and out of very conscience will denounce a method so calm, so ironical. These cries of hysteria are confused with many others — the voices of war and statecraft and religion — in the fermenting vat. But Boötes, we may be sure, thinks nothing of such cries, eager as ever at that ancient business of leading his hunting-dogs across the zenith 'in their leash of sidereal fire'.[3]

[1] Joyce's attribution of 'magical' powers to the imagination is probably indebted to Yeats, who often insisted on the word.

[2]   *For every true-born mysticist*
        A Dante is, unprejudiced.
        'The Holy Office', p. 150 below.

[3] 'These fringes of lamplight, struggling up through the smoke and thousand-fold exhalation, some fathoms into the ancient reign of Night, what thinks Boötes of them, as he leads his Hunting-Dogs over the Zenith in their leash of sidereal fire?' Carlyle, *Sartor Resartus*, Bk. 1, chapter 3.

101

16

The Soul of Ireland[1]

1903

Lady Gregory was one of the Irish writers whose help Joyce sought in November 1902, *when he was about to go to Paris to study medicine. She obligingly persuaded Longworth, the editor of the* Daily Express, *to take Joyce on as a reviewer. Possibly because of this connection, Longworth sent Joyce her* Poets and Dreamers *to review. No doubt the delight of Yeats and Lady Gregory in 'the folk' had become a little wearing to others by* 1903, *and Joyce, at any rate, was impatient with folklore. Shortly before his departure he had rebuked Yeats for his peasant plays, and he recklessly took the occasion now to rebuke Lady Gregory, who was not pleased by his review.*

Read today, Joyce's strictures on her pleasant book seem captious; but they were preliminary skirmishings in his battle for artistic independence. The pejorative comparison of Poets and Dreamers *with Yeats's* The Celtic Twilight *is gratuitous, but suggests how all-important the artist's shaping power was for Joyce. When, in his own last book, he deigned at last to make use of the materials of Irish folklore, he showed himself to be as much in tune with them as either Lady Gregory or Yeats.*

Lady Gregory's book had the virtue of forcing Joyce into a more personal and individual review than any of the other books that Longworth sent him. The covert national feeling implied in the final paragraph is rare in Joyce's essays of this time; it becomes prominent later in his Irish articles in the Piccolo della Sera *and in the lectures he delivered in Trieste.*

---

[1] A review of Lady Gregory's *Poets and Dreamers*, published in the *Daily Express*, Dublin, March 26, 1903. The review appeared over Joyce's initials, as Stanislaus Joyce points out, because Longworth wished to disclaim any personal responsibility for it.

Aristotle finds at the beginning of all speculation the feeling of wonder, a feeling proper to childhood, and if speculation be proper to the middle period of life it is natural that one should look to the crowning period of life for the fruit of speculation, wisdom itself. But nowadays people have greatly confused childhood and middle life and old age; those who succeed in spite of civilization in reaching old age seem to have less and less wisdom, and children who are usually put to some business as soon as they can walk and talk, seem to have more and more 'common sense'; and, perhaps, in the future little boys with long beards will stand aside and applaud, while old men in short trousers play handball against the side of a house.

This may even happen in Ireland, if Lady Gregory has truly set forth the old age of her country. In her new book she has left legends and heroic youth far behind, and has explored in a land almost fabulous in its sorrow and senility. Half of her book is an account of old men and old women in the West of Ireland. These old people are full of stories about giants and witches, and dogs and black-handled knives, and they tell their stories one after another at great length and with many repetitions (for they are people of leisure) by the fire or in the yard of a workhouse. It is difficult to judge well of their charms and herb-healing, for that is the province of those who are learned in these matters and can compare the customs of countries, and, indeed, it is well not to know these magical-sciences, for if the wind changes while you are cutting wild camomile you will lose your mind.

But one can judge more easily of their stories. These stories appeal to some feeling which is certainly not that feeling of wonder which is the beginning of all speculation. The story-tellers are old, and their imagination is not the imagination of childhood. The story-teller preserves the strange machinery of fairyland, but his mind is feeble and sleepy. He begins one story and wanders from it into another story, and none of the stories has any satisfying imaginative wholeness, none of them is like Sir John Daw's poem that cried tink in the close.[1] Lady Gregory is conscious of this, for she often tries to lead the speaker back to his story by questions, and when the story has become hopelessly involved, she tries to

[1] Ben Jonson, *Epicoene*, II, ii. While in Paris Joyce was reading through Jonson's works.

establish some wholeness by keeping only the less involved part; sometimes she listens 'half interested and half impatient'. In fine, her book, wherever it treats of the 'folk', sets forth in the fulness of its senility a class of mind which Mr. Yeats has set forth with such delicate scepticism in his happiest book, 'The Celtic Twilight'.

Something of health and naturalness, however, enters with Raftery, the poet. He had a terrible tongue, it seems, and would make a satirical poem for a very small offence. He could make love-poems, too (though Lady Gregory finds a certain falseness in the western love-poems), and repentant poems. Raftery, though he be the last of the great bardic procession, has much of the bardic tradition about him. He took shelter one day from the rain under a bush: at first the bush kept out the rain, and he made verses praising it, but after a while it let the rain through, and he made verses dispraising it.

Lady Gregory translates some of his verses, and she also translates some West Irish ballads and some poems by Dr. Douglas Hyde. She completes her book with translations of four one-act plays by Dr. Douglas Hyde, three of which have for their central figure that legendary person, who is vagabond and poet, and even saint at times, while the fourth play is called a 'nativity' play. The dwarf-drama (if one may use that term) is a form of art which is improper and ineffectual, but it is easy to understand why it finds favour with an age which has pictures that are 'nocturnes', and writers like Mallarmé and the composer of 'Récapitulation'.[1] The dwarf-drama is accordingly to be judged as an entertainment, and Dr. Douglas Hyde is certainly entertaining in the 'Twisting of the Rope', and Lady Gregory has succeeded better with her verse-translations here than elsewhere, as these four lines may show:

[1] The untutored linking of Whistler and Mallarmé with Catulle Mendès implies that they are freakish and soft. Mendès' trivial poem scarcely merits so much attention:

RÉCAPITULATION

Rose, Emmeline,	*Artémidore,*
Marguéridette,	*Myrrha, Myrrhine,*
Odette,	*Périne,*
Alix, Aline,	*Näis, Eudore.*
Paule, Hippolyte,	*Zulma, Zélie,*
Lucy, Lucile,	*Régine, Reine,*
Cécile,	*Irène!...*
Daphné, Melite.	*Et j'en oublie.*

I have heard the melodious harp
On the streets of Cork playing to us;
More melodious by far I thought your voice,
More melodious by far your mouth than that.

This book, like so many other books of our time, is in part picturesque and in part an indirect or direct utterance of the central belief of Ireland. Out of the material and spiritual battle which has gone so hardly with her Ireland has emerged with many memories of beliefs, and with one belief — a belief in the incurable ignobility of the forces that have overcome her[1] — and Lady Gregory, whose old men and women seem to be almost their own judges when they tell their wandering stories, might add to the passage from Whitman which forms her dedication,[2] Whitman's ambiguous word for the vanquished — 'Battles are lost in the spirit in which they are won.'[3]

J. J.

[1] In attitude and phrase Joyce is here close to Yeats, who also based his nationalism on a reaction to the vulgar materialism of the British, and celebrated Irish idealism in all its forms, including superstition, as a counter to it.

[2] *Will you seek afar off? You surely come back at last,*
In things best known to you finding the best, or as
good as the best;
In folks nearest to you finding the sweetest, strongest,
lovingest,
Happiness, knowledge not in another place but this place —
not for another hour but this hour.
[from 'A Song for Occupations']

The lines may have sounded admonitory to the young Irishman off in Paris.

[3] Joyce is distorting the meaning of Whitman's 'Song of Myself',
Have you heard that it was good to gain the day?
I also say it is good to fall, battles are lost in the same spirit
in which they are won,
to say that Ireland has been depressed to her conqueror's level of ignobility

17

The Motor Derby[1]

1903

What turned out to be Joyce's last money-making scheme in Paris was his notion of interviewing for the Irish Times *a French racing-car driver named Henri Fournier, who was scheduled to come to Dublin in July to compete in the second James Gordon Bennett cup race. A few days after this interview, which probably took place on April 5, Joyce received a telegram from his father, 'Mother dying come home. Father', and went back to Dublin on Good Friday, April 12. When the Bennett cup race took place, Joyce did not bother, according to his brother, to attend it, but he used his memories of Fournier in the story 'After the Race'. Though Joyce never thought highly of this story, it embodies, like 'The Dead' and 'A Little Cloud', his favourite theme of the conflict of native and exotic, and underneath the ironical plainness of his interview with Fournier it is not difficult to see in embryo something of the same conflict.*

In the Rue d'Anjou, not far from the Church of the Madeleine, is M. Henri Fournier's[2] place of business. 'Paris-Automobile' — a company of which M. Fournier is the manager — has its headquarters there. Inside the gateway is a big square court, roofed over, and on the floor of the court and on great shelves extending from the floor to the roof are ranged motor-cars of all sizes, shapes, and colours. In the afternoon this court is full of noises — the voices of workmen, the voices of buyers talking in half-a-dozen

---

[1] An article, subtitled 'Interview with the French Champion (from a correspondent)', published in the *Irish Times*, Dublin, April 7, 1903.

[2] Fournier, besides being French champion was one of the best racers of his time. He did not, however, win the Cup in Ireland.

languages, the ringing of telephone bells, the horns sounded by the 'chauffeurs' as the cars come in and go out — and it is almost impossible to see M. Fournier unless one is prepared to wait two or three hours for one's turn. But the buyers of 'autos' are, in one sense, people of leisure. The morning, however, is more favourable, and yesterday morning, after two failures, I succeeded in seeing M. Fournier.

M. Fournier is a slim, active-looking young man, with dark reddish hair. Early as the hour was our interview was now and again broken in upon by the importunate telephone.

'You are one of the competitors for the Gordon-Bennett Cup, M. Fournier?'

'Yes, I am one of the three selected to represent France.'

'And you are also a competitor, are you not, for the Madrid prize?'

'Yes.'

'Which of the races comes first—the Irish race or the Madrid race?'

'The Madrid race. It takes place early in May, while the race for the International Cup does not take place till July.'

'I suppose that you are preparing actively for your races?'

'Well, I have just returned from a tour to Monte Carlo and Nice.'

'On your racing machine?'

'No, on a machine of smaller power.'

'Have you determined what machine you will ride in the Irish race?'

'Practically.'

'May I ask the name of it — is it a Mercedes?'

'No, a Mors.'

'And its horse-power?'

'Eighty.'

'And on this machine you can travel at a rate of ——?'

'You mean its highest speed?'

'Yes.'

'Its highest speed would be a hundred and forty kilometres an hour.'

'But you will not go at that rate all the time during the race?'

'Oh, no. Of course its average speed for the race would be lower than that.'

'An average speed of how much?'

'Its average speed would be a hundred kilometres an hour, perhaps a little more than that, something between a hundred and a hundred and ten kilometres an hour.'

'A kilometre is about a half-mile, is it not?'

'More than that, I should think. There are how many yards in your mile?'

'Seventeen hundred and sixty, if I am right.'

'Then your half-mile has eight hundred and eighty yards. Our kilometre is just equal to eleven hundred yards.'

'Let me see. Then your top speed is nearly eighty-six miles an hour, and your average speed is sixty-one miles an hour?'

'I suppose so, if we calculate properly.'

'It is an appalling pace! It is enough to burn our roads. I suppose you have seen the roads you are to travel?'

'No.'

'No? You don't know the course, then?'

'I know it slightly. I know it, that is, from some sketches that were given of it in the Paris newspapers.'

'But, surely, you will want a better knowledge than that?'

'Oh, certainly. In fact, before the month is over, I intend to go to Ireland to inspect the course. Perhaps I shall go in three weeks' time.'

'Will you remain any time in Ireland?'

'After the race?'

'Yes.'

'I am afraid not. I should like to, but I don't think I can.'

'I suppose you would not like to be asked your opinion of the result?'

'Hardly.'

'Yet, which nation do you fear most?'

'I fear them all — Germans, Americans, and English. They are all to be feared.'

'And how about Mr. Edge?'

No answer.

'He won the prize the last time, did he not?'

'O, yes.'

'Then he should be your most formidable opponent?'

'O, yes . . . . But, you see, Mr. Edge won, of course, but . . . a man who was last of all, and had no chance of winning might win if the other machines broke.'

Whatever way one looks at this statement it appears difficult to challenge its truth.

18

Aristotle on Education[1]

1903

This book is compiled from the first three books of the Ethics, and the tenth book, with some extracts from the Politics. Unfortunately, the compilation is not a complete treatise on education, nor is it even exhaustive so far as it goes. The Ethics is seized upon by admirers and opponents alike as the weak part of the peripatetic philosophy. The modern notion of Aristotle as a biologist[2] — a notion popular among advocates of 'science' — is probably less true than the ancient notion of him as a metaphysician; and it is certainly in the higher applications of his severe method that he achieves himself. His theory of education is, however, not without interest, and is subordinate to his theory of the state. Individualism, it would seem, is not easily recommended to the Greek mind, and in giving his theory of education Aristotle has endeavoured to recruit for a Greek state rather than to give a final and absolute solution to questions of the greatest interest. Consequently this book can hardly be considered a valuable addition to philosophical literature, but it has a contemporary value in view of recent developments in France,[3] and at the present time, when the scientific specialists and the whole cohort of Materialists are cheapening the good name of philosophy, it is

[1] A review of John Burnet's *Aristotle on Education*, published in the *Daily Express*, Dublin, September 3, 1903. The review has no title.

[2] Joyce is glancing at Burnet, who twice calls Aristotle 'first and foremost a biologist' (pp. 2, 129).

[3] This judgment is not Joyce's but Burnet's (p. 106): 'The sort of question that Aristotle raises here is really the same as that which divides France at the present moment. The objection of the French government to the teaching of the religious orders is just that it does not produce a "Republican spirit" in the pupils, that it is not, in Aristotelian phrase, an education in conformity with the constitution.' Burnet is referring to the efforts of Émile Combes to secularize French education.

very useful to give heed to one who has been wisely named 'maestro di color che sanno.'[1]

[1] Dante's description of Aristotle in the fourth canto of the *Inferno* is used again by Joyce at the beginning of the Proteus episode of *Ulysses*, where he shows Stephen Dedalus wrestling with the problems of Aristotle's *De Anima*. As his review makes clear, Aristotle's consideration of man as a political animal interested Joyce far less than his metaphysics and aesthetics.

19

A Ne'er-Do-Well[1]

1903

Joyce returned to Dublin in April to find his mother dying slowly of cancer. Ireland pleased him no better, and he did not see clearly what to do next. After his mother's death on August 13, he had a flurry of assiduousness or monetary need which impelled him to write fourteen reviews from the end of August until late November, when he stopped reviewing altogether.

Of his notice of A Ne'er-Do-Well, *by 'Valentine Caryl', whose real name was Valentine Hawtrey, Stanislaus Joyce remarks: 'In dismissing this novel cursorily, my brother condemns pseudonyms; however, when a year later his own first stories were published, he yielded to the suggestion (not mine)[2] and used a pseudonym, "Stephen Daedalus", but then bitterly regretted the self-concealment. He did not feel that he had perpetrated bad literature of which he ought to be ashamed. He had taken the name from the central figure in the novel "Stephen Hero", which he had already begun to write. Against that name I had protested in vain; but it was, perhaps, his use of the name as a pseudonym that decided him finally on its adoption. He wished to make up for a momentary weakness; in fact, in order further to identify himself with his hero, he announced his intention of appending to the end of the novel the signature "Stephanus Daedalus pinxit".'[3]*

---

[1] Published in the *Daily Express*, Dublin, September 3, 1903. The review has no title.

[2] An undated letter to Joyce from George Russell, editor of the *Irish Homestead*, in which Joyce's first three short-stories were published, suggested that he could sign any name he liked as a pseudonym if he didn't mind 'playing to the common understanding and liking once in a way'. The letter is quoted in John J. Slocum, 'Notes on Joyce After Ten Years', *N. Y. Herald Tribune Book Review*, January 28, 1951, p. 8.

[3] *Book Reviews*, p. 25.

After all a pseudonym library has its advantages; to acknowledge bad literature by signature is, in a manner, to persevere in evil. 'Valentine Caryl' 's book is the story of a gypsy genius, whose monologues are eked out by accompaniments on the violin — a story told in undistinguished prose. The series in which this volume appears, the production of the book, and the scantiness of its matter have an air of pretentiousness which is ill justified by perusal.

20

Empire Building[1]

1903

About a month after his mother's death on August 13, 1903, Joyce wrote what appears to have been intended as a letter to the editor of an Irish newspaper.[2] He refers in it to Jacques Lebaudy, a wealthy young French adventurer, who had been cruising around North Africa in his yacht Frasquita *during the summer, letting it be known that he was founding a new empire of the Sahara and as Jacques I would be its first emperor. Lebaudy went so far as to seize the territory between Cape Juby and Cape Bojador, which was under no clear rule at that time. The French government disavowed any connection with his activities, but when five of his sailors were captured by natives at the beginning of September, had to send the cruiser* Galilée, *under Captain Jaurès, to release them. A dispatch to* The Times *of September 8, 1903, comments, 'The tone in which the Paris Press treats the whole affair only confirms the impression it produced from the very first — namely, that there is nothing in it.' Joyce was annoyed at the mistreatment of the sailors, a subject to which he refers again in* Ulysses *in a different context, and wrote this ironic comment.*

1903

Empire building does not appear to be as successful in Northern, as it has been in Southern Africa. While his cousins are astonish-

---

[1] This letter is in a holograph manuscript in Stanislaus Joyce's diary at the Cornell University Library.

[2] A search of Irish newspapers, kindly carried out by Mr. Patrick Henchy, Keeper of Books of the National Library, Dublin, indicates that the letter was never published.

ing the Parisian public by excursions in the air[1] M Jacques Lebaudy, the new Emperor of the Sahara, is preparing to venture into the heavier and more hazardous atmosphere of the Palais.[2] He has been summoned to appear before M André at the suit of two sailors, Jean Marie Bourdiec and Joseph Cambrai, formerly of the *Frosquetta*. They claim 100,000 francs damages on account of the hardships and diseases which they have contracted owing to M Lebaudy's conduct. The new emperor, it would seem, is not over-careful of the bodily welfare of his subjects. He leaves them unprovided for in a desert, bidding them wait until he returns. They are made captive by a party of natives and suffer the agonies of hunger and thirst during their captivity. They remain prisoners for nearly two months and are finally rescued by a French man-o'-war under the command of M Jaurès. One of them is subsequently an inmate of a hospital at the Havre and after a month's treatment there is still only convalescent. Their appeals for redress have been all disregarded and now they are having recourse to law. Such is the case of the sailors for the defence of which Maître Aubin and Maître Labori have been retained. The emperor, acting through a certain Benoit, one of his officers, has entered a plea for arbitration. He considers that the case is between the French Republic and the Saharan empire and that in consequence it should be tried before a tribunal of some other national. He petitions, therefore, that the case should be submitted for judgment to England, Belgium or Holland. However the case goes (and it is plain that the peculiar circumstances attending it render it an extremely difficult one to try) it cannot be that the new empire will gain either materially or in *prestige* by its trial. The dispute, in fact, tends to reduce what was, perhaps, a colonising scheme into a commercial concern but indeed, when one considers how little the colonising spirit appeals to the French people, it is not easy to defend M Lebaudy against the accusation of faddism. The new scheme does not seem to have the State behind it; the new empire does not seem to be entering on its career under any such capable management as reared up the Southern Empire out of the Bechuanaland Commission. But, however this may be, the enterprise is certainly sufficiently novel to excite an international

[1] Paul and Pierre Lebaudy's experimental flights in semirigid dirigibles were attracting considerable attention at this time.
[2] The Palais de Justice.

interest in this new candidate for nationhood and the hearing of a case, in which such singular issues are involved, will doubtless divide the attention of the Parisians with such comparatively minor topics as Réjane[1] and *les petits oiseaux.*

JAMES A. JOYCE
7 S. Peter's Terrace
Cabra, Dublin

[1] Gabrielle Charlotte Reju (1856–1920), the French actress.

21

New Fiction[1]

1903

This little volume is a collection of stories dealing chiefly with Indian life. The reader will find the first five stories — the adventures of Prince Aga Mirza — the more entertaining part of the book, if he is to any extent interested in tales of Indian magic. The appeal, however, of such stories is, frankly, sensational, and we are spared the long explanations which the professional occultists use. The stories that treat of camp life are soundly seasoned with that immature brutality which is always so anxious to be mistaken for virility. But the people who regulate the demand for fiction are being day by day so restricted by the civilization they have helped to build up that they are not unlike the men of Mandeville's time, for whom enchantments, and monsters, and deeds of prowess were so liberally purveyed.[2]

[1] A review of Aquila Kempster's *The Adventures of Prince Aga Mirza*, published in the *Daily Express*, Dublin, September 17, 1903.

[2] For Joyce, there was no need of external manifestations of magic. In *Ulysses*, while he takes occasion to parody the magical tricks of Mandeville, Monk Lewis, and other fabulists in the 'Oxen of the Sun', he also shows in the 'Circe' episode the more miraculous changes and evocations that go on *within* the mind.

22

The Mettle of the Pasture[1]

1903

In his treatment of a novel of James Lane Allen, Joyce is unexpectedly indulgent. Allen, a Kentuckian, had hit upon themes that were of extraordinary interest to Joyce, even when treated in Allen's old-fashioned manner. In The Mettle of the Pasture, *Allen's hero confesses his immoral past to his fiancée, who promptly throws him over and returns to him only when he is dying. The same theme of utter honesty between man and woman is developed in* Exiles. *Joyce was predisposed in Allen's favour by an earlier novel,* The Increasing Purpose (1900), *which he evidently read with the utmost sympathy. The novel describes the emotional and intellectual development of a young man who, while attending a Kentucky Bible College, discovers Darwinism; his resultant quarrels with his professors and with his parents seem like an artistically inferior, Protestant parallel to those of Stephen Dedalus. Finally, he admired Allen's unusual verbal dexterity and delight in prose cadences; and he did not mind the long discursive passages hung on a thin narrative thread, of which the* Portrait *also has its share.*

A book written by the author of 'The Increasing Purpose' is sure of a kind hearing from a public which can be thankful to those who serve it well. Mr. Allen has not yet written any work of extraordinary merit, but he has written many which are, so far as they go, serious and patient interpretations of his people. Whether it be in the writer or in his theme, one cannot fail to recognize here the quality of self-reliant sanity — the very mettle

[1] A review of James Lane Allen's *The Mettle of the Pasture*, published in the *Daily Express*, Dublin, September 17, 1903, under the same heading as that of item 21.

(to employ the Shakespearian phrase which serves him for the title)[1] of the pasture. The style is nearly always clean and limpid, and is at fault only where it assumes ornateness. The method is psychological, very slightly narrative, and though that epithet has been used to cover a multitude of literary sins, it can be as safely applied to Mr. Allen as *longo intervallo* to Mr. Henry James.

It is a tragedy of scandal, the story of a love affair, which is abruptly terminated by a man's confession, but which is renewed again years later when it has passed through the trials which the world proposes to such as would renew any association and so offer offence to time and change. This story is surrounded with two or three other love affairs, all more or less conventional. But the characterization is often very original — as in the case of old Mrs. Conyers — and the general current of the book arrests the reader by its suggestion of an eager lively race working out its destiny among other races under the influence of some vague pantheistic spirit which is at times strangely mournful. 'For her', he says somewhere in a passage of great charm, 'for her it was one of the moments when we are reminded that our lives are not in our keeping, and that whatsoever is to befall us originates in sources beyond our power. Our wills may indeed reach the length of our arms, or as far as our voices can penetrate space; but without us and within us moves one universe that saves us or ruins us only for its own purposes;[2] and we are no more free amid its laws than the leaves of the forest are free to decide their own shapes and seasons of unfolding, to order the showers by which they are to be nourished, and the storms which shall scatter them at last.'[3]

[1]
> *And you good yeomen,*
> *Whose limbs were made in England, show us here*
> *The mettle of your pasture.*
>
> *Henry V*, III, i, 28–30.

[2] 'Throb always without you and the throb always within. Your heart you sing of. I between them. Where? Between two roaring worlds where they swirl.' *Ulysses*, p. 238 (229).

[3] Allen, p. 125; Joyce is quoting from memory.

23

A Peep Into History[1]

1903

One may have no satirical reference either to the subject of this book, or to its treatment by Mr. Pollock, in saying that this account of the Popish Plot is far more diverting than many works of fiction. Mr. Pollock, though he seems thoroughly initiated into the mysteries of the historical method, has set forth an account of the 'Plot' which is clear, detailed, and (so far as it is critical) liberal-minded.

By far the most interesting part of the book is the story of the murder of Sir Edmund Godfrey[2] — a murder so artistically secret that it evoked the admiration of De Quincey,[3] a murder so little documented, yet so overwhelmed with false testimonies, that Lord Acton declared it an insoluble mystery.[4] But justice was freely dealt out in those days of political and religious rancour, and Green and Berry suffered the last penalty for a crime of which posterity (unanimous in this one thing at least) has acquitted them.

As for those who swore against the poor wretches, Prance and Bedloe cannot be accorded the same condemnation. Prance, after all, was only lying himself out of a very awkward position,[5] but Bedloe was a more enterprising ruffian, second only to his monstrous, moon-faced leader,[6] the horrible Oates. It is bewildering

[1] A review of John Pollock's *The Popish Plot*, published in the *Daily Express*, Dublin, September 17, 1903.
[2] The magistrate before whom Titus Oates had sworn to the truth of his information concerning a Popish plot.
[3] Joyce is paraphrasing Pollock (p. 3).
[4] Joyce's memory falters here. Pollock quotes Hume's remark that the mystery was 'insoluble' (p. 83) and Lord Acton's that it was 'quite unravelled' (p. vii).
[5] Joyce resists the opportunity to expound Pollock's argument that Prance was a Jesuit agent, which the book develops at considerable length.
[6] The word is misleading; Oates and Bedloe were not connected.

to read all the charges and counter-charges made in connection with the Plot, and it is with a sigh of sympathy that we read of Charles's conduct. 'In the middle of the confusion the King suddenly left for the races at Newmarket, scandalizing all by his indecent levity.'[1] Nevertheless he conducted the examination of Oates in a very skilful manner, and he described Oates very succinctly as 'a most lying knave'.

Mr. Pollock's treatment of those who have been accused as instigators justifies him in citing a concise phrase from Mabillon on his title page,[2] and the reader will know how patient and scholarly this book is if he compares it with the garbled, ridiculous account set down by L'Estrange.[3]

[1] Joyce garbles the text here, which says simply: 'To add to the general confusion the king left for the races at Newmarket . . .' (p. 80).

[2] 'Donner pour certain ce qui est certain, pour faux ce qui est faux, pour douteux ce qui est douteux.'

[3] Joyce's knowledge of L'Estrange's account of the plot was gained from Pollock's quotations.

24

A French Religious Novel[1]

1903

Of all Joyce's reviews, by far the most laudatory is that of Marcelle Tinayre's novel. Its account of a young man who half-revolts against his Jansenist upbringing and half-yields to it, who accepts life and love only to reject them finally, was close enough to his own theme to interest Joyce deeply. His review suggests that he was moving towards two original elements of his own work. In criticizing Tinayre's plot of the naïve young man and the worldly woman as a little stale, he perhaps had in mind the plot he was developing for Stephen Hero *and the* Portrait, *in which the hero, overwhelmed by the shows of neither this world nor the next, embraces art rather than woman or religion. Where Tinayre's hero disintegrates, sadly but surely, from his conflict, Stephen Dedalus achieves a joyful unity. The second original element of Joyce's work, which he heralds here in his excessive praise of Tinayre's style, is his conception of style as an expression of the subject-matter rather than of the author; he would develop this idea to a previously unknown extreme in* Ulysses.

This novel, reprinted from the pages of one of the leading French reviews, and now very successfully translated into English, seems to have attracted more attention in London than in Paris. It deals with the problem of an uncompromising orthodoxy, beset by a peculiarly modern, or (as the Churchmen would say) morbid scepticism, and sorely tried by that alluring, beautiful, mysterious spirit of the earth,[2] whose voice is for ever breaking in upon, and sometimes tempering, the prayers of the saints.

[1] A review of Marcelle Tinayre's *The House of Sin*, published in the *Daily Express*, Dublin, October 1, 1903.
[2] Ibsen's phrase in *When We Dead Awaken*, which Joyce also uses in the essay on Mangan; see pp. 61 and 83 above.

Augustine Chanteprie, the descendant of an old Catholic family, many of whose members have been disciples of Pascal, has been brought up in an atmosphere of rigid, practical belief, and is destined, if not for a clerical life, at least for such a life in the world as may be jealously guarded from the snares of the devil, sacrificing as little as may be of innocence and piety. Among his ancestors, however, there was one who forsook the holy counsel given him in youth, and assumed the excellent foppery of the world. He built, in protest against the gloomy house of his family, a pleasant folly, which afterwards came to be known as 'The House of Sin'. Augustine, unfortunately for himself, inherits the double temperament, and little by little the defences of the spiritual life are weakened, and he is made aware of human love as a subtle, insinuating fire. The intercourse of Augustine and Madame Manole is finely conceived, finely executed, enveloped in a glow of marvellous tenderness. A simple narration has always singular charm when we divine that the lives it offers us are themselves too ample, too complex, to be expressed entirely:

'Augustine and Fanny were now alone. They retraced their steps toward Chene-Pourpre, and suddenly stopping in the middle of the road, they kissed each other .... There was neither light nor sound. Nothing lived under the vault of heaven but the man and the woman intoxicated by their kiss. From time to time, without disengaging their hands, they drew away and looked at each other.'[1]

The last chapters of the book, the chapters in which the tradition of generations overcomes the lover, but so remorselessly that the mortal temple of all those emotions is shattered into fragments, show an admirable adjustment of style and narrative, the prose pausing more and more frequently with every lessening of vitality, and finally expiring (if one may reproduce the impression somewhat fantastically) as it ushers into the unknown, amid a murmur of prayers, the poor trembling soul.

[1] Tinayre had written (p. 163): 'There was neither light nor sound. Nothing to reveal the presence of the beings who slept behind those walls. The frogs no longer croaked. Nothing lived under the vault of heaven but the man and woman intoxicated by their kiss. From time to time, without disengaging their hands, they drew away and looked at each other with a rapturous expression. Taking a few steps at a time along the moonlit path, they stopped again and again to unite their lips.' Joyce accepted 'the vault of heaven' and 'intoxicated by their kiss' but boggled at 'with a rapturous expression'.

The interest in the politico-religious novel is, of course, an interest of the day, and, perhaps, it is because Huysmans is daily growing more formless and more obviously comedian in his books that Paris has begun to be wearied by the literary oblate. The writer of 'The House of Sin', again, is without the advantage of a perverted career, and is not to be reckoned among the converts. The complication of an innocent male and a woman of the world is, perhaps, not very new, but the subject receives here very striking treatment, and the story gains much by a comparison with Bourget's 'Mensonges' — a book that is crude, however detailed and cynical.

'Marcelle Tinayre', who seems to have a finer sympathy with Catholicism than most of the neo-Catholics have, is a lover of life and of the fair shows of the world; and though piety and innocence are interwoven with every change of affection and every mood of our manifold nature in these pages, one is conscious that the writer has suspended over her tragedy, as a spectre of sorrow and desolation, the horrible image of the Jansenist Christ.[1]

---

[1] This image appears literally on a crucifix which the lovers banish from their bedchamber; as a symbol of religion it is comparable to the 'shadowed face' of the priest in the *Portrait* who invites Stephen to enter the priesthood.

25

Unequal Verse[1]

1903

Mr. Langbridge, in his preface to this volume of his verses, has confessed to so great a number of literary discipleships that one is well prepared for the variety of styles and subjects of which the book is full. Mr. Langbridge's worst manner is very bad indeed; here the worst vices of Browning are united with a disease of sentiment of which the 'Master' cannot be justly accused; here 'tears splash on ground', blind beggars, mothers' girlies, pathetic clerks, and cripples are huddled together in dire confusion, and the colloquial style, half American half Cockney, is employed to adorn their easily-imagined adventures. Anything more lamentable than the result would be difficult to conceive; and the result is all the more lamentable because the few sonnets which Mr. Langbridge has inserted in his volume are evidences of some care and a not inconsiderable technical power. The lines, 'To Maurice Maeterlinck', are, therefore, curiously out of place in this farrago of banal epics, so dignified are they in theme, so reserved in treatment,[2] and one can only hope that Mr. Langbridge, when he

---

[1] A review of *Ballads and Legends* by Frederick Langbridge, published in the *Daily Express*, Dublin, October 1, 1903.

[2] Joyce's admiration for this sonnet, page 3 of Langbridge's book, may be due to its echoes of Yeats:

TO MAURICE MAETERLINCK

Ah, you who dwell in a dim, haunted place,
Where flesh is halfway spirit, where young eyes
Are large and heavy with innocent tragedies,
Where a strange, wistful twilight veils a space
Of ominous water, breaking round the base
Of an undated tower, in human-wise
Sad, and old woods in questions and replies
Rumour the sorrow of a fated race:—

124

publishes again, will see fit to sacrifice his taste for 'comédie larmoyante', and attest in serious verse that love which he professes for the muse.

Hardly I dare to carry to the feet
  Of your presaging dreams, occult, apart,
My book of rhymes, where clamorous wants compete,
  And all the air is venal with the mart:
And yet, like you, I hear the white wings beat,
  And the dark waters, and the breaking heart.

26

Mr. Arnold Graves' New Work[1]

1903

Joyce delighted in reproving his distinguished elders, and both Arnold Graves and Professor R. Y. Tyrrell, who introduced Graves' book, were well-known Irishmen. The review continues Joyce's battle, waged steadily while he was at University College, against art with a moral slant, and he upholds here, as in a famous passage in the Portrait, *the artist's 'indifferent sympathy' with his characters, whether they commit infidelity or murder.*

In the introduction which Dr. Tyrrell has written for Mr. Graves's tragedy, it is pointed out that 'Clytemnæstra'[2] is not a Greek play in English, like 'Atalanta in Calydon', but rather a Greek story treated from the standpoint of a modern dramatist — in other words it claims to be heard on its own merits merely, and not at all as a literary curio. To leave aside for the moment the subordinate question of language it is not easy to agree with Dr. Tyrrell's opinion that the treatment is worthy of the subject. On the contrary there would appear to be some serious flaws in the construction. Mr. Graves has chosen to call his play after the faithless wife of Agamemnon, and to make her nominally the cardinal point of interest. Yet from the tenor of the speeches, and inasmuch as the play is almost entirely a drama of the retribution which follows crime, Orestes being the agent of Divine vengeance, it is plain that the criminal nature of the queen has not engaged Mr. Graves's sympathies.

[1] A review of *Clytæmnestra: A Tragedy*, by Arnold F. Graves, published in the *Daily Express*, Dublin, October 1, 1903.

[2] Joyce misspells Clytæmnestra throughout as Clytemnæstra.

The play, in fact, is solved according to an ethical idea, and not according to that indifferent sympathy with certain pathological states which is so often anathematized by theologians of the street. Rules of conduct can be found in the books of moral philosophers, but 'experts' alone can find them in Elizabethan comedy. Moreover, the interest is wrongly directed when Clytemnæstra, who is about to imperil everything for the sake of her paramour, is represented as treating him with hardly disguised contempt, and again where Agamemnon, who is about to be murdered in his own palace by his own queen on his night of triumph, is made to behave towards his daughter Electra with a stupid harshness which is suggestive of nothing so much as of gout. Indeed, the feeblest of the five acts is the act which deals with the murder. Nor is the effect even sustained, for its second representation during Orestes' hypnotic trance[1] cannot but mar the effect of the real murder in the third act in the mind of an audience which has just caught Clytemnæstra and Egisthus red-handed.

These faults can hardly be called venial, for they occur at vital points of the artistic structure, and Mr. Graves, who might have sought to cover all with descriptive writing, has been honest enough to employ such a studiously plain language as throws every deformity into instant relief. However, there are fewer offences in the verse than in most of the verse that is written nowadays, and it is perhaps only an indication of the mental confusion incident upon seership when Tiresias, the prophet, is heard exclaiming:

Beware! beware!
The stone you started rolling down the hill
Will crush you if you do not change your course.[2]

[1] Joyce's scientific phrase refers to Orestes' divinely inspired vision at Delphi.

[2] Joyce delighted in collecting absurdities of this kind, and annoyed John Synge in Paris in 1902 by showing him the solecisms he had turned up in the works of Yeats and other contemporaries.

27

A Neglected Poet[1]

1903

The revival of interest in common life in the late eighteenth century was inevitably of special interest to Joyce, whose struggles to be prosaic and observant can be seen in some of the stories of Dubliners. Although in this review he lauds Crabbe over Goldsmith as a realist, he was later to hail Goldsmith as one of the great Irish writers of English;[2] and in Finnegans Wake he is fond of quoting him. The perceptive allusion to the Dutchmen at the end of the review is one of Joyce's few references to painting, an art in which he had little interest; the 'splendour' he finds in them and occasionally in Crabbe suggests that his own realism would not be content with mere fidelity.

Tennyson is reported to have said that if God made the country and man made the city, it must have been the devil that made the country town.[3] The dreary monotonousness, the squalor, the inevitable moral decay — all, in fine, that has been called 'provincial' — is the constant theme of Crabbe's verse. Patronized in his own day by Edmund Burke and Charles James Fox, the friend of Scott, and Rogers, and Bowles, the literary godfather of Fitz-Gerald, Crabbe has so far fallen in our day from his high estate that it is only by a favour that he is accorded mention in some manual of literature.

This neglect, though it can be easily explained, is probably not a final judgment. Of course, much of Crabbe's work is dull and

---

[1] A review of Alfred Ainger's *George Crabbe*, published in the *Daily Express*, Dublin, October 15, 1903.

[2] Pp. 170 and 177 below.

[3] 'Reported' in Ainger (p. 118).

undistinguished, and he never had such moments as those which Wordsworth can always plead in answer to his critics.[1] On the contrary, it is his chief quality that he employs the metre of Pope so evenly, and with so little of Pope's brilliancy that he succeeds admirably as narrator of the obscure tragedies of the provinces. His tales are, therefore, his claim to a place in the history of English fiction. At a time when false sentiment and the 'genteel' style were fashionable, and when country life was seized upon for exploitation as eagerly as by any of the modern Kailyard[2] school, Crabbe appeared as the champion of realism. Goldsmith had preceded him in treating rural subjects, treating them with an Arcadian grace, it is true, but with what remoteness and lack of true insight and sympathy a comparison of Auburn with 'The Village', 'The Borough', and 'The Parish Register' will show. These latter are no more than names in the ears of the present generation, and it is the purpose of the present monograph to obtain a hearing, at least, for one of the most neglected of English writers.

The name of its author is one of the most honourable and painstaking in contemporary criticism, and amid a multitude of schools and theories perhaps he may succeed in securing a place for one like Crabbe, who, except for a few passages wherein the world of opinion is divided, is an example of sane judgment and sober skill, and who has set forth the lives of villagers with appreciation and fidelity, and with an occasional splendour reminiscent of the Dutchmen.

[1] This comparison was suggested by Ainger.
[2] This epithet, meaning 'cabbage patch', was applied to a school of fiction that presented common life in Scotland, with much use of dialect, in the eighteen-nineties.

28

Mr. Mason's Novels[1]

1903

Faced with the obligation to review popular novels, Joyce contents himself with a few gentle sarcasms. The allusion to Leonardo with which he begins is ironically heavy in its context, but in the 'Scylla and Charybdis' episode of Ulysses *Joyce evolves a similar theory to expound Shakespeare's use of his life in his plays.*

These novels, much as they differ in their subjects and styles, are curiously illustrative of the truth of one of Leonardo's observations. Leonardo, exploring the dark recesses of consciousness in the interests of some semi-pantheistic psychology, has noted the tendency of the mind to impress its own likeness upon that which it creates. It is because of this tendency, he says, that many painters have cast as it were a reflection of themselves over the portraits of others.[2] Mr. Mason, perhaps, in like manner, has allowed these stories to fit themselves into what is doubtless one of the 'moulds of his understanding'.

Among Mr. Mason's 'properties' the reader will not fail to notice the early, effaceable husband. In 'The Courtship of Morrice Buckler' it is Julian Harwood, in 'The Philanderers' it is the outcast Gorley, in 'Miranda of the Balcony' it is Ralph Warriner. In all three books a previously-implicated girl of wayward habits

[1] A review of three novels by A. E. W. Mason: *The Courtship of Morrice Buckler*, *The Philanderers*, and *Miranda of the Balcony*, published in the *Daily Express*, Dublin, October 15, 1903.

[2] Joyce has in mind such statements of Leonardo as this one from the *Notebooks* (McCurdy ed., II, 261): 'you may readily deceive yourself by selecting such faces as bear a resemblance to your own, since it would often seem that such similarities please us; and if you were ugly you would not select beautiful faces, but would be creating ugly faces like many faces whose types often resemble their master.'

is associated with a young man, who is a type of class common enough in novels — the sturdy, slow-witted Englishman. It is curious to watch this story reproducing itself without the author's assent, one imagines, through scenes and times differing so widely.

A minor phenomenon is the appearance of Horace in each story. In 'The Courtship of Morrice Buckler' the plan of the castle in the Tyrol, which is the centre of gravity of the story, is made on a page of a little Elzevir copy of Horace. In 'The Philanderers' Horace is laid under tribute more than once for a simile worthy of the classical beauty of Clarice. And once again in 'Miranda of the Balcony' that interesting figure 'Major' Wilbraham is represented as engaged on a translation of Horace in the intervals of marauding and blackmailing.

Mr. Mason is much more successful when he is writing of a time or scene somewhat remote from big towns. The Belgravian atmosphere of 'The Philanderers' (a title which Mr. Mason has to share with Mr. George Bernard Shaw)[1] is not enlivened by much wit or incident, but 'Miranda of the Balcony' has a pleasing sequence of Spanish and Moorish scenes. Mr. Mason's best book, however, is certainly 'The Courtship of Morrice Buckler'. The story is of the cape and sword order, and it passes in the years after Sedgemoor. Germany is an excellent place for castles and intrigues; and in the adventurous air of this romance those who have read too many novels of modern life may recreate themselves at will. The writing is often quite pretty, too. Isn't 'Miranda of the Balcony' a pretty name?

[1] Shaw's play was presented in 1893; Joyce followed his career attentively.

29

The Bruno Philosophy[1]

1903

According to his brother, James Joyce once considered becoming an actor, and went so far as to choose a stage name. It was Gordon Brown, a tribute to his respect for Giordano Bruno. By the time he wrote this review, Joyce was familiar with Bruno's work and had quoted it in The Day of the Rabblement. *He had discussed Bruno with his Italian professor, Father Ghezzi, at University College, Ghezzi maintaining that Bruno was a terrible heretic and Joyce that he was terribly burned.*

Bruno, who died in 1600, was neglected for two centuries, then was much noticed again during the nineteenth century. In 1889 a statue to him was unveiled in Rome in the Campo dei Fiori, where he was burned at the stake. Joyce was impressed by both his character and philosophy: by the heroic tenacity with which Bruno held to his ideas in the face of imprisonment, by his break with the joylessness of scholastic philosophy and monastic life, and by his theory of the coincidence of contraries, which underlies the Shem-Shawn relationship in Finnegans Wake. *But as usual in that book Joyce renders Bruno the Nolan Irish by relating him to the Dublin booksellers, Browne and Nolan.*

E<small>XCEPT</small> for a book in the English and Foreign Philosophical Library,[2] a book the interest of which was chiefly biographical, no considerable volume has appeared in England to give an account of the life and philosophy of the heresiarch martyr of Nola.

[1] A review of J. Lewis McIntyre's *Giordano Bruno*, published in the *Daily Express*, Dublin, October 30, 1903.

[2] I. Frith, *Life of Giordano Bruno* (London, 1887), a book which Joyce appears to have read; see footnote 3, p. 69 above.

Inasmuch as Bruno was born about the middle of the sixteenth century, an appreciation of him — and that appreciation the first to appear in England — cannot but seem somewhat belated now. Less than a third of this book is devoted to Bruno's life, and the rest of the book to an exposition and comparative survey of his system. That life reads like a heroic fable in these days of millionaires. A Dominican monk, a gipsy professor, a commentator of old philosophies and a deviser of new ones, a playwright, a polemist, a counsel for his own defence, and, finally, a martyr burned at the stake in the Campo dei Fiori — Bruno, through all these modes and accidents (as he would have called them) of being, remains a consistent spiritual unity.

Casting away tradition with the courage of early humanism, Bruno has hardly brought to his philosophical enquiry the philosophical method of a peripatetic. His active brain continually utters hypotheses; his vehement temper continually urges him to recriminate; and though the hypothesis may be validly used by the philosopher in speculation and the countercheck quarrelsome be allowed him upon occasion, hypotheses and recriminations fill so many of Bruno's pages that nothing is easier than to receive from them an inadequate and unjust notion of a great lover of wisdom. Certain parts of his philosophy — for it is many-sided — may be put aside. His treatises on memory, commentaries on the art of Raymond Lully, his excursions into that treacherous region from which even ironical Aristotle did not come undiscredited, the science of morality, have an interest only because they are so fantastical and middle-aged.

As an independent observer, Bruno, however, deserves high honour. More than Bacon or Descartes must he be considered the father of what is called modern philosophy.[1] His system by turns rationalist and mystic, theistic and pantheistic is everywhere impressed with his noble mind and critical intellect, and is full of that ardent sympathy with nature as it is — *natura naturata* — which is the breath of the Renaissance. In his attempt to reconcile the matter and form of the Scholastics — formidable names, which in his system as spirit and body retain little of their metaphysical character — Bruno has hardly put forward an hypothesis, which is a curious anticipation of Spinoza.[2] Is it not strange,

[1] McIntyre's judgment (p. 324).
[2] McIntyre's view (p. 338).

then, that Coleridge should have set him down a dualist, a later Heraclitus, and should have represented him as saying in effect: 'Every power in nature or in spirit must evolve an opposite as the sole condition and means of its manifestation; and every opposition is, therefore, a tendency to reunion.'[1]

And yet it must be the chief claim of any system like Bruno's that it endeavours to simplify the complex. That idea of an ultimate principle, spiritual, indifferent, universal, related to any soul or to any material thing, as the Materia Prima of Aquinas is related to any material thing, unwarranted as it may seem in the view of critical philosophy, has yet a distinct value for the historian of religious ecstasies. It is not Spinoza, it is Bruno, that is the god-intoxicated man.[2] Inwards from the material universe, which, however, did not seem to him, as to the Neoplatonists the kingdom of the soul's malady, or as to the Christians a place of probation, but rather his opportunity for spiritual activity, he passes, and from heroic enthusiasm to enthusiasm to unite himself with God. His mysticism is little allied to that of Molinos or to that of St. John of the Cross; there is nothing in it of quietism or of the dark cloister: it is strong, suddenly rapturous, and militant. The death of the body is for him the cessation of a mode of being, and in virtue of this belief and of that robust character 'prevaricating yet firm', which is an evidence of that belief, he becomes of the number of those who loftily do not fear to die. For us his vindication of the freedom of intuition must seem an enduring monument, and among those who waged so honourable a war, his legend must seem the most honourable, more sanctified, and more ingenuous than that of Averroes or of Scotus Erigena.[3]

---

[1] Joyce is quoting, with slight variations, a footnote to Essay XIII in Coleridge's *The Friend*. Coleridge anticipated Joyce's interest in both Bruno and Vico.

[2] McIntyre's remark (p. 110).

[3] McIntyre makes this comparison (p. 110) without drawing so forceful a conclusion.

30

Humanism[1]

1903

Barbarism, says Professor Schiller,[2] may show itself in philosophy in two guises, as barbarism of style and as barbarism of temper, and what is opposed to barbarism is Professor Schiller's philosophical creed: Humanism, or, as he sometimes names it, Pragmatism. One, therefore, who has been prepared to expect courteous humanism both in temper and in style, will read with some surprise statements such as — 'The *a priori* philosophies have all been found out'; 'Pragmatism . . . has . . . reached the "Strike, but hear me!" stage'; 'It [the Dragon of Scholasticism] is a spirit . . . that grovels in muddy technicality, buries itself in the futile burrowings of valueless researches, and conceals itself from human insight [but not from humane insight, Professor Schiller!] by dust-clouds of desiccated rubbish which it raises.'[3]

But these are details. Pragmatism is really a very considerable thing. It reforms logic, it shows the absurdity of pure thought, it establishes an ethical basis for metaphysic, makes practical usefulness the criterion of truth, and pensions off the Absolute once and for all. In other words, pragmatism is common-sense.

[1] A review of *Humanism: Philosophical Essays*, by F. C. S. Schiller, published in the *Daily Express*, Dublin, November 12, 1903. Stanislaus Joyce writes: 'My brother's interest in Pragmatism was slight, hardly more than a certain curiosity regarding a school of philosophy . . . which, he held, avoided philosophical difficulties by sidestepping nimbly. The asserted relativity of truth and the practical test of knowledge by its usefulness to an end ran counter not only to his Aristotelian principles of logic, but still more to his character . . . . In Trieste he once told me that he preferred the Italian to the British Encyclopedia because it contained so much useless knowledge that interested him . . . .' *Book Reviews*, p. 43.

[2] Schiller was the leading European exponent of William James's philosophy.

[3] As his review of Bruno indicates, Joyce was no unqualified adherent of scholasticism; but he seems to have preferred that philosophy to the new one, as he preferred Catholicism to Protestantism, without believing in either.

The reader, accordingly, will not be surprised to find that in the post-Platonic dialogue, which is called ' "Useless" Knowledge,' a disciple of William James utterly routs and puts to shame the ghostly forms of Plato and Aristotle. Emotional psychology is made the starting-point, and the procedure of the philosopher is to be regulated in accordance. If Professor Schiller had sought to establish rational psychology as a starting-point, his position would have been well-grounded, but rational psychology he has either never heard of or considers unworthy of mention. In his essay on the desire of immortality he establishes one fact — that the majority of human beings are not concerned as to whether or not their life is to end with the dissolution of the body. And yet, after having set up efficiency as the test of truth and the judgment of humanity as the final court of appeal, he concludes by pleading on behalf of the minority, by advocating the claims of the Society for Psychical Research,[1] of which, it seems, he has been for many years a member.

Was it so well done, after all, to reform logic so radically? But your pragmatist is nothing if not an optimist, and though he himself denies philosophies by the score, he declares that pessimism is 'der Geist der stets verneint.'[2] The Mephistopheles of Goethe is the subject of one of the most entertaining essays in the book. 'The subtlest of his disguises,' says Prof. Schiller in a characteristic sentence, 'his most habitual mask, is one which deceives all the other characters in Faust, except the Lord, and has, so far as I know, utterly deceived all Goethe's readers except myself.'[3] But surely Professor Schiller can hardly derive much satisfaction from the knowledge that he shares his discovery with the Lord in Goethe's Faust, a being which (to quote the phrase of the English sceptic upon a term of the English sensationalist-theologians)[4] is taken for God because we do not know what the devil it can be, a being, moreover, which is closely allied to such inefficient and pragmatically annihilated entities as the Absolute of Mr. Bradley and the Unknowable of Mr. Spencer.[5]

[1] In 1914 Schiller became president of this society, as William James had been before him.

[2] Joyce plays on this phrase from *Faust* (I, i, 1808) in a letter to Frank Budgen, which describes Molly Bloom as 'der Fleisch der stets bejaht'. *Letters*, p. 170.

[3] This quotation, taken from p. 168, is one of the few in Joyce's twenty-two reviews that is altogether correct.

[4] F. H. Bradley, whose remark on Spencer's Unknowable is quoted on p. 191.

[5] Bradley and Spencer are Schiller's targets throughout.

31

Shakespeare Explained[1]

1903

In a short prefatory note the writer of this book states that he has not written it for Shakespearian scholars, who are well provided with volumes of research and criticism, but has sought to render the eight plays more interesting and intelligible to the general reader. It is not easy to discover in the book any matter for praise. The book itself is very long — nearly five hundred pages of small type — and expensive. The eight divisions of it are long drawn out accounts of some of the plays of Shakespeare — plays chosen, it would seem, at haphazard. There is nowhere an attempt at criticism, and the interpretations are meagre, obvious, and commonplace. The passages 'quoted' fill up perhaps a third of the book, and it must be confessed that the writer's method of treating Shakespeare is (or seems to be) remarkably irreverent. Thus he 'quotes' the speech made by Marullus in the first act of 'Julius Caesar', and he has contrived to condense the first sixteen lines of the original with great success, omitting six of them without any sign of omission.

Perhaps it is a jealous care for the literary digestion of the general public that impels Mr. Canning to give them no more than ten-sixteenths of the great bard. Perhaps it is the same care which dictates sentences such as the following: 'His noble comrade fully rivals Achilles in wisdom as in valour.[2] Both are supposed to utter their philosophic speeches during the siege of Troy, which they are conducting with the most energetic ardour. They evidently

---

[1] A review of A. S. Canning's *Shakespeare Studied in Eight Plays*, published in the *Daily Express*, Dublin, November 12, 1903.

[2] Canning wrote (p. 6): 'His noble comrade Ulysses rivals Achilles in wisdom as in valour.' For Joyce now, as later, the wise Ulysses had nothing in common with the bullying Achilles.

turn aside from their grand object for a brief space to utter words of profound wisdom . . . .' It will be seen that the substance of this book is after the manner of ancient playbills. Here is no psychological complexity, no cross-purpose, no interweaving of motives such as might perplex the base multitude. Such a one is a 'noble character', such a one a 'villain'; such a passage is 'grand', 'eloquent', or 'poetic'. One page in the account of 'Richard the Third' is made up of single lines or couplets and such non-committal remarks as 'York says then', 'Gloucester, apparently surprised, answers', 'and York replies', 'and Gloucester replies', 'and York retorts'. There is something very naïve about this book, but (alas!) the general public will hardly pay sixteen shillings for such *naïveté*. And the same Philistine public will hardly read five hundred pages of 'replies', and 'retorts' illustrated with misquotations. And even the pages are wrongly numbered.

32

Borlase and Son[1]

1903

'Borlase and Son' has the merit, first of all, of 'actuality'. As the preface is dated for May last, one may credit the author with prophetic power, or at least with that special affinity for the actual, the engrossing topic, which is a very necessary quality in the melodramatist. The scene of the story is the suburban district about Peckham Rye, where the Armenians have just fought out a quarrel,[2] and, moreover, the epitasis (as Ben Jonson would call it)[3] of the story dates from a fall of stocks incident upon a revolution among the Latin peoples of America.[4]

But the author has an interest beyond that derivable from such allusions. He has been called the Zola of Camberwell, and, inappropriate as the epithet is, it is to Zola we must turn for what is, perhaps, the supreme achievement in that class of fiction of which 'Borlase and Son' is a type. In 'Au Bonheur des Dames' Zola has set forth the intimate glories and shames of the great warehouse — has, in fact, written an epic for drapers; and in 'Borlase and Son', a much smaller canvas, our author has drawn very faithfully the picture of the smaller 'emporium', with its sordid avarice, its underpaid labour, its intrigue, its 'customs of trade'.

The suburban mind is not invariably beautiful, and its working is here delineated with unsentimental vigour. Perhaps the unc-

---

[1] A review of *Borlase and Son* by T. Baron Russell, published in the *Daily Express*, Dublin, November 19, 1903. The review has no title.

[2] On October 26, 1903, Sagouni, president of the Armenian Revolutionary Society, was murdered at Peckham as a result of feuds among the Armenians in exile.

[3] *The Magnetic Lady*, Epilogue to Act I. Compare 'protasis, epitasis, catastasis, catastrophe' in *Ulysses*, p. 209 (200).

[4] On November 3, a long-expected revolution broke out when Panama declared her independence from Colombia.

tuousness of old Borlase is somewhat overstated, and the land-ladies may be reminiscent of Dickens. In spite of its 'double circle' plot, 'Borlase and Son' has much original merit, and the story, a little slender starveling of a story, is told very neatly and often very humorously. For the rest, the binding of the book is as ugly as one could reasonably expect.

33

Aesthetics

1903/04

Impelled in part by his ambition to establish the relation of drama to other genres, Joyce went heroically on to compound his own aesthetic. He inevitably began with Aristotle, then turned, surprisingly, to Thomas Aquinas, and ended, more predictably, with Flaubert.[1] His earliest formulations were made during his second trip to Paris,[2] in February and March 1903; he wrote them down in a notebook and signed his name and the date after each observation as if to guarantee its importance as well as to identify its authorship. He continued his speculations in Pola (then Austrian), in November 1904, while teaching at the Berlitz school there. Between March and July of the following year he brought together his early essays and his notebook statements for Stephen Hero. *The discussion of aesthetics in the* Portrait *was written several years later. He moves, then, from bald statement in the Paris and Pola notebooks to a mixture of narrative essay and dramatic presentation of his theories in* Stephen Hero, *and finally to the sheerly dramatic presentation in the* Portrait.

In the Paris notebook Joyce grandly follows the manner as well as the topics of Aristotle. Unleashing, like Stephen Dedalus later, his

[1] Flaubert, in a letter to Mlle. Leroyer de Chantepie, March 18, 1857, writes 'Avec une lectrice telle que vous, Madame, at aussi sympathique, la franchise est un devoir. Je vais donc répondre à vos questions: *Madame Bovary* n'a rien de vrai. C'est une histoire *totalement inventée*; je n'y ai rien mis ni de mes sentiments ni de mon existence. L'illusion (s'il y en a une) vient au contraire de *l'impersonnalité* de l'oeuvre. C'est un de mes principes: qu'il ne faut pas s'écrire. L'artiste doit être dans son oeuvre comme Dieu dans la Création, invisible et tout-puissant, qu'on le sente partout, mais qu'on ne le voie pas.

Et puis l'art doit s'élever au-dessus des affections personnelles et des suscepti-bilités nerveuses! Il est temps de lui donner, par une méthode impitoyable, la prévision des sciences physiques! La difficulté capitale, pour moi, n'en reste pas moins le style; la forme, la beau indéfinissable résultant de la conception même et qui est la splendeur du vrai, comme disait Platon.'

[2] Joyce returned to Dublin for the Christmas holidays in 1902.

'*dagger definitions*', *he elaborates in pat contrast the differences between tragedy and comedy. He argues for the superiority of comedy over tragedy on the grounds that comedy makes for joy and tragedy for sorrow, and that the sense of deprivation is imperfect, and therefore, he implies, inferior to the sense of possession. With more originality he expertly re-defines pity and terror and finds in the arrest of these emotions, as in that of joy, the stasis necessary to art. He then distinguishes between the lyrical, epical, and dramatic modes, covertly awarding the palm to drama as the most impersonal. Finally he insists that art moves towards an aesthetic, and not a moral end.*

The moral question is the one he next takes up, at Pola. Using a sentence from Thomas Aquinas[1] *for text, he argues that, since the good is what is desirable, and since the true and the beautiful are most persistently desired, then they must be considered good. This is his only concession to the ethical aspect of art, but it is sufficient to make clear that he regards the good, the true, and the beautiful as intertwined. That art is not didactic does not mean that it should be pornographic; in fact he rejects pornography in the Paris notebook as equally offensive. It is not immoral nor amoral, but its purposes so far transcend conventional morality that it is better to forget morality altogether.*

He then asks what things are beautiful, and draws upon another sentence of Aquinas to establish that those things are beautiful the apprehension of which pleases. Beautiful must be taken to include what is colloquially termed ugly, he insists, probably with his own future subject-matter in mind. He is anxious to avoid the degeneration of beauty into mere prettiness. He turns now to the three stages in the apprehension of the beautiful, a prelude to his isolation, in Stephen Hero, *of the three elements of beauty.*

Later, in Stephen Hero, *Joyce focuses the aesthetic theory on the artist, and uses his essays on Mangan and on 'Drama and Life' to display his hero's speculations on the role of the artist. Echoing Shelley, he insists that every age must look for its sanction to its poets and philosophers, but makes clear that art has no explicit didactic purpose. In* integritas, consonantia, *and* claritas, *three terms from Aquinas, he discovers the three aspects of beauty, and illustrates how*

[1] For a different view of Joyce's relation to Aquinas, see: William T. Noon, *Joyce and Aquinas* (New Haven, 1957); Thomas E. Connolly, 'Joyce's Aesthetic Theory', *University of Kansas City Review*, v. 23 no. 1 (Oct. 1956) 47–50; and Maurice Beebe, 'Joyce and Aquinas: The Theory of Aesthetics', *Philological Quarterly*, v. 36 (1957) 20–35.

they may be apprehended in three stages which imitate their mounting intensity. He borrows from Christianity the term 'epiphany' to describe the thing of beauty in its most vivid manifestation.

Finally, in the Portrait, *Joyce makes a new blend of the notebooks and* Stephen Hero. *He removes the early essays, and allows Stephen to develop his aesthetic theory in its original theoretical terms; but he also enables him to promulgate it with much more wit and force, and to bring it to a climax with the fine image of the artist as god that Joyce took over from Flaubert's correspondence. It has become fashionable recently to describe Stephen as a mere aesthete, but this is to misunderstand him. He is as interested in truth as he is in beauty, and omits discussing the good because he assumes it rather than because he ignores it. When at the* Portrait's *end he announces that he will forge the conscience of his race, he is perfectly consistent with the aesthetic he has formulated.*

I. Paris Notebook[1]

Desire is the feeling which urges us to go to something and loathing is the feeling which urges us to go from something: and that art is improper which aims at exciting these feelings in us whether by comedy or by tragedy. Of comedy later. But tragedy aims at exciting in us feelings of pity and terror. Now terror is the feeling which arrests us before whatever is grave in human fortunes and unites us with its secret cause and pity is the feeling which arrests us before whatever is grave in human fortunes and unites us with the human sufferer. Now loathing, which in an improper art aims at exciting[2] in the way of tragedy, differs, it will be seen, from the feelings which are proper to tragic art, namely terror and pity. For loathing urges us from rest because it urges us to go from something, but terror and pity hold us in rest, as it were, by fascination. When tragic art makes my body to shrink terror is not my feeling because I am urged from rest, and moreover this art does not show me what is grave, I mean what is constant and

[1] Published in Gorman, pp. 96–9. The manuscripts from which Gorman was working no longer exist. The Slocum Collection of the Yale University Library contains in one holograph manuscript sheet, written on both sides, what probably is an earlier draft of the first two items printed below (dated February 13 and March 6). While essentially the same as the printed version, this text contains minor variations in diction, of which the most important are noted below.

[2] Yale MS. reads: 'which an improper art aims at exciting . . . .'

irremediable in human fortunes nor does it unite me with any secret cause for it shows me only what is unusual and remediable[1] and it unites me with a cause only too manifest. Nor is an art properly tragic which would move me to prevent human suffering any more than an art is properly tragic which would move me in anger against some manifest cause of human suffering. Terror and pity, finally, are aspects of sorrow comprehended in sorrow[2] — the feeling which the privation of some good excites in us.

And now of comedy. An improper art aims at exciting in the way of comedy the feeling of desire but the feeling which is proper to comic art is the feeling of joy. Desire, as I have said, is the feeling which urges us to go to something but joy is the feeling which the possession of some good excites in us. Desire, the feeling which an improper art seeks to excite in the way of comedy, differs, it will be seen, from joy. For desire urges us from rest that we may possess something but joy holds us in rest so long as we possess something. Desire, therefore, can only be excited in us by a comedy (a work of comic art) which is not sufficient in itself inasmuch as it urges us to seek something beyond itself; but a comedy (a work of comic art) which does not urge us to seek anything beyond itself excites in us the feeling of joy. All art which excites in us the feeling of joy is so far comic and according as this feeling of joy is excited by whatever is substantial or accidental[3] in human fortunes the art is to be judged more or less excellent: and even tragic art may be said to participate in the nature of comic art so far as the possession of a work of tragic art (a tragedy) excites in us the feeling of joy. From this it may be seen that tragedy is the imperfect manner and comedy the perfect manner in art. All art, again, is static for the feelings of terror and pity on the one hand and of joy on the other hand are feelings which arrest us.[4] It will be seen afterwards how this rest is necessary for the apprehension of the beautiful — the end of all art, tragic or comic — for this rest is the only condition under which the images, which are to

[1] Yale MS. does not contain 'nor does it unite me with any secret cause for it shows me only what is unusual and remediable'.

[2] Yale MS. reads 'germane to sorrow' instead of 'aspects of sorrow comprehended in sorrow'.

[3] Yale MS. adds after this word: 'general or fortuitous.'

[4] Joyce substitutes stasis for catharsis. That joy may result from tragedy as well as from comedy does not follow well from what he has said. In the *Portrait* he confines the discussion almost completely to tragedy and changes 'joy' to 'the luminous silent stasis of aesthetic pleasure.'

excite in us terror or pity or joy, can be properly presented to us and properly seen by us. For beauty is a quality of something seen but terror and pity and joy are states of mind.

JAMES A. JOYCE, 13 Feb., 1903.

. . . There are three conditions of art: the lyrical, the epical and the dramatic. That art is lyrical whereby the artist sets forth the image in immediate relation to himself; that art is epical whereby the artist sets forth the image in mediate relation to himself and to others; that art is dramatic whereby the artist sets forth the image in immediate relation to others . . . .

JAMES A. JOYCE, 6 March, 1903, Paris.

Rhythm seems to be the first or formal relation of part to part in any whole or of a whole to its part or parts, or of any part to the whole of which it is a part . . . . Parts constitute a whole as far as they have a common end.

JAMES A. JOYCE, 25 March, 1903, Paris.

e tekhne mimeitai ten physin — This phrase is falsely rendered as 'Art is an imitation of Nature'. Aristotle does not here define art; he says only, 'Art imitates Nature' and means that the artistic process is like the natural process[1]. . . . It is false to say that sculpture, for instance, is an art of repose if by that be meant that sculpture is unassociated with movement. Sculpture is associated with movement in as much as it is rhythmic; for a work of sculptural art must be surveyed according to its rhythm and this surveying is an imaginary movement in space. It is not false to say that sculpture is an art of repose in that a work of sculptural art cannot be presented as itself moving in space and remain a work of sculptural art.

JAMES A. JOYCE, 27 March, 1903, Paris.

Art is the human disposition of sensible or intelligible matter for an aesthetic end.

JAMES A. JOYCE, 28 March, 1903, Paris.

[1] Perhaps an anticipation of Stephen's theory that the making of a work of art includes the three stages of 'artistic conception, artistic gestation, and artistic reproduction' (*Portrait*, p. 475 [238]), an idea that he continues when he says that 'the mystery of aesthetic like that of material creation is accomplished' (*Portrait*, p. 481 [244–5]).

Question: Why are not excrements, children, and lice works of art?

Answer: Excrements, children, and lice are human products — human dispositions of sensible matter. The process by which they are produced is natural and non-artistic; their end is not an aesthetic end: therefore they are not works of art.

Question: Can a photograph be a work of art?

Answer: A photograph is a disposition of sensible matter and may be so disposed for an aesthetic end but it is not a human disposition of sensible matter. Therefore it is not a work of art.

Question: If a man hacking in fury at a block of wood make there an image of a cow (say) has he made a work of art?

Answer: The image of a cow made by a man hacking in fury at a block of wood is a human disposition of sensible matter but it is not a human disposition of sensible matter for an aesthetic end. Therefore it is not a work of art.

Question: Are houses, clothes, furniture, etc., works of art?

Answer: Houses, clothes, furniture, etc., are not necessarily works of art. They are human dispositions of sensible matter. When they are so disposed for an aesthetic end they are works of art.

II. Pola Notebook[1]

Bonum est in quod tendit appetitus.[2] S. Thomas Aquinas.

The good is that towards the possession of which an appetite tends: the good is the desirable. The true and the beautiful are the most persistent orders of the desirable.[3] Truth is desired by

[1] Published in Gorman, pp. 133–5. The manuscripts that Gorman was working with no longer exist, but there is a single holograph manuscript sheet in the Slocum Collection of the Yale University Library that is probably a first draft of the first item printed below (dated 7 XI 04). Except for two small changes in diction, this text is identical with the printed version.

[2] *Summa Contra Gentiles*, Ch. III. Aquinas is developing the opening sentence of Aristotle's *Nicomachean Ethics*.

[3] Compare Shelley's *Defence of Poetry*: '. . . to be a poet is to apprehend the true and the beautiful, in a word, the good which exists in the relation, subsisting, first between existence and perception, and secondly between perception and expression.' Joyce uses a phrase from this essay in his discussion of aesthetics in the *Portrait*.

the intellectual appetite which is appeased by the most satisfying relations of the intelligible; beauty is desired by the aesthetic appetite which is appeased by the most satisfying relations of the sensible. The true and the beautiful are spiritually possessed; the true by intellection, the beautiful by apprehension, and the appetites which desire to possess them, the intellectual and aesthetic appetites, are therefore spiritual appetites . . . .

J. A. J. Pola, 7 XI 04.

Pulchra sunt quae visa placent.[1] S. Thomas Aquinas.

Those things are beautiful the apprehension of which pleases. Therefore beauty is that quality of a sensible object in virtue of which its apprehension pleases or satisfies the aesthetic appetite which desires to apprehend the most satisfying relations of the sensible. Now the act of apprehension involves at least two activities, the activity of cognition or simple perception and the activity of recognition. If the activity of simple perception is, like every other activity, itself pleasant, every sensible object that has been apprehended can be said in the first place to have been and to be in a measure beautiful; and even the most hideous object can be said to have been and to be beautiful in so far as it has been apprehended. In regard then to that part of the act of apprehension which is called the activity of simple perception there is no sensible object which cannot be said to be in a measure beautiful.

With regard to the second part of the act of apprehension which is called the activity of recognition it may further be said that there is no activity of simple perception to which there does not succeed in whatsoever measure the activity of recognition. For by the activity of recognition is meant an activity of decision; and in accordance with this activity in all conceivable cases a sensible object is said to be satisfying or dissatisfying. But the activity of recognition is, like every other activity, itself pleasant and therefore every object that has been apprehended is secondly in whatsoever measure beautiful. Consequently even the most hideous object may be said to be beautiful for this reason as it is *a priori* said to be beautiful in so far as it encounters the activity of simple perception.

[1] The exact phrase is 'pulchra enim dicuntur ea quae visa placent'. *Summa Theologica* I, q. 5, art. 4. To consider this statement apart from final causes is good Joyce but bad Aquinas.

Sensible objects, however, are said conventionally to be beautiful or not for neither of the foregoing reasons but rather by reason of the nature, degree and duration of the satisfaction resulting from the apprehension of them and it is in accordance with these latter merely that the words 'beautiful' and 'ugly' are used in practical aesthetic philosophy. It remains then to be said that these words indicate only a greater or less measure of resultant satisfaction and that any sensible object, to which the word 'ugly' is practically applied, an object, that is, the apprehension of which results in a small measure of aesthetic satisfaction, is, in so far as its apprehension results in any measure of satisfaction whatsoever, said to be for the third time beautiful . . . .

J. A. J. Pola, 15 XI 04.

The Act of Apprehension

It has been said that the act of apprehension involves at least two activities — the activity of cognition or simple perception and the activity of recognition. The act of apprehension, however, in its most complete form involves three activities — the third being the activity of satisfaction.[1] By reason of the fact that these three activities are all pleasant themselves every sensible object that has been apprehended must be doubly and may be trebly beautiful. In practical aesthetic philosophy the epithets 'beautiful' and 'ugly' are applied with regard chiefly to the third activity, with regard, that is, to the nature, degree and duration of the satisfaction resultant from the apprehension of any sensible object and therefore any sensible object to which in practical aesthetic philosophy the epithet 'beautiful' is applied must be trebly beautiful, must have encountered, that is, the three activities which are involved in the act of apprehension in its most complete form. Practically then the quality of beauty in itself must involve three constituents to encounter each of these three activities . . . .

J. A. J. Pola. 16 XI 04.

[1] Joyce here goes beyond Aquinas, who speaks of 'pleasing' and not 'satisfying'. Joyce is bridging from his theory of *stasis* in drama to his theory of *claritas* as both the final quality of a work of art and the highest aspect of response to it. Satisfaction, which implies rest and calm, is therefore essential to his theory of apprehension.

34

The Holy Office[1]

1904

Joyce composed this satirical broadside about two months before he left Dublin in 1904. He had it printed but could not afford to pay for it, so the following year, in Pola, he had it printed again and sent the sheets to his brother Stanislaus for distribution to the butts of his satire in Dublin.

In the poem he lumps together Yeats and Russell and their follow-ers, accusing them all of hypocrisy and self-deception. One would hardly suspect from their writings that they had bodies at all; their spirituality has its analogue in female prudery. Joyce, who had always prided himself on his candour and honesty, and was now demonstrating these qualities in Stephen Hero *and the first stories of* Dubliners, *yokes Aristotle to Christian ritual to claim that his own office is Katharsis, the revelation of what the mummers hide. Then, elevating his metaphor, he condemns them from the mountain-top to which Ibsen and Nietzsche had helped to bring him.*

Myself unto myself will give
This name, Katharsis-Purgative.
I, who dishevelled ways forsook
To hold the poets' grammar-book,[2]
Bringing to tavern and to brothel
The mind of witty Aristotle,

[1] The title refers ironically to (1) the office of confession, and (2) the department of the church that launched the Inquisition, and that today exercises the function of censorship. There are also overtones of 'the holy office an ostler does for the stallion', *Ulysses*, p. 200 (191).

[2] Joyce collected the solecisms in the works of his eminent contemporaries; see footnote 2, p. 127 above.

149

Lest bards in the attempt should err
Must here be my interpreter:
Wherefore receive now from my lip
Peripatetic scholarship.

To enter heaven, travel hell,
Be piteous or terrible,
One positively needs the ease
Of plenary indulgences.

For every true-born mysticist
A Dante is, unprejudiced,[1]
Who safe at ingle-nook, by proxy,
Hazards extremes of heterodoxy,
Like him who finds a joy at table,
Pondering the uncomfortable.
Ruling one's life by commonsense
How can one fail to be intense?

But I must not accounted be
One of that mumming company[2] —
With him[3] who hies him to appease
His giddy dames'[4] frivolities
While they console him when he whinges
With gold-embroidered Celtic fringes[5] —
Or him who sober all the day
Mixes a naggin in his play[6] —
Or him whose conduct 'seems to own'
His preference for a man of 'tone'[7] —

---

[1] Repeated from 'Catilina', p. 101 above.

[2]
> Know that I would accounted be
> True brother of a company
> That sang, to sweeten Ireland's wrong . . .
> Yeats, 'Address to Ireland in the Coming Times'.

The 'mumming company' is used as a general derogatory label, but has also a specific reference to the Abbey Theatre, which received its patent in August, 1904. Sponsored financially by Annie E. Horniman, headed by Lady Augusta Gregory, and artistically dominated by Yeats, it had grown out of the earlier Irish National Theatre, and almost all the young Irish writers except Joyce had some share in one group or the other.

[3] Yeats.

[4] Lady Gregory and Miss Horniman, and perhaps Maud Gonne MacBride.

[5] An allusion to the gilt decorations on the books that Yeats published in the 1890's.

[6] John Synge.

[7] Oliver Gogarty.

Or him who plays the ragged patch
To millionaires in Hazelhatch
But weeping after holy fast
Confesses all his pagan past[1] —
Or him who will his hat unfix
Neither to malt nor crucifix
But show to all that poor-dressed be
His high Castilian courtesy[2] —
Or him who loves his Master dear[3] —
Or him who drinks his pint in fear[4] —
Or him who once when snug abed
Saw Jesus Christ without his head
And tried so hard to win for us
The long-lost works of Eschylus.[5]
But all these men of whom I speak
Make me the sewer of their clique.
That they may dream their dreamy dreams
I carry off their filthy streams
For I can do those things for them
Through which I lost my diadem,
Those things for which Grandmother Church
Left me severely in the lurch.
Thus I relieve their timid arses,
Perform my office of Katharsis.
My scarlet leaves them white as wool.[6]
Through me they purge a bellyful.
To sister mummers one and all
I act as vicar-general,[7]
And for each maiden, shy and nervous,
I do a similar kind service.
For I detect without surprise
That shadowy beauty in her eyes,
The 'dare not' of sweet maidenhood

[1] Padraic Colum.
[2] W. K. Magee ('John Eglinton').
[3] George Roberts, a devoted follower of George Russell, who addressed Russell in this way in a poem.
[4] James S. Starkey ('Seumas O'Sullivan').
[5] George Russell.
[6] 'Though your sins be as scarlet, they shall be as white as snow.' Isaiah 1:18.
[7] A bishop's assistant, who handles operational details of the diocese.

That answers my corruptive 'would'.[1]
Whenever publicly we meet
She never seems to think of it;
At night when close in bed she lies
And feels my hand between her thighs
My little love in light attire
Knows the soft flame that is desire.
But Mammon places under ban
The uses of Leviathan[2]
And that high spirit ever wars
On Mammon's countless servitors,
Nor can they ever be exempt
From his taxation of contempt.
So distantly I turn to view
The shamblings of that motley crew,
Those souls that hate the strength that mine has
Steeled in the school of old Aquinas.
Where they have crouched and crawled and prayed
I stand the self-doomed, unafraid,
Unfellowed, friendless and alone,
Indifferent as the herring-bone,
Firm as the mountain-ridges where
I flash my antlers on the air.[3]
Let them continue as is meet
To adequate the balance-sheet.
Though they may labour to the grave
My spirit shall they never have
Nor make my soul with theirs as one
Till the Mahamanvantara[4] be done:
And though they spurn me from their door
My soul shall spurn them evermore.

[1] Letting 'I dare not' wait upon 'I would',
  Like the poor cat i' the adage.
          Macbeth, I, vii, 44–5.

[2] The heroic, individualistic Satan; here Joyce.

[3] 'There was his ground and he flung them disdain from flashing antlers.'
Stephen Hero, p. 35 (27).

[4] The Hindu great year.

35

Ireland, Island of Saints and Sages[1]

1907

Joyce left Dublin in October 1904, *with Nora Barnacle, and spent
the next two and a half years in Pola, Trieste, and Rome. He returned
to Trieste in March* 1907, *after nine unhappy months in Rome as a
bank clerk. By this time, his command of the Tuscan dialect had
advanced so far that he was invited to deliver three public lectures in
Italian at the Università Popolare, a kind of adult education centre
in Trieste. He devoted his first lecture, on April* 27, *to Irish political
and cultural history, his second to Mangan, and the third, which he
promised his audience in the Mangan lecture* (*but which has not
survived*), *to the Irish literary renaissance.*

*His Triestine audience was anticlerical and mostly agnostic,
attracted by the Irredentist movement which wanted to oust the
Austrians and return the city to Italy, but not wholly carried away by
it. Joyce had no need to point up the parallel between Ireland and
Trieste, both living under foreign domination, both claiming a
language distinct from the conqueror's, both Catholic. But he felt
compelled to point out that his country had its history of betrayals,
of eloquent inactivity, of absurd and narrow belief. His attitude,
though he calls it objective, wavers between affectionate fascination
with Ireland and distrust of her.*

*Joyce was advised to give his lectures extempore, but he did not
want to risk mistakes and so read them from his manuscript. His
delivery was by Italian standards rather cool and unemotional, but*

---

[1] Translated from the Italian of 'Irlanda, Isola dei Santi e dei Savi', a holograph
manuscript of forty-six pages, heavily revised by Joyce, in the Slocum Collection
of the Yale University Library. It also bears some corrections in another hand,
perhaps that of Joyce's friend, Alessandro Francini-Bruni.

his audience, composed in part of his language pupils and friends, applauded him vigorously.

Nations have their ego, just like individuals. The case of a people who like to attribute to themselves qualities and glories foreign to other people has not been entirely unknown in history, from the time of our ancestors, who called themselves Aryans and nobles, or that of the Greeks, who called all those who lived outside the sacrosanct land of Hellas barbarians. The Irish, with a pride that is perhaps less easy to explain, love to refer to their country as the island of saints and sages.

This exalted title was not invented yesterday or the day before. It goes back to the most ancient times, when the island was a true focus of sanctity and intellect, spreading throughout the continent a culture and a vitalizing energy. It would be easy to make a list of the Irishmen who carried the torch of knowledge from country to country as pilgrims and hermits, as scholars and wisemen. Their traces are still seen today in abandoned altars, in traditions and legends where even the name of the hero is scarcely recognizable, or in poetic allusions, such as the passage in Dante's *Inferno* where his mentor points to one of the Celtic magicians tormented by infernal pains and says:

> *Quel'altro, che ne' fianchi è così poco,*
> *Michele Scotto fu, che veramente*
> *Delle magiche frode seppe il gioco.*[1]

In truth, it would take the learning and patience of a leisurely Bollandist[2] to relate the acts of these saints and sages. We at least remember the notorious opponent of St. Thomas, John Duns Scotus (called the Subtle Doctor to distinguish him from St. Thomas, the Angelic Doctor, and from Bonaventura, the Seraphic Doctor) who was the militant champion of the doctrine of the Immaculate Conception, and, as the chronicles of that period

---

[1]   *That other one so meagre in the flanks,*
             Was Michael Scott, who really knew the tricks
             Of false magic.

Canto XX, 115–17.

[2] The Bollandist fathers perform the enormous labour of compiling and editing the *Acta Sanctorum*.

tell us, an unbeatable dialectician. It seems undeniable that Ireland at that time was an immense seminary, where scholars gathered from the different countries of Europe, so great was its renown for mastery of spiritual matters. Although assertions of this kind must be taken with great reservations, it is more than likely (in view of the religious fervour that still prevails in Ireland, of which you, who have been nourished on the food of scepticism in recent years, can hardly form a correct idea) that this glorious past is not a fiction based on the spirit of self-glorification.

If you really wish to be convinced, there are always the dusty archives of the Germans. Ferrero[1] now tells us that the discoveries of these good professors of Germany, so far as they deal with the ancient history of the Roman republic and the Roman empire, are wrong from the beginning — almost completely wrong. It may be so. But, whether or not this is so, no one can deny that, just as these learned Germans were the first to present Shakespeare as a poet of world significance to the warped eyes of his compatriots (who up to that time had considered William a figure of secondary importance, a fine fellow with a pleasant vein of lyric poetry, but perhaps too fond of English beer), these very Germans were the only ones in Europe to concern themselves with Celtic languages and the history of the five Celtic nations. The only Irish grammars and dictionaries that existed in Europe up until a few years ago, when the Gaelic League was founded in Dublin, were the works of Germans.

The Irish language, although of the Indo-European family, differs from English almost as much as the language spoken in Rome differs from that spoken in Teheran. It has an alphabet of special characters, and a history almost three thousand years old. Ten years ago, it was spoken only by the peasants in the western provinces on the coast of the Atlantic and a few in the south, and on the little islands that stand like pickets of the vanguard of Europe, on the front of the eastern hemisphere. Now the Gaelic League[2] has revived its use. Every Irish newspaper, with the exception of the Unionist organs, has at least one special headline printed in Irish. The correspondence of the principal cities is written in Irish, the Irish language is taught in most of the primary

[1] Guglielmo Ferrero, the Italian historian, whose *Grandezza e Decadenza di Roma* was published in 1901.
[2] Founded in 1893.

and secondary schools, and, in the universities, it has been set on a level with the other modern languages, such as French, German, Italian, and Spanish. In Dublin, the names of the streets are printed in both languages. The League organizes concerts, debates, and socials at which the speaker of *beurla* (that is, English) feels like a fish out of water, confused in the midst of a crowd that chatters in a harsh and guttural tongue. In the streets, you often see groups of young people pass by speaking Irish, perhaps a little more emphatically than is necessary. The members of the League write to each other in Irish, and often the poor postman, unable to read the address, must turn to his superior to untie the knot.

This language is oriental in origin, and has been identified by many philologists with the ancient language of the Phoenicians, the originators of trade and navigation, according to historians. This adventurous people, who had a monopoly of the sea, established in Ireland a civilization that had decayed and almost disappeared before the first Greek historian took his pen in hand. It jealously preserved the secrets of its knowledge, and the first mention of the island of Ireland in foreign literature is found in a Greek poem of the fifth century before Christ, where the historian repeats the Phoenician tradition. The language that the Latin writer of comedy, Plautus, put in the mouth of Phoenicians in his comedy *Poenulus* is almost the same language that the Irish peasants speak today, according to the critic Vallancey.[1] The religion and civilization of this ancient people, later known by the name of Druidism, were Egyptian. The Druid priests had their temples in the open, and worshipped the sun and moon in groves of oak trees. In the crude state of knowledge of those times, the Irish priests were considered very learned, and when Plutarch mentions Ireland, he says that it was the dwelling place of holy men. Festus Avienus in the fourth century was the first to give Ireland the title of *Insula Sacra*; and later, after having undergone the invasions of the Spanish and Gaelic tribes, it was converted to Christianity by St. Patrick and his followers, and again earned the title of 'Holy Isle'.

I do not propose to give a complete history of the Irish church

[1] Charles Vallancey (1721–1812), whose identification of Irish with the language of the Phoenicians Joyce mentions above, published several works on Irish language and history. He had long since been discredited as an authority when it became apparent that he had little knowledge of Irish.

in the first centuries of the Christian era. To do so would be beyond the scope of this lecture, and, in addition, not overly interesting. But it is necessary to give you some explanation of my title 'Island of Saints and Sages', and to show you its historical basis. Leaving aside the names of the innumerable churchmen whose work was exclusively national, I beg you to follow me for a few minutes while I expose to your view the traces that the numerous Celtic apostles in almost every country have left behind them. It is necessary to recount briefly events that today seem trivial to the lay mind, because in the centuries in which they occurred and in all the succeeding Middle Ages, not only history itself, but the sciences and the various arts were all completely religious in character, under the guardianship of a more than maternal church. And, in fact, what were the Italian scientists and artists before the Renaissance if not obedient handmaids of God, erudite commentators of sacred writings, or illustrators in verse or painting of the Christian fable?

It will seem strange that an island as remote as Ireland from the centre of culture could excel as a school for apostles, but even a superficial consideration will show us that the Irish nation's insistence on developing its own culture by itself is not so much the demand of a young nation that wants to make good in the European concert as the demand of a very old nation to renew under new forms the glories of a past civilization. Even in the first century of the Christian era, under the apostleship of St. Peter, we find the Irishman Mansuetus, who was later canonized, serving as a missionary in Lorraine, where he founded a church and preached for half a century. Cataldus had a cathedral and two hundred theologians at Geneva, and was later made bishop of Taranto. The great heresiarch Pelagius, a traveller and tireless propagandist, if not an Irishman, as many contend, was certainly either Irish or Scottish, as was his right hand, Caelestius. Sedulius traversed a great part of the world, and finally settled at Rome, where he composed the beauties of almost five hundred theological tracts, and many sacred hymns that are used even today in Catholic ritual. Fridolinus Viator, that is, the Voyager, of royal Irish stock, was a missionary among the Germans, and died at Seckingen in Germany, where he is buried. Fiery Columbanus[1]

---

[1] 'You were going to do wonders, what? Missionary to Europe after fiery Columbanus.' *Ulysses*, p. 43 (39).

had the task of reforming the French church, and, after having started a civil war in Burgundy by his preaching, went to Italy, where he became the apostle of the Lombards and founded the monastery at Bobbio. Frigidian, son of the king of northern Ireland, occupied the bishopric of Lucca. St. Gall, who at first was the student and companion of Columbanus, lived among the Grisons in Switzerland as a hermit, hunting, and fishing, and cultivating his fields by himself. He refused the bishopric of the city of Constance, which was offered to him, and died at the age of ninety-five. On the site of his hermitage an abbey rose, and its abbot became prince of the canton by the grace of God, and greatly enriched the Benedictine library, whose ruins are still shown to those who visit the ancient town of St. Gall.

Finnian, called the Learned, founded a school of theology on the banks of the river Boyne in Ireland, where he taught Catholic doctrine to thousands of students from Great Britain, France, Armorica, and Germany, giving them all (O happy time!) not only their books and instruction but also free room and board. However, it seems that some of them neglected to fill their study lamps, and one student whose lamp went out suddenly had to invoke the divine grace, which made his fingers shine miraculously in such a way that by running his luminous fingers through the pages, he was able to satisfy his thirst for knowledge. St. Fiacre,[1] for whom there is a commemorative plaque in the church of St. Mathurin in Paris, preached to the French and conducted extravagant funerals at the expense of the court. Fursey founded monasteries in five countries, and his feast day is still celebrated at Peronne, the place where he died in Picardy.

Arbogast built sanctuaries and chapels in Alsace and Lorraine, and ruled the bishop's see at Strasbourg for five years until, feeling that he was near his end (according to his Dauphin) he went to live in a hut at the place where criminals were put to death and where later the great cathedral of the city was built. St. Verus became champion of the cult of the Virgin Mary in France, and Disibod, bishop of Dublin, travelled here and there through all of Germany for more than forty years, and finally founded a Benedictine monastery named Mount Disibod, now called Disenberg. Rumold became bishop of Mechlin in France, and the

---

[1] 'Fiacre and Scotus on their creepystools in heaven spilt from their pintpots ....'
Ulysses, p. 43 (39).

martyr Albinus, with Charlemagne's help, founded an institute of science at Paris and another which he directed for many years in ancient Ticinum (now Pavia). Kilian, the apostle of Franconia, was consecrated bishop of Würzburg, in Germany, but, trying to play the part of John the Baptist between Duke Gozbert and his mistress, he was killed by cut-throats. Sedulius the younger was chosen by Gregory II for the mission of settling the quarrels of the clergy in Spain, but when he arrived there, the Spanish priests refused to listen to him, on the grounds that he was a foreigner. To this Sedulius replied that since he was an Irishman of the ancient race of Milesius, he was in fact a native Spaniard. This argument so thoroughly convinced his opponents that they allowed him to be installed in the bishop's palace at Oreto.

In sum, the period that ended in Ireland with the invasion of the Scandinavian tribes in the eighth century is nothing but an unbroken record of apostleships, and missions, and martyrdoms. King Alfred, who visited the country and left us his impressions of it in the verses called 'The Royal Journey', tells us in the first stanza:

> *I found when I was in exile*
> *In Ireland the beautiful*
> *Many ladies, a serious people,*
> *Laymen and priests in abundance*

and it must be admitted that in twelve centuries the picture has not changed much; although, if the good Alfred, who found an abundance of laymen and priests in Ireland at that time, were to go there now, he would find more of the latter than the former.

Anyone who reads the history of the three centuries that precede the coming of the English must have a strong stomach, because the internecine strife, and the conflicts with the Danes and the Norwegians, the black foreigners and the white foreigners, as they were called, follow each other so continuously and ferociously that they make this entire era a veritable slaughterhouse. The Danes occupied all the principal ports on the east coast of the island and established a kingdom at Dublin, now the capital of Ireland, which has been a great city for about twenty centuries. Then the native kings killed each other off, taking well-earned rests from time to time in games of chess. Finally, the bloody victory of the usurper Brian Boru over the nordic hordes on the sand dunes outside the walls of Dublin put an end to the Scandinavian raids. The Scandinavians, however, did not leave the country, but were gradually assimilated into the community, a fact that we must keep in mind if we want to understand the curious character of the modern Irishman.[1]

During this period, the culture necessarily languished, but Ireland had the honour of producing the three great heresiarchs John Duns Scotus, Macarius, and Vergilius Solivagus. Vergilius was appointed by the French king to the abbey at Salzburg and later was made bishop of that diocese, where he built a cathedral. He was a philosopher, mathematician, and translator of the writings of Ptolemy. In his tract on geography, he held the theory, which was subversive at that time, that the earth was round, and for such audacity was declared a sower of heresy by Popes Boniface and Zacharias. Macarius lived in France, and the monastery of St. Eligius still preserves his tract *De Anima*, in which he taught the doctrine later known as Averroism, of which Ernest Renan, himself a Breton Celt, has left us a masterful examination. Scotus Erigena, Rector of the University of Paris, was a mystical pantheist, who translated from the Greek the books of mystical theology of Dionysius, the pseudo-Areopagite, patron saint of the French nation.[2] This translation presented to Europe for the first time the transcendental philosophy of the Orient, which had as much influence on the course of European religious thought as later the translations of Plato, made in the time of Pico della Mirandola, had on the development of the profane Italian civilization. It goes without saying that such an innovation (which seemed like a life-giving breath resurrecting the dead bones of orthodox theology piled up in an inviolable churchyard, a field of Ardath)[3] did not have the sanction of the Pope, who invited Charles the Bald to send both the book and the author to Rome under escort, probably because he wanted to have them taste the delights of papal courtesy. However, it seems that Scotus had kept a grain of good sense in his exalted brain, because he pretended not to hear this courteous invitation and departed in haste for his native land.

[1] In *Finnegans Wake* Joyce emphasizes the Scandinavian origin of his hero, Earwicker.

[2] Joyce is confusing Dionysius the pseudo-Areopagite with Dionysius the Areopagite (St. Denis, or Dionysius, of Athens), and with St. Denis, or Dionysius, of Paris, the patron saint of France.

[3] Where the prophet Ezra ate flowers and had visions. 2 Esdras 9:26

From the time of the English invasion to our time, there is an interval of almost eight centuries, and if I have dwelt rather at length on the preceding period in order to make you understand the roots of the Irish temperament, I do not intend to detain you by recounting the vicissitudes of Ireland under the foreign occupation. I especially will not do so because at that time Ireland ceased to be an intellectual force in Europe. The decorative arts, at which the ancient Irish excelled, were abandoned, and the sacred and profane culture fell into disuse.

Two or three illustrious names shine here like the last few stars of a radiant night that wanes as dawn arrives. According to legend, John Duns Scotus, of whom I have spoken before, the founder of the school of Scotists, listened to the arguments of all the Doctors of the University of Paris for three whole days, then rose and, speaking from memory, refuted them one by one; Joannes de Sacrobosco, who was the last great supporter of the geographical and astronomical theories of Ptolemy, and Petrus Hibernus, the theologian who had the supreme task of educating the mind of the author of the scholastic apology *Summa contra Gentiles*, St. Thomas Aquinas, perhaps the keenest and most lucid mind known to human history.

But while these last stars still reminded the European nations of Ireland's past glory, a new Celtic race was arising, compounded of the old Celtic stock and the Scandinavian, Anglo-Saxon, and Norman races. Another national temperament rose on the foundation of the old one, with the various elements mingling and renewing the ancient body. The ancient enemies made common cause against the English aggression, with the Protestant inhabitants (who had become *Hibernis Hiberniores*, more Irish than the Irish themselves) urging on the Irish Catholics in their opposition to the Calvinist and Lutheran fanatics from across the sea, and the descendants of the Danish and Norman and Anglo-Saxon settlers championing the cause of the new Irish nation against the British tyranny.

Recently, when an Irish member of parliament was making a speech to the voters on the night before an election, he boasted that he was one of the ancient race and rebuked his opponent for being the descendant of a Cromwellian settler. His rebuke provoked a general laugh in the press, for, to tell the truth, to exclude from the present nation all who are descended from foreign

161

families would be impossible, and to deny the name of patriot to all those who are not of Irish stock would be to deny it to almost all the heroes of the modern movement — Lord Edward Fitzgerald, Robert Emmet, Theobald Wolfe Tone and Napper Tandy, leaders of the uprising of 1798, Thomas Davis and John Mitchel, leaders of the Young Ireland movement, Isaac Butt, Joseph Biggar, the inventor of parliamentary obstructionism, many of the anticlerical Fenians, and, finally, Charles Stewart Parnell, who was perhaps the most formidable man that ever led the Irish, but in whose veins there was not even a drop of Celtic blood.

In the national calendar, two days, according to the patriots, must be marked as ill-omened — that of the Anglo-Saxon and Norman invasion, and that, a century ago, of the union of the two parliaments. Now, at this point, it is important to recall two piquant and significant facts. Ireland prides itself on being faithful body and soul to its national tradition as well as to the Holy See. The majority of the Irish consider fidelity to these two traditions their cardinal article of faith. But the fact is that the English came to Ireland at the repeated requests of a native king,[1] without, needless to say, any great desire on their part, and without the consent of their own king, but armed with the papal bull of Adrian IV and a papal letter of Alexander.[2] They landed on the east coast with seven hundred men, a band of adventurers against a nation; they were received by some native tribes, and in less than a year, the English King Henry II celebrated Christmas with gusto in the city of Dublin. In addition, there is the fact that parliamentary union[3] was not legislated at Westminster but at Dublin, by a parliament elected by the vote of the people of Ireland, a parliament corrupted and undermined with the greatest ingenuity by the agents of the English prime minister, but an Irish parliament nevertheless. From my point of view, these two facts must be thoroughly explained before the country in which they occurred has the most rudimentary right to persuade one of

[1] Dermot MacMurrogh, King of Leinster, whom Mr. Deasy confuses with Tiernan O'Rourke in *Ulysses*, p. 35 (32).

[2] The Bull of *Laudabiliter* (1156) granting the sovereignty of Ireland to Henry II; the authenticity of the document is doubtful. See Joyce's bull-play in *Ulysses*, p. 393 (381–3). Three letters and a papal privilege of Pope Alexander III confirmed the English hold on Ireland.

[3] The act of 1800 that united the kingdoms of England and Ireland, dissolved the Irish parliament, and gave the Irish representation in the parliament at Westminster in its place.

her sons to change his position from that of an unprejudiced observer to that of a convinced nationalist.

On the other hand, impartiality can easily be confused with a convenient disregard of facts, and if an observer, fully convinced that at the time of Henry II Ireland was a body torn by fierce strife and at the time of William Pitt was a venal and wicked mess of corruption, draws from these facts the conclusion that England does not have many crimes to expiate in Ireland, now and in the future, he is very much mistaken. When a victorious country tyrannizes over another, it cannot logically be considered wrong for that other to rebel. Men are made this way, and no one who is not deceived by self-interest or ingenuousness will believe, in this day and age, that a colonial country is motivated by purely Christian motives. These are forgotten when foreign shores are invaded, even if the missionary and the pocket Bible precede, by a few months, as a routine matter, the arrival of the soldiers and the uplifters. If the Irishmen at home have not been able to do what their brothers have done in America, it does not mean that they never will, nor is it logical on the part of English historians to salute the memory of George Washington and profess themselves well content with the progress of an independent, almost socialist, republic in Australia while they treat the Irish separatists as madmen.

A moral separation already exists between the two countries. I do not remember ever having heard the English hymn 'God Save the King' sung in public without a storm of hisses, shouts, and shushes that made the solemn and majestic music absolutely inaudible. But to be convinced of this separation, one should have been in the streets when Queen Victoria entered the Irish capital the year before her death.[1] Above all, it is necessary to notice that when an English monarch wants to go to Ireland, for political reasons, there is always a lively flurry to persuade the mayor to receive him at the gates of the city. But, in fact, the last monarch who entered[2] had to be content with an informal reception by the sheriff, since the mayor had refused the honour. (I note here merely as a curiosity that the present mayor of Dublin is an Italian, Mr. Nannetti.)[3]

---

[1] April 4–26, 1900. Joyce was eighteen at the time of her visit.

[2] An allusion to the visit of Edward VII and Queen Alexandra, July 21–August 1, 1903.

[3] J. P. Nannetti was born in Florence.

Queen Victoria had been in Ireland only once, fifty years before,[1] [nine years] after her marriage. At that time, the Irish (who had not completely forgotten their fidelity to the unfortunate Stuarts, nor the name of Mary Stuart, Queen of Scots, nor the legendary fugitive, Bonnie Prince Charlie) had the wicked idea of mocking the Queen's consort as though he were an abdicated German prince,[2] amusing themselves by imitating the way he was said to lisp English, and greeting him exuberantly with a cabbage stalk just at the moment when he set foot on Irish soil.

The Irish attitude and the Irish character were antipathetic to the queen, who was fed on the aristocratic and imperialistic theories of Benjamin Disraeli, her favourite minister, and showed little or no interest in the lot of the Irish people, except for disparaging remarks, to which they naturally responded in a lively way. Once, it is true, when there was a horrible disaster in county Kerry which left most of the county without food or shelter, the queen, who held on tightly to her millions, sent the relief committee, which had already collected thousands of pounds from benefactors of all social classes, a royal grant in the total amount of ten pounds.[3] As soon as the committee noticed the arrival of such a gift, they put it in an envelope and sent it back to the donor by return mail, together with their card of thanks. From these little incidents, it would appear that there was little love lost between Victoria and her Irish subjects, and if she decided to visit them in the twilight of her years, such a visit was most certainly motivated by politics.

The truth is that she did not come; she was sent by her advisers. At that time, the English debacle in South Africa in the war against the Boers had made the English army an object of scorn in the European press, and if it took the genius of the two commanders-in-chief, Lord Roberts and Lord Kitchener (both of them Irishmen, born in Ireland) to redeem its threatened prestige (just as in 1815 it took the genius of another Irish soldier to overcome the renewed might of Napoleon at Waterloo), it also took Irish recruits and volunteers to demonstrate their renowned valour on the field of battle. In recognition of this fact, when the war was over, the English government allowed the Irish regiments to wear

[1] In 1849.

[2] A similar attack on the German origin of the English royal family is made in *Ulysses*, pp. 324–5 (314–5).

[3] Joyce is here following a popular tradition; Queen Victoria donated five hundred pounds to the relief fund during the famine of 1878–80.

the shamrock, the patriotic emblem, on St. Patrick's Day. In fact, the Queen came over for the purpose of capturing the easy-going sympathies of the country, and adding to the lists of the recruiting sergeants.

I have said that to understand the gulf that still separates the two nations, one should have been present at her entry into Dublin. Along the way were arrayed the little English soldiers[1] (because, since the time of James Stephens' Fenian revolt, the government had never sent Irish regiments to Ireland), and behind this barrier stood the crowd of citizens. In the decorated balconies were the officials and their wives, the unionist employees and their wives, the tourists and their wives. When the procession appeared, the people in the balconies began to shout greetings and wave their handkerchiefs. The Queen's carriage passed, carefully protected on all sides by an impressive body of guards with bared sabres, and within was seen a tiny lady, almost a dwarf, tossed and jolted by the movements of the carriage, dressed in mourning, and wearing horn-rimmed glasses on a livid and empty face. Now and then she bowed fitfully, in reply to some isolated shout of greeting, like one who has learned her lesson badly. She bowed to left and right, with a vague and mechanical movement. The English soldiers stood respectfully at attention while their patroness passed, and behind them, the crowd of citizens looked at the ostentatious procession and the pathetic central figure with curious eyes and almost with pity; and when the carriage passed, they followed it with ambiguous glances. This time there were no bombs or cabbage stalks, but the old Queen of England entered the Irish capital in the midst of a silent people.

The reasons for this difference in temperament, which has now become a commonplace of the phrase-makers of Fleet Street, are in part racial and in part historical. Our civilization is a vast fabric, in which the most diverse elements are mingled, in which nordic aggressiveness and Roman law, the new bourgeois conventions and the remnant of a Syriac religion[2] are reconciled. In such a fabric, it is useless to look for a thread that may have remained pure and virgin without having undergone the influence of a neighbouring thread. What race, or what language (if we except

[1] Joyce's pencilled note is in the margin: 'Explain why the soldiers were English', with the parenthetical explanation below it.
[2] That is, Christianity.

the few whom a playful will seems to have preserved in ice, like the people of Iceland) can boast of being pure today? And no race has less right to utter such a boast than the race now living in Ireland. Nationality (if it really is not a convenient fiction like so many others to which the scalpels of present-day scientists have given the coup de grâce) must find its reason for being rooted in something that surpasses and transcends and informs changing things like blood and the human word. The mystic theologian who assumed the pseudonym of Dionysius, the pseudo-Areopagite, says somewhere, 'God has disposed the limits of nations according to his angels', and this probably is not a purely mystical concept. Do we not see that in Ireland the Danes, the Firbolgs, the Milesians from Spain, the Norman invaders, and the Anglo-Saxon settlers have united to form a new entity, one might say under the influence of a local deity? And, although the present race in Ireland is backward and inferior, it is worth taking into account the fact that it is the only race of the entire Celtic family that has not been willing to sell its birthright for a mess of pottage.

I find it rather naïve to heap insults on England for her misdeeds in Ireland. A conqueror cannot be casual, and for so many centuries the Englishman has done in Ireland only what the Belgian is doing today in the Congo Free State, and what the Nipponese dwarf will do tomorrow in other lands. She enkindled its factions and took over its treasury. By the introduction of a new system of agriculture, she reduced the power of the native leaders and gave great estates to her soldiers. She persecuted the Roman church when it was rebellious and stopped when it became an effective instrument of subjugation. Her principal preoccupation was to keep the country divided, and if a Liberal English government that enjoyed the full confidence of the English voters were to grant a measure of autonomy to Ireland tomorrow, the conservative press of England would immediately begin to incite the province of Ulster against the authority in Dublin.

She was as cruel as she was cunning. Her weapons were, and still are, the battering-ram, the club, and the rope; and if Parnell was a thorn in the English side, it was primarily because when he was a boy in Wicklow he heard stories of the English ferocity from his nurse. A story that he himself told was about a peasant who had broken the penal laws and was seized at the order of a colonel, stripped, bound to a cart, and whipped by the troops. By the colonel's orders, the whipping was administered on his abdomen in such a way that the miserable man died in atrocious pain, his intestines falling out onto the roadway.

The English now disparage the Irish because they are Catholic, poor, and ignorant; however, it will not be so easy to justify such disparagement to some people. Ireland is poor because English laws ruined the country's industries, especially the wool industry, because the neglect of the English government in the years of the potato famine allowed the best of the population to die from hunger,[1] and because under the present administration, while Ireland is losing its population and crimes are almost non-existent, the judges receive the salary of a king, and governing officials and those in public service receive huge sums for doing little or nothing. In Dublin alone, to take an example, the Lord Lieutenant receives a half-million francs a year. For each policeman, the Dublin citizens pay 3,500 francs a year (twice as much, I suppose, as a high school teacher receives in Italy), and the poor fellow who performs the duties of chief clerk of the city is forced to get along as well as he can on a miserable salary of 6 pounds sterling a day. The English critic is right, then, Ireland is poor, and moreover it is politically backward. For the Irish, the dates of Luther's Reformation and the French Revolution mean nothing. The feudal struggles of the nobles against the king, known in England as the Barons' War, had their counterpart in Ireland. If the English barons knew how to slaughter their neighbours in a noble manner, the Irish barons did, too. At that time in Ireland, there was no lack of ferocious deeds, the fruit of aristocratic blood. The Irish prince, Shane O'Neill, was so strongly blessed by nature that they had to bury him up to his neck in his mother earth every so often, when he had a desire for carnal pleasure. But the Irish barons, cunningly divided by the foreign politician, were never able to act in a common plan. They indulged in childish civil disputes among themselves, and wasted the vitality of the country in wars, while their brothers across St. George's Channel forced King John to sign the Magna Charta (the first chapter of modern liberty) on the field of Runnymede.

[1] Compare the Citizen's remarks in *Ulysses* (p. 320 [310]): 'Where are our missing twenty millions of Irish should be here today instead of four, our lost tribes? And our potteries and textiles, the finest in the whole world! And our wool that was sold in Rome in the time of Juvenal and our flax and our damask from the looms of Antrim and our Limerick lace . . . .

The wave of democracy that shook England at the time of Simon de Montfort, founder of the House of Commons, and later, at the time of Cromwell's protectorate, was spent when it reached the shores of Ireland; so that now Ireland (a country destined by God to be the everlasting caricature of the serious world) is an aristocratic country without an aristocracy. Descendants of the ancient kings (who are addressed by their family names alone, without a prefix) are seen in the halls of the courts of justice, with wig and affidavits, invoking in favour of some defendant the laws that have suppressed their royal titles. Poor fallen kings, recognizable even in their decline as impractical Irishmen. They have never thought of following the example of their English brothers in a similar plight who go to wonderful America to ask the hand of the daughter of some other king, even though he may be a Varnish King or a Sausage King.

Nor is it any harder to understand why the Irish citizen is a reactionary and a Catholic, and why he mingles the names of Cromwell and Satan when he curses. For him, the great Protector of civil rights is a savage beast who came to Ireland to propagate his faith by fire and sword. He does not forget the sack of Drogheda and Waterford, nor the bands of men and women hunted down in the furthermost islands by the Puritan, who said that they would go 'into the ocean or into hell', nor the false oath that the English swore on the broken stone of Limerick.[1] How could he forget? Can the back of a slave forget the rod? The truth is that the English government increased the moral value of Catholicism when they banished it.

Now, thanks partly to the endless speeches and partly to Fenian violence, the reign of terror is over. The penal laws have been revoked. Today, a Catholic in Ireland can vote, can become a government employee, can practise a trade or profession, can teach in a public school, can sit in parliament, can own his own land for longer than thirty years, can keep in his stalls a horse worth more than 5 pounds sterling, and can attend a Catholic mass, without running the risk of being hanged, drawn, and quartered by the common hangman. But these laws have been revoked such a short time ago that a Nationalist member of parliament

[1] The treaty of Limerick (1691), which ended the Williamite wars, guaranteed to Ireland the religious freedom that had been granted her by Charles II, but the English oppression of Irish Catholics in the eighteenth century was the worst in her history.

who is still living was actually sentenced by an English jury to be hanged, drawn, and quartered for the crime of high treason by the common hangman (who is a mercenary in England, chosen by the sheriff from among his mercenary colleagues for conspicuous merit in diligence or industry.)

The Irish populace, which is ninety per cent Catholic, no longer contributes to the maintenance of the Protestant church, which exists only for the well-being of a few thousand settlers. It is enough to say that the English treasury has suffered some loss, and that the Roman church has one more daughter. With regard to the educational system, it allows a few streams of modern thought to filter slowly into the arid soil. In time, perhaps there will be a gradual reawakening of the Irish conscience, and perhaps four or five centuries after the Diet of Worms, we will see an Irish monk throw away his frock, run off with some nun, and proclaim in a loud voice the end of the coherent absurdity that was Catholicism and the beginning of the incoherent absurdity that is Protestantism.[1]

But a Protestant Ireland is almost unthinkable. Without any doubt, Ireland has been up to now the most faithful daughter of the Catholic church. It is perhaps the only country that received the first Christian missionaries with courtesy and was converted to the new doctrine without spilling a drop of blood. And, in fact, the ecclesiastical history of Ireland completely lacks a martyrology, as the Bishop of Cashel had occasion to boast in a reply to the mocker, Giraldus Cambrensis. For six or eight centuries it was the spiritual focus of Christianity. It sent its sons to every country in the world to preach the gospel, and its Doctors to interpret and renew the holy writings.

Its faith was never once shaken seriously, if we except a certain doctrinal tendency of Nestorius in the fifth century concerning the hypostatic union of the two natures in Jesus Christ, some negligible differences in ritual noticeable at the same time, such as the kind of clerical tonsure and the time of celebrating Easter, and finally, the defection of some priests at the urging of the reform emissaries of Edward VII. But at the first intimation that the church was running into danger, a veritable swarm of Irish

[1] Compare Stephen's words in the *Portrait* (p. 514 [277]): 'What kind of liberation would that be to forsake an absurdity which is logical and coherent and to embrace one which is illogical and incoherent?'

envoys left at once for all the coasts of Europe, where they attempted to stir up a strong general movement among the Catholic powers against the heretics.

Well, the Holy See has repaid this fidelity in its own way. First, by means of a papal bull and a ring, it gave Ireland to Henry II of England, and later, in the papacy of Gregory XIII, when the Protestant heresy raised its head, it repented having given faithful Ireland to the English heretics, and to redeem the error, it named a bastard of the papal court[1] as supreme ruler of Ireland. He naturally remained a king *in partibus infidelium*, but the pope's intention was none the less courteous because of this. On the other hand, Ireland's compliance is so complete that it would hardly murmur if tomorrow the pope, having already turned it over to an Englishman and an Italian, were to turn their island over to some *hidalgo* of the court of Alphonso[2] who found himself momentarily unemployed, because of some unforseen complication in Europe. But the Holy See was more chary of its ecclesiastical honours, and although Ireland in the past has enriched the hagiographic archives in the manner that we have seen, this was scarcely recognized in the councils of the Vatican, and more than fourteen hundred years passed before the holy father thought of elevating an Irish bishop to a cardinal.

Now, what has Ireland gained by its fidelity to the papacy and its infidelity to the British crown? It has gained a great deal, but not for itself. Among the Irish writers who adopted the English language in the seventeenth and eighteenth centuries, and almost forgot their native land, are found the names of Berkeley, the idealist philosopher, Oliver Goldsmith, author of *The Vicar of Wakefield*, two famous playwrights, Richard Brinsley Sheridan and William Congreve, whose comic masterpieces are admired even today on the sterile stages of modern England, Jonathan Swift, author of *Gulliver's Travels*, which shares with Rabelais the place of the best satire in world literature, and Edmund Burke, whom the English themselves called the modern Demosthenes and considered the most profound orator who had ever spoken in the House of Commons.

---

[1] Presumably Joyce is referring to Gregory's illegitimate son, Giacomo Buoncompagno. The incident is not dwelt on in papal histories, and the source of Joyce's information is not known.

[2] Alfonso XIII, King of Spain.

Even today, despite her heavy obstacles, Ireland is making her contribution to English art and thought. That the Irish are really the unbalanced, helpless idiots about whom we read in the lead articles of the *Standard* and the *Morning Post* is denied by the names of the three greatest translators in English literature — FitzGerald, translator of the *Rubaiyat* of the Persian poet Omar Khayyam, Burton, translator of the Arabian masterpieces, and Cary, the classic translator of the *Divine Comedy*. It is also denied by the names of other Irishmen — Arthur Sullivan, the dean of modern English music, Edward O'Connor,[1] founder of Chartism, the novelist George Moore, an intellectual oasis in the Sahara of the false spiritualistic, Messianic, and detective writings whose name is legion in England,[2] by the names of two Dubliners, the paradoxical and iconoclastic writer of comedy, George Bernard Shaw, and the too well known Oscar Wilde, son of a revolutionary poetess.

Finally, in the field of practical affairs this pejorative conception of Ireland is given the lie by the fact that when the Irishman is found outside of Ireland in another environment, he very often becomes a respected man. The economic and intellectual conditions that prevail in his own country do not permit the development of individuality. The soul of the country is weakened by centuries of useless struggle and broken treaties, and individual initiative is paralysed by the influence and admonitions of the church, while its body is manacled by the police, the tax office, and the garrison. No one who has any self-respect stays in Ireland, but flees afar as though from a country that has undergone the visitation of an angered Jove.

From the time of the Treaty of Limerick,[3] or rather, from the time that it was broken by the English in bad faith, millions of Irishmen have left their native land. These fugitives, as they were centuries ago, are called the wild geese. They enlisted in all the foreign brigades of the powers of Europe — France, Holland, and Spain, to be exact — and won on many battlefields the laurel of victory for their adopted masters. In America, they found another native land. In the ranks of the American rebels was heard the old Irish language, and Lord Mountjoy himself said in 1784, 'We have

---

[1] Feargus Edward O'Connor.
[2] Compare Joyce's judgment of Moore in 'The Day of the Rabblement', (p. 71 above).
[3] 1691.

lost America through the Irish emigrants.' Today, these Irish emigrants in the United States number sixteen million, a rich, powerful, and industrious settlement. Maybe this does not prove that the Irish dream of a revival is not entirely an illusion!

If Ireland has been able to give to the service of others men like Tyndall, one of the few scientists whose name has spread beyond his own field, like the Marquess of Dufferin,[1] Governor of Canada and Viceroy of India, like Charles Gavin Duffy, and Hennessey,[2] colonial governors, like the Duke de Tetuan,[3] the recent Spanish minister, like Bryan, candidate for president of the United States, like Marshal MacMahon, president of the French Republic, like Lord Charles Beresford, virtual head of the English navy, just recently placed in command of the Channel Fleet, like the three most renowned generals of the English army — Lord Wolseley, the commander-in-chief, Lord Kitchener, victor of the Sudan campaign and at present commanding general of the army in India, and Lord Roberts, victor of the war in Afghanistan and South Africa — if Ireland has been able to give all this practical talent to the service of others, it means that there must be something inimical, unpropitious, and despotic in its own present conditions, since her sons cannot give their efforts to their own native land.

Because, even today, the flight of the wild geese continues. Every year, Ireland, decimated as she already is, loses 60,000 of her sons. From 1850 to the present day, more than 5,000,000 emigrants have left for America, and every post brings to Ireland their inviting letters to friends and relatives at home. The old men, the corrupt, the children, and the poor stay at home, where the double yoke wears another groove in the tamed neck; and around the death bed where the poor, anaemic, almost lifeless, body lies in agony, the rulers give orders and the priests administer last rites.

Is this country destined to resume its ancient position as the Hellas of the north some day?[4] Is the Celtic mind, like the Slavic

---

[1] Frederick Temple Blackwood, Marquess of Dufferin and Ava (1826–1902).

[2] John Bobanau Nickerlieu Hennessey (1829–1910), Deputy Surveyor–General of India.

[3] Leopold O'Donnell, Duke of Tetuan (1809–67), who served as war minister of Spain, and was several times premier.

[4] 'God, Kinch, if you and I could only work together we might do something for the island. Hellenise it.' *Ulysses.* p. 9 (5).

mind which it resembles in many ways, destined to enrich the civil conscience with new discoveries and new insights in the future? Or must the Celtic world, the five Celtic nations, driven by stronger nations to the edge of the continent, to the outermost islands of Europe, finally be cast into the ocean after a struggle of centuries? Alas, we dilettante sociologists are only second-class augurers. We look and peer into the innards of the human animal, and, after all, confess that we see nothing there. Only our supermen know how to write the history of the future.

It would be interesting, but beyond the scope I have set myself tonight, to see what might be the effects on our civilization of a revival of this race. The economic effects of the appearance of a rival island near England, a bilingual, republican, self-centred, and enterprising island with its own commercial fleet, and its own consuls in every port of the world. And the moral effects of the appearance in old Europe of the Irish artist and thinker — those strange spirits, frigid enthusiasts, sexually and artistically untaught, full of idealism and unable to yield to it, childish spirits, ingenuous and satirical, 'the loveless Irishmen', as they are called. But in anticipation of such a revival, I confess that I do not see what good it does to fulminate against the English tyranny while the Roman tyranny occupies the palace of the soul.

I do not see the purpose of the bitter invectives against the English despoiler, the disdain for the vast Anglo-Saxon civilization, even though it is almost entirely a materialistic civilization, nor the empty boasts that the art of miniature in the ancient Irish books, such as the *Book of Kells*, the *Yellow Book of Lecan*, the *Book of the Dun Cow*, which date back to a time when England was an uncivilized country, is almost as old as the Chinese, and that Ireland made and exported to Europe its own fabrics for several generations before the first Fleming arrived in London to teach the English how to make bread. If an appeal to the past in this manner were valid, the fellahin of Cairo would have all the right in the world to disdain to act as porters for English tourists.[1] Ancient Ireland is dead just as ancient Egypt is dead. Its death chant has been sung, and on its gravestone has been placed the seal. The old national soul that spoke during the centuries through the mouths of fabulous seers, wandering minstrels, and Jacobite

---

[1] 'Kingdoms of this world. The masters of the Mediterranean are fellaheen today.' *Ulysses*, p. 142 (134).

poets disappeared from the world with the death of James Clarence Mangan.[1] With him, the long tradition of the triple order of the old Celtic bards ended; and today other bards, animated by other ideals, have the cry.

One thing alone seems clear to me. It is well past time for Ireland to have done once and for all with failure. If she is truly capable of reviving, let her awake, or let her cover up her head and lie down decently in her grave forever. 'We Irishmen', said Oscar Wilde one day to a friend of mine,[2] 'have done nothing, but we are the greatest talkers since the time of the Greeks.' But though the Irish are eloquent, a revolution is not made of human breath and compromises. Ireland has already had enough equivocations and misunderstandings. If she wants to put on the play that we have waited for so long, this time let it be whole, and complete, and definitive. But our advice to the Irish producers is the same as that our fathers gave them not so long ago — hurry up! I am sure that I, at least, will never see that curtain go up, because I will have already gone home on the last train.

[1] This looks forward to the lecture on Mangan that was to follow.
[2] Yeats.

36

James Clarence Mangan [2][1]

1907

Joyce's second Italian lecture, on Mangan, wrestles frankly with the problem of Mangan's limitations which, in his paper on Mangan read at University College five years before, he had glossed over. He now concedes that Mangan had not sufficiently freed himself from 'the idols without and within'. Mangan no longer appears to him primarily as a great poet; rather he is a great symbolic figure, whose verse enshrines the griefs and aspirations and limitations of his people. In some parts of his lecture Joyce retains and translates his earlier essay, but in other parts, notably the beginning, he is much more muscular, and clearly dissociates his own personality from Mangan's fainting rhythms.

There are certain poets who, in addition to the virtue of revealing to us some phase of the human conscience unknown until their time, also have the more doubtful virtue of summing up in themselves the thousand contrasting tendencies of their era, of being, so to speak, the storage batteries of new forces. For the most part, it is in the latter role rather than the former that they come to be appreciated by the masses, who are by nature unable to evaluate any work of true self-revelation, and so hasten to

---

[1] Translated from the Italian of 'Giacomo Clarenzio Mangan', an incomplete heavily corrected holograph manuscript of twenty-four pages in the Slocum Collection of the Yale University Library. In the Joyce papers at the Cornell University Library there is a typed manuscript version of this lecture that was copied, with a number of errors, from the holograph manuscript at a time when page four was missing from it. Page four is one of two pages found separately by John Slocum and added to the manuscript at some time before his collection went to Yale. The other page is unnumbered, and, as indicated in footnote 1, p. 186 below, apparently is not a part of this manuscript.

recognize by some act of grace the incalculable aid that the individual affirmation of a poet gives to a popular movement. The most popular act of grace in such cases is a monument, because it honours the dead while it flatters the living. It has also the supreme advantage of finality, since, to tell the truth, it is the most polite and effective way to assure a lasting oblivion of the deceased. In logical and serious countries, it is customary to finish the monument in a decent manner, and have the sculptor, the city officials, orators, and a great crowd of people attend the unveiling. But in Ireland, a country destined by God to be the eternal caricature of the serious world,[1] even when the monuments are for the most popular men, whose character is most amenable to the will of the people, they rarely get beyond the laying of the foundation stone. In the light of the foregoing, perhaps I can give you an idea of the Cimmerian night that enfolds the name of Clarence Mangan when I say that, to the detriment of the noted generosity of the Emerald Isle, up to now no ardent spirit has thought of laying the restless ghost of the national poet with the foundation stone and the usual wreaths. Perhaps the unbroken peace in which he lies will have become so pleasant for him that he will be offended (if mortal accents ever come to that world beyond the grave) at hearing his spectral quiet disturbed by a countryman in exile,[2] at hearing an amateur talk about him in a strange tongue before well-wishing foreigners.

Ireland's contribution to European literature can be divided into five periods and into two large parts, that is, literature written in the Irish language and literature written in the English language. Of the first part, which includes the first two periods, the more remote is almost lost in the night of the times in which all the ancient sacred books, the epics, the legal codes, and the topographic histories and legends were written. The more recent period lasted a long time after the invasion of the Anglo-Saxons and Normans under Henry II and King John, the age of the wandering minstrels, whose symbolic songs carried on the tradition of the triple order of the old Celtic bards, and of this period I had occasion to speak to you several nights ago.[3] The second part, that of Irish literature written in the English language, is divided

---

[1] Repeated from 'Ireland, Island of Saints and Sages' (p. 168 above).
[2] This is the only recorded time that Joyce describes himself as an 'exile'.
  A reference to his lecture 'Ireland, Island of Saints and Sages'.

into three periods. The first is the eighteenth century, which includes among other Irishmen the glorious names of Oliver Goldsmith,[1] author of the famous novel *The Vicar of Wakefield*, of the two famous writers of comedy, Richard Brinsley Sheridan and William Congreve, whose masterpieces are admired even today on the sterile stage of modern England, of the Rabelaisian Dean, Jonathan Swift, author of *Gulliver's Travels*, of the so-called English Demosthenes, Edmund Burke, whom even his English critics consider the most profound orator that ever spoke in the House of Commons and one of the wisest statesmen, even among the astute band of politicians of fair Albion. The second and third periods belong to the last century. One is the literary movement of Young Ireland in '42 and '45, and the other the literary movement of today, of which I intend to speak to you in my next lecture.[2]

The literary movement of '42 dates from the establishment of the separatist newspaper *The Nation*, founded by the three leaders Thomas Davis, John Blake Dillon (father of the former leader of the Irish parliamentary party)

[one page missing]

of the middle class, and after a childhood passed in the midst of domestic cruelties, misfortunes, and misery, he became a clerk in a third-rate notary's office. He had always been a child of quiet and unresponsive nature, secretly given to the study of various languages, retiring, silent, preoccupied with religious matters, without friends or acquaintances. When he began to write, he immediately attracted the attention of the cultured, who recognized in him an exalted lyrical music and a burning idealism that revealed themselves in rhythms of extraordinary and unpremeditated beauty, to be found, perhaps, nowhere else in the range of English literature except in the inspired songs of Shelley. Thanks to the influence of some literary men, he obtained a position as assistant in the great library of Trinity College, Dublin, a rich treasure of books three times as large as the Victor Emmanuel Library in Rome,[3] and the place where such ancient Irish books as *The Book of the Dun Cow*, *The Yellow Book of Lecan* (a famous

---

[1] Joyce is less impressed with Goldsmith in the review of Ainger's *George Crabbe*, p. 129 above, but speaks equally well of him in 'Ireland, Island of Saints and Sages', p. 170 above.

[2] This lecture on the Irish literary renaissance has not survived.

[3] The National Library of Italy.

legal treatise, the work of the learned king Cormac the Magnificent,[1] who was called the Irish Solomon) and *The Book of Kells* are kept, books that date back to the first century of the Christian era, and in the art of miniature are as old as the Chinese.[2] There it was that his biographer and friend Mitchel[3] saw him for the first time, and in the preface to the poet's works, he describes the impression made on him by this thin little man with the waxen countenance and the pale hair, who was sitting on the top of a ladder with his legs crossed, deciphering a huge, dusty volume in the dim light.

In this library Mangan passed his days in study and became a competent linguist. He knew well the Italian, Spanish, French and German languages and literatures, as well as those of England and Ireland, and it appears that he had some knowledge of oriental languages, probably some Sanskrit and Arabic. From time to time he emerged from that studious quiet to contribute some poems to the revolutionary newspaper, but he took little interest in the nightly meetings of the party. He passed his nights far away. His dwelling was a dark and dingy room in the old city, a quarter of Dublin that even today has the significant name 'The Liberties'.[4] His nights were so many Stations of the Cross among the disreputable dives of 'The Liberties', where he must have made a very strange figure in the midst of the choice flower of the city's low-life — petty thieves, bandits, fugitives, pimps and inexpensive harlots. It is strange to say (but it is the consensus of opinion among his countrymen, who are always ready to testify in such matters) that Mangan had nothing but purely formal intercourse with this underworld. He drank little, but his health was so weakened that drinking produced an extraordinary effect on him. The death mask that is left to us shows a refined, almost aristocratic face, in whose delicate lines it is impossible to discover anything but melancholy and great weariness.

I understand that pathologists deny the possibility of combining

---

[1] Cormac Mac Art was not called, like Lorenzo, 'the Magnificent', and while his reign in the third century was the most splendid of all the pagan kings of Ireland it was a far cry from the high Italian Renaissance. Joyce is confusing the *Yellow Book of Lecan*, which is not a legal treatise, with the *Book of Aicill*, which is thought to be a collection of Cormac's legal opinions.

[2] Repeated from 'Ireland, Island of Saints and Sages', (p. 173 above).

[3] John Mitchel (1815–75), a leader in the Young Ireland movement.

[4] 'Outside *la Maison Claire* Blazes Boylan waylaid Jack Mooney's brother-in-law, humpty, tight, making for the liberties.' *Ulysses*, p. 243 (233).

the pleasures of alcohol with those of opium, and it seems that Mangan soon became convinced of this fact, because he began to take narcotic drugs immoderately. Mitchel tells us that toward the end of his life Mangan looked like a living skeleton. His face was fleshless, barely covered with a skin as transparent as fine China. His body was gaunt, his eyes, behind whose infrequent glimmerings seemed to be hidden the horrible and voluptuous memories of his visions, were large, fixed, and vacant, his voice slow, weak, and sepulchral. He descended the last steps toward the grave with frightening rapidity. He became mute and ragged. He ate hardly enough to keep body and soul together, until one day he collapsed suddenly while he was walking in the street. When he was carried to the hospital, a few coins and a worn book of German poetry were found in his pockets. When he died, his miserable body made the attendants shudder, and some charitable friends paid the cost of his sordid burial.

So lived and died the man that I consider the most significant poet of the modern Celtic world, and one of the most inspired singers that ever used the lyric form in any country. It is too early, I think, to assert that he must live forever in the drab fields of oblivion, but I am firmly convinced that if he finally emerges into the posthumous glory to which he has a right, it will not be by the help of any of his countrymen. Mangan will be accepted by the Irish as their national poet on the day when the conflict will be decided between my native land and the foreign powers — Anglo-Saxon and Roman Catholic, and a new civilization will arise, either indigenous or completely foreign. Until that time, he will be forgotten or remembered rarely on holidays as

[*one page missing*]

The question that Wagner put into the mouth of the innocent Parsifal[1] must come to mind when we read from time to time certain English criticism, due for the most part to the influence of the blind and bitter spirit of Calvinism. It is easy to explain these critics when they deal with a powerful and original genius, because the appearance of such a genius is always a signal for all the corrupt and vested interests to join together in defence of the old

---

[1] 'Who is good?' While the lecture has been original to this point, this entire paragraph is merely an inflated version of a similar paragraph in the original Mangan essay, p. 76 above.

order. For instance, anyone who has understood the destructive and fiercely self-centred tendency of all of Henrik Ibsen's works will not be astonished to hear the most influential critics in London inveighing against the playwright on the morning after one of Ibsen's first nights, calling him (I quote the exact words of the deceased critic of the *Daily Telegraph*) a filthy, muck-ferreting dog.[1] But the case in which the poor condemned man is some more or less innocuous poet whose fault is that of not having been able to adhere scrupulously to the cult of respectability is less explainable. And[2] so it happens that when Mangan's name is mentioned in his native land (and I must admit that he is sometimes spoken of in literary circles) the Irish lament that such poetic talent was found joined in him to such licence, and they are naïvely surprised to find evidence of the poetic faculty in a man whose vices were exotic and whose patriotism was not very ardent.

Those who have written about him have been scrupulous in holding the balance between the drunkard and the opium-eater, and have taken great pains to determine whether learning or imposture was hidden behind such phrases as 'translated from the Ottoman', 'translated from the Coptic'; and save for this poor remembrance, Mangan has been a stranger in his native land, a rare and bizarre figure in the streets, where he is seen going sadly and alone, like one who does penance for some ancient sin. Surely life, which Novalis has called a malady of the spirit, is a heavy penance for Mangan, for him who has, perhaps, forgotten the sin that laid it on him, an inheritance so much the more sorrowful, too, because of the delicate artist in him who reads so well the lines of brutality and of weakness in the faces of men that look at him with hate and scorn. In the short biographical sketch that he has left us, he speaks only of his early life, his infancy and childhood, and tells us that as a child he knew nothing but sordid misery and coarseness, that his acquaintances defiled his person with their

[1] See footnote 1 to 'Ibsen's New Drama', p. 48 above. The original epithet 'educated and muck-ferreting dogs', applied to Ibsen's admirers, appeared anonymously in a magazine named *Truth*, and was repeated, with a protest, in the *Pall Mall Gazette*, and later in Shaw's *Quintessence of Ibsenism*. Joyce alters the phrase to impress his audience.

[2] From this point on Joyce follows his early essay on Mangan, but with sizeable interpolations that provide a measure of Joyce's growth in the five years between 1902 and 1907. We have used the diction of the early essay wherever it is clear that Joyce is translating it. The footnotes to the early essay are not repeated here.

hateful venom, that his father was a human rattlesnake. In these violent assertions we recognize the effects of the oriental drug, but nevertheless, those who think that his story is only the figment of a disordered brain have never known, or have forgotten what keen pain contact with gross natures inflicts on a sensitive boy. His sufferings drove him to become a hermit, and in fact he lived the greater part of his life almost in a dream, in that sanctuary of the mind where for many centuries the sad and the wise have elected to be. When a friend remarked to him that the tale mentioned above was wildly exaggerated and partly false, Mangan answered, 'Maybe I dreamed it.' The world has evidently become somewhat unreal for him, and not very significant.

What, then, will become of those dreams, which, for every young and simple heart are garbed in such dear reality? One whose nature is so sensitive cannot forget his dreams in a secure and strenuous life. He doubts them for the first time and rejects them, but when he hears someone deride and curse them, he would acknowledge them proudly; and where sensitivity has induced weakness, or, as with Mangan, refined an innate weakness, would even compromise with the world to win at least the favour of silence, as for something too frail to bear a violent disdain, for that desire of the heart so cynically derided, that cruelly abused idea. His manner is such that none can say whether it is pride or humility that looks out of his vague face, which seems to live only in the clear and shining eyes, and in the fair and silken hair, of which he is a little vain. This reserve is not without dangers, and in the end it is only his excesses that save him from indifference. There is some talk of an intimate relation between Mangan and a pupil of his to whom he gave instruction in German, and later, it seems, he took part in a love-comedy of three, but if he is reserved with men, he is timid with women, and he is too self-conscious, too critical, knows too little of the flattering lie ever to be a gallant. In his strange dress — the high conical hat, the baggy trousers three times too big for his little legs, and the old umbrella shaped like a torch — we can see an almost comical expression of his diffidence. The learning of many lands goes with him always, eastern tales and the remembrance of curiously printed medieval books which have rapt him out of his time, gathered day by day and woven into a fabric. He knows twenty languages, more or less, and sometimes makes a liberal show of them, and has read in many literatures, crossing how many seas, even penetrating into the land of Peristan, which is found in no atlas. He is very much interested in the life of the seeress of Prevorst, and in all the phenomena of the middle nature, and here, where most of all the sweetness and resoluteness of soul have power, he seems to seek in a fictitious world, but how different from that in which Watteau (in Pater's happy phrase) may have sought, both with a certain characteristic inconstancy, what is found there in no satisfying measure or not at all.

His writings, which have never been collected in a definitive edition, are completely without order and often without thought. His essays in prose are perhaps interesting on the first reading, but, in truth, they are insipid attempts. The style is conceited, in the worst sense of the word, strained, and banal, the subject trivial and inflated, the kind of prose, in fact, in which the bits of local news are written in a bad rural newspaper. It must be remembered that Mangan wrote without a native literary tradition, and wrote for a public that was interested only in the events of the day, and insisted that the only task of the poet was to illustrate these events. He was unable to revise his work, except in unusual cases, but, aside from the so-called humorous burlesques, and the occasional poems, which are obvious and unpolished, the best part of his work makes a genuine appeal; because it was conceived in the imagination, which he himself calls, I think, the mother of things, whose dream we are, who images us to herself, and to us, and images herself in us, that power before whose breath the mind in creation becomes (to use Shelley's phrase) a fading coal. Though in that which he has written best the presence of alien emotions is often felt, the presence of an imaginative personality reflecting the light of imaginative beauty is felt even more vividly. East and West meet in that personality (we now know how), images interweave there like soft luminous scarves, the words shine and ring like the links in a coat of mail, and whether he sings of Ireland or of Istamboul, his prayer is always the same, that peace may come again to her who has lost it, the pearl of his soul, as he calls her, Ameen.

This figure which he adores recalls the spiritual yearnings and the imaginary loves of the Middle Ages, and Mangan has placed his lady in a world full of melody, of lights and perfumes, a world that grows fatally to frame every face that the eyes of a poet have gazed on with love. There is only one chivalrous idea, only one male devotion, that lights up the faces of Vittoria Colonna, Laura, and Beatrice, just as the bitter disillusion and the self-disdain that end the chapter are one and the same. But the world in which Mangan wishes his lady to dwell is different from the marble temple built by Buonarotti, and from the peaceful oriflamme[1] of the Florentine theologian. It is a wild world, a world of night in the orient. The mental activity that comes from opium has scattered this world of magnificent and terrible images, and all the orient that the poet recreated in his flaming dream, which is the paradise of the opium-eater, pulsates in these pages in Apocalyptic phrases and similes and landscapes. He speaks of the moon that languishes in the midst of a riot of purple colours, of the magic book of heaven red with fiery signs, of the sea foaming over saffron sands, of the lonely cedar on the peaks of the Balkans, of the barbaric hall shining with golden crescents luxuriously permeated with the breath of roses from the gulistan of the king.

The most famous of Mangan's poems, those in which he sings hymns of praise to his country's fallen glory under a veil of mysticism, seem like a cloud that covers the horizon on a summer's day, thin, impalpable, ready to disperse, and suffused with little points of light. Sometimes the music seems to waken from its lethargy and shouts with the ecstasy of combat. In the final stanzas of the *Lament for the Princes of Tir-Owen and Tirconnell*,[2] in long lines full of tremendous force, he has put all the energy of his race:

[1] Compare *Ulysses*, p. 137 (129): 'quella pacifica oriafiamma'. The phrase, from *Paradiso*, XXXI, 127, refers to the Virgin Mary, not to Dante's Lady, Beatrice.

[2] These lines are actually from Mangan's *O'Hussey's Ode to The Maguire*. Joyce's Italian translation is as follows:

> Benchè stanotte il gelo cristallizi la ruggiada limpida
> dei suoi occhi,
> Benchè manipoli candidi di ghiaccio inguantino le sue dita
> nobili, fini, sottili e pallide,
> Vestito caldo è per lui quello che portò sempre, vestito
> di lampo,
> Lampo dell'anima e non dei cieli.
>
> Ugo andò alla battaglia. Piansi al vederlo partir così,
> Ed, ahimè, stanotte erra senza speme, moribondo sotto la
> pioggia algente.
> Ma la memoria delle magioni nivee che la sua mano mise
> In ceneri effoca il cuor del prode.

And though frost glaze to-night the clear dew of his eyes,
And white gauntlets glove his noble fair fine fingers o'er,
A warm dress is to him that lightning-garb he ever wore,
The lightning of the soul, not skies.

Hugh marched forth to the fight — I grieved to see him so depart;
And lo! to-night he wanders frozen, rain-drenched, sad, betrayed —
But the memory of the lime-white mansions his right hand
    hath laid
In ashes warms the hero's heart.

I do not know any other passage in English literature in which the spirit of revenge has been joined to such heights of melody. It is true that sometimes this heroic note becomes raucous, and a troop of unmannerly passions echoes it derisively, but a poet like Mangan who sums up in himself the soul of a country and an era does not so much try to create for the entertainment of some dilettante as to transmit to posterity the animating idea of his life by the force of crude blows. On the other hand, it cannot be denied that Mangan always kept his poetic soul spotless. Although he wrote such a wonderful English style, he refused to collaborate with the English newspapers or reviews; although he was the spiritual focus of his time, he refused to prostitute himself to the rabble or to make himself the loud-speaker of politicians. He was one of those strange abnormal spirits who believe that their artistic life should be nothing more than a true and continual revelation of their spiritual life, who believe that their inner life is so valuable that they have no need of popular support, and thus abstain from proffering confessions of faith, who believe, in sum, that the poet is sufficient in himself, the heir and preserver of a secular patrimony, who therefore has no urgent need to become a shouter, or a preacher, or a perfumer.

Now what is this central idea that Mangan wants to hand down to posterity? All his poetry records injustice and tribulation, and the aspiration of one who is moved to great deeds and rending cries when he sees again in his mind the hour of his grief. This is the theme of a large part of Irish poetry, but no other Irish poems are full, as are those of Mangan, of misfortune nobly suffered, of vastation of soul so irreparable. Naomi wished to change her name to Mara, because she had known too well how bitter is the existence of mortals, and is it not perhaps a profound sense of sorrow and bitterness that explains in Mangan all the names and titles that he gives himself, and the fury of translation in which he tried to hide himself? For he did not find in himself the faith of the solitary, or the faith that in the Middle Ages sent the spires in the air like triumphant songs, and he waits his hour, the hour that will end his sad days of penance. Weaker than Leopardi, for he has not the courage of his own despair, but forgets every ill and forgoes all scorn when someone shows him a little kindness, he has, perhaps for this reason, the memorial that he wished, a ['constant presence with those that love me'.][1]

[*one page missing*]

[Poetry, even when apparently most fantastic, is always a revolt against artifice, a revolt, in][1] a certain sense, against actuality. It speaks of that which seems unreal and fantastic to those who have lost the simple intuitions which are the tests of reality. Poetry considers many of the idols of the market place unimportant — the succession of the ages, the spirit of the age, the mission of the race. The poet's central effort is to free himself from the unfortunate influence of these idols that corrupt him from without and within, and certainly it would be false to assert that Mangan has always made this effort. The history of his country encloses him so straitly that even in his hours of extreme individual passion he can barely reduce its walls to ruins. He cries out in his life and in his mournful verses against the injustice of despoilers, but almost never laments a loss greater than that of buckles and banners. He inherits the latest and worst part of a tradition upon which no divine hand has ever traced a boundary, a tradition which is loosened and divided against itself as it moves down the cycles. And precisely because this tradition has become an obsession with him, he has accepted it with all its regrets and failures and would pass it on just as it is. The poet who hurls his lightning against tyrants would establish upon the future an intimate and crueller tyranny. The figure that he adores has the appearance of an abject queen to whom, because of the bloody crimes that she has committed and the no less bloody crimes committed against her by the hands of others, madness has come and death is about to come, but who does not wish to believe that she is about to die, and

[1] Supplied from the early Mangan essay.

remembers only the rumour of voices that besiege her sacred garden and her lovely flowers that have become *pabulum aprorum*, food for wild boars. Love of grief, despair, high-sounding threats — these are the great traditions of the race of James Clarence Mangan, and in that impoverished figure, thin and weakened, an hysterical nationalism receives its final justification.

In what niche of the temple of glory should we place his image? If he has never won the sympathy of his own countrymen, how can he win that of foreigners? Doesn't it seem probable that the oblivion that he would almost have desired awaits him? Certainly he did not find in himself the force to reveal to us triumphant beauty, the splendour of truth that the ancients deify. He is a romantic, a herald manqué, the prototype of a nation manqué, but with all that, one who has expressed in a worthy form the sacred indignation of his soul cannot have written his name in water. In those vast courses of multiplex life that surround us, and in that vast memory which is greater and more generous than ours, probably no life, no moment of exaltation is ever lost; and all those who have written in noble disdain have not written in vain, although, weary and [desperate, they have never heard the silver laughter of wisdom.][1]

[*The manuscript ends here.*]

[1] Supplied from the early Mangan essay. Joyce has very nearly reached the end of that essay, and the tone of this lecture seems to be moving to a similar conclusion. An additional unnumbered page inserted in this essay by John Slocum discusses the struggle in Ireland between the party of violence and the party of non-violence. It does not fit any of the single-page lacunae in the manuscript, and since Mangan had very little to do with politics of any kind, it is difficult to see how the lecture could have continued from this point in a direction that would encompass the extra page.

37

Fenianism

THE LAST FENIAN[1]

1907

In Joyce's time in Trieste the most important newspaper was Il Piccolo della Sera, *founded in 1881 by Teodoro Mayer. The* Piccolo *made no secret of its desire to see Trieste under Italian instead of Austrian rule, and Mayer's zeal in the Irredentist cause was rewarded after the First World War when he was made an Italian Senator. He had chosen for his editor a clever, dapper journalist, Roberto Prezioso, to whom Joyce taught English early in his Triestine stay. Prezioso liked Joyce and knew of his financial difficulties, which, after his return from Rome in March 1907, were worse than before. Having heard Joyce talk about Ireland, Prezioso proposed that he write a series of articles about his country, expecting that the display of the evils of British imperial rule in Ireland would have its lesson for the imperial ruler of Trieste. Joyce was pleased with the pay, which Prezioso agreed to make higher than that of his other contributors, and also liked to display his graceful and idiomatic Italian.*

The first three articles ('Fenianism', 'Home Rule Comes of Age', 'Ireland at the Bar'), written in 1907, surveyed the Irish political situation, finding fault with the Irish as well as the British, but supporting Sinn Fein *and the independence movement. The third is written in a tone quite different from the first two, as if, having said all he wished about the defects of the Irish, Joyce wanted now to defend their position as eloquently as he could.*

The next two articles ('Oscar Wilde: the Poet of Salomé', 'Bernard Shaw's Battle with the Censor'), written in 1909, were occasional.

[1] Translated from the Italian of 'Il Fenianismo. L'Ultimo Feniano', *Il Piccolo della Sera*, Trieste, March 22, 1907.

The first was written in connection with the first production in Trieste of Strauss's Salomé, *based on Oscar Wilde's play; Joyce took the opportunity to represent Wilde as the type of the betrayed artist. The second was written in Dublin, where Joyce was visiting in the summer of 1909; he attended the première there of Shaw's* The Shewing-Up of Blanco Posnet, *which had been forbidden in England, and, while disliking the play, admired the attack on censorship of the theatre.*

In his next two articles ('The Home Rule Comet', 'The Shade of Parnell'), written in 1910 and 1912, Joyce treats with equal indignation the British delays of the Irish Home Rule bills, and the Irish abandonment of their greatest leader, Parnell. Then, in his last two articles ('The City of the Tribes', 'The Mirage of the Fisherman of Aran'), which are travel pieces, he changes his tone and writes deftly and attractively about Galway and about the Aran Islands, to which he went in 1912 for the first time.

With the recent death of John O'Leary in Dublin on St. Patrick's Day,[1] the Irish national holiday, went perhaps the last actor in the turbid drama of Fenianism, a time-honoured name derived from the old Irish language (in which the word 'fenians' means the King's bodyguard) which came to designate the Irish insurrectionist movement. Anyone who studies the history of the Irish revolution during the nineteenth century finds himself faced with a double struggle — the struggle of the Irish nation against the English government, and the struggle, perhaps no less bitter, between the moderate patriots and the so-called party of physical force. This party under different names: 'White Boys', 'Men of '98', 'United Irishmen', 'Invincibles', 'Fenians', has always refused to be connected with either the English political parties or the Nationalist parliamentarians. They maintain (and in this assertion history fully supports them) that any concessions that have been granted to Ireland, England has granted unwillingly, and, as it is usually put, at the point of a bayonet. The intransigent press never ceases to greet the deeds of the Nationalist representatives at Westminster with virulent and ironic comments, and although it recognizes that in view of England's power armed revolt has

[1] March 17, 1907.

now become an impossible dream, it has never stopped inculcating in the minds of the coming generation the dogma of separatism.

Unlike Robert Emmet's foolish uprising[1] or the impassioned movement of Young Ireland in '45, the Fenianism of '67 was not one of the usual flashes of Celtic temperament that lighten the shadows for a moment and leave behind a darkness blacker than before. At the time that the movement arose, the population of the Emerald Isles was more than eight million, while that of England was no more than seventeen million. Under the leadership of James Stephens, head of the Fenians, the country was organized into circles composed of a Sergeant and twenty-five men, a plan eminently fitted to the Irish character because it reduces to a minimum the possibility of betrayal. These circles formed a vast and intricate net, whose threads were in Stephens' hands. At the same time, the American Fenians were organized in the same way, and the two movements worked in concert. Among the Fenians there were many soldiers in the English Army, police spies, prison guards, and jailers.

Everything seemed to go well, and the Republic was on the point of being established (it was even proclaimed openly by Stephens), when O'Leary and Luby, editors of the party newspaper, were arrested. The government put a price on Stephens' head, and announced that it knew all the locations where the Fenians held their military drills by night. Stephens was arrested and imprisoned, but succeeded in escaping, thanks to the loyalty of a Fenian prison guard; and while the English agents and spies were under cover at every port, watching the departing ships, he left the capital in a gig, disguised as a bride (according to legend) with a white crepe veil and orange blossoms.[2] Then he was taken aboard a little charcoal boat[3] that quickly set sail for France. O'Leary was tried and condemned to twenty years of forced labour, but later he was pardoned and exiled from Ireland for fifteen years.

[1] In 1803. Joyce's attitude toward Emmet is reflected in the burlesque execution in the 'Cyclops' episode of *Ulysses* (pp. 301–5 [291–5]), which is reminiscent of Emmet's execution, and in his treatment of Emmet's speech from the dock, (*Ulysses* p. 286 [276]).

[2] 'How the head centre got away, authentic version. Got up as a young bride, man, veil, orangeblossoms . . . .' *Ulysses*, p. 44 (40).

[3] Stanislaus Joyce in *My Brother's Keeper* pp. 77–8 (93), says that his father was a friend of the captain of this boat; but the expression, 'There's the man that got away James Stephens,' was a catchphrase in Dublin.

And why this disintegration of a movement so well organized? Simply because in Ireland, just at the right moment, an informer always appears.[1]

* * * *

After the dispersal of the Fenians, the tradition of the doctrine of physical force shows up at intervals in violent crimes. The Invincibles blow up the prison at Clerkenwell,[2] snatch their friends from the hands of the police at Manchester and kill the escort,[3] stab to death in broad daylight the English Chief Secretary, Lord Frederick Cavendish, and the Under-secretary, Burke, in Phoenix Park, Dublin.[4]

After each one of these crimes, when the general indignation has calmed a little, an English minister proposes to the House some reform measure for Ireland, and the Fenians and Nationalists revile each other with the greatest scorn, one side attributing the measure to the success of parliamentary tactics and the other attributing it to the persuasive faculty of the knife or the bomb. And as a backdrop to this sad comedy is the spectacle of a population which diminishes year by year with mathematical regularity, of the uninterrupted emigration to the United States or Europe of Irishmen for whom the economic and intellectual conditions of their native land are unbearable. And almost as if to set in relief this depopulation there is a long parade of churches, cathedrals, convents, monasteries, and seminaries to tend to the spiritual needs of those who have been unable to find courage or money enough to undertake the voyage from Queenstown to New York. Ireland, weighed down by multiple duties, has fulfilled what has hitherto been considered an impossible task — serving both God and Mammon, letting herself be milked by England and yet increasing Peter's pence (perhaps in memory of Pope Adrian IV, who made a gift of

[1] There were contributing factors: in 1863 Stephens founded a newspaper, the *Irish People*, to be the mouthpiece of a secret movement, its banner announced that '65 was the year of action, and all the leaders of the movement worked on the paper, conveniently located within a stone's throw of Dublin Castle, the centre of British authority.

[2] In an attempt to release Fenian prisoners, the wall of the prison at Clerkenwell, London, was blown up on December 13, 1867. 'Lover, for her love he prowled with colonel Richard Burke, tanist of his sept, under the walls of Clerkenwell, and crouching, saw a flame of vengeance hurl them upward in the fog.' *Ulysses*, p. 44(40).

[3] November 1867.

[4] May 6, 1882, the year of Joyce's birth. This event is referred to frequently in *Ulysses*.

the island to the English King Henry II about 800 years ago, in a moment of generosity).

Now, it is impossible for a desperate and bloody doctrine like Fenianism to continue its existence in an atmosphere like this, and in fact, as agrarian crimes and crimes of violence have become more and more rare, Fenianism too has once more changed its name and appearance. It is still a separatist doctrine but it no longer uses dynamite. The new Fenians are joined in a party which is called Sinn Fein (We Ourselves).[1] They aim to make Ireland a bi-lingual Republic, and to this end they have established a direct steamship service between Ireland and France. They practise boycotts against English goods; they refuse to become soldiers or to take the oath of loyalty to the English crown; they are trying to develop industries throughout the entire island; and instead of paying out a million and a quarter annually for the maintenance of eighty representatives in the English Parliament, they want to inaugurate a consular service in the principal ports of the world for the purpose of selling their industrial products without the intervention of England.

*   *   *   *

From many points of view, this last phase of Fenianism is perhaps the most formidable. Certainly its influence has once more remodelled the character of the Irish people, and when the old leader O'Leary returned to his native land after years spent in study while an exile in Paris, he found himself among a generation animated by ideals quite different from those of '65. He was received by his compatriots with marks of honour, and from time to time appeared in public to preside over some separatist conference or some banquet. But he was a figure from a world which had disappeared. He would often be seen walking along the river, an old man dressed in light-coloured clothes, with a shock of very white hair hanging down to his shoulders, almost bent in two from old age and suffering. He would stop in front of the gloomy shops of the old-book dealers, and having made some purchase, would return along the river. Aside from this, he had little reason to be happy. His plots had gone up in smoke, his friends had died, and in his own native land, very few knew who he was and what he had

---

[1] Founded by Arthur Griffith in 1899.

done.[1] Now that he is dead, his countrymen will escort him to his tomb with great pomp. Because the Irish, even though they break the hearts of those who sacrifice their lives for their native land, never fail to show great respect for the dead.

JAMES JOYCE

[1] This account of O'Leary as a broken and lonely figure after his return to Dublin in 1885 is at variance with that of Yeats, who saw him as one of the chief begetters of the Irish literary revival of the 1890's.

38

Home Rule Comes of Age[1]

1907

Twenty-one years ago, on the evening of April 9, 1886, the streets that led to the office of the Nationalist newspaper in Dublin were jammed with people. From time to time, a bulletin printed in four-inch letters would appear on the wall, and in this way the crowd was able to participate in the scene unfolding at Westminster, where the galleries had been crammed full since dawn. The Prime Minister's speech which had begun at four o'clock lasted until eight. A few minutes later the final bulletin appeared on the wall: 'Gladstone concluded with a magnificent peroration declaring that the English Liberal party would refuse to legislate for England until she granted a measure of autonomy to Ireland.' At this news, the crowd in the street burst into enthusiastic cries. On all sides was heard, 'Long live Gladstone', 'Long live Ireland'. People who were complete strangers shook hands to ratify the new national pact, and old men wept for sheer joy.[2]

Seven years pass, and we are at the second Home Rule Act.[3] Gladstone, having in the meantime completed the moral assassination of Parnell with the help of the Irish bishops, reads his measure to the House for a third time. This speech is shorter than the other; it lasts hardly an hour and a half. Then the Home Rule Bill is passed. The happy news traverses the wires to the Irish capital, where it arouses a new burst of enthusiasm. In the main room of the Catholic Club, it is the subject of joyous conversations, discussions, toasts and prophecies.

[1] Translated from the Italian of 'Home Rule Maggiorenne', *Il Piccolo della Sera*, Trieste, May 19, 1907.

[2] However, the first Home Rule Act was defeated.

[3] The second Home Rule Act was also defeated.

Fourteen more years pass and we are at 1907. Twenty-one years have passed since 1886; therefore the Gladstonian measure has come of age, according to English custom. But in the interval Gladstone himself has died and his measure is not yet born. As he well foresaw, immediately after his third reading, the alarm sounded in the upper House, and all the Lords spiritual and temporal gathered at Westminster in a solid phalanx to give the bill the coup de grâce. The English Liberals forgot their commitments. A fourth-rate politician who voted for every coercive measure against Ireland from 1881 to 1886[1] dons the mantle of Gladstone. The position of Chief Secretary of Ireland, a position which the English themselves have called the tomb of political reputations, is occupied by a literary jurist,[2] who probably hardly knew the names of the Irish counties when he was presented to the electors of Bristol two years ago. Despite their pledges and promises, despite the support of the Irish vote during a quarter of a century, despite its enormous majority (which is without precedent in the parliamentary history of England), the English Liberal ministry introduces a measure of devolution which does not go beyond the proposals made by the imperialist Chamberlain in 1885, which the conservative press in London openly refused to take seriously. The bill is passed on the first reading with a majority of almost 300 votes, and while the yellow journals break out in shudders of pretended anger, the Lords consult each other to decide whether this wavering scarecrow about to enter the lists is really worthy of their sword.

Probably the Lords will kill the measure, since this is their trade, but if they are wise, they will hesitate to alienate the sympathy of the Irish for constitutional agitation; especially now that India and Egypt are in an uproar and the overseas colonies are asking for an imperial federation. From their point of view, it would not be advisable to provoke by an obstinate veto the reaction of a people who, poor in everything else and rich only in political ideas, have perfected the strategy of obstructionism and made the word 'boycott' an international war-cry.

On the other hand, England has little to lose. The measure (which is not the twentieth part of the Home Rule measure) gives the Executive Council at Dublin no legislative power, no power

---

[1] The Earl of Rosebery, who formed his cabinet in March 1894.
[2] John Morley (1838–1923).

to impose or regulate taxes, no control over 39 of the 47 government offices, including the police, the supreme court, and the agrarian commission. In addition, the Unionist interests are jealously safeguarded. The Liberal minister has been careful to insert in the first line of his speech the fact that the English electorate must disburse more than a half million pounds sterling each year as the price of the measure; and, understanding their countryman's intentions, the journalists and the Conservative speakers have made good use of this statement, appealing in their hostile comments to the most vulnerable part of the English electorate — their pocketbook. But neither the Liberal ministers nor the journalists will explain to the English voters that this expense is not a disbursement of English money, but rather a partial settlement on account of England's debt to Ireland. Nor will they cite the report of the English Royal Commission which established the fact that Ireland was overtaxed 88 million francs in comparison with her senior partner. Nor will they recall the fact that the statesmen and scientists who inspected the vast central swamp of Ireland asserted that the two spectres that sit at every Irish fireplace, tuberculosis and insanity, deny all that the English claim; and that the moral debt of the English government to Ireland for not having reforested this pestiferous swamp during an entire century amounts to 500 million francs.

Now, even from a hasty study of the history of Home Rule, we can make two deductions, for what they are worth. The first is this: the most powerful weapons that England can use against Ireland are no longer those of Conservatism, but those of Liberalism and Vaticanism. Conservatism, though it may be tyrannical, is a frankly and openly inimical doctrine. Its position is logical; it does not want a rival island to arise near Great Britain, or Irish factories to create competition for those in England, or tobacco and wine again to be exported from Ireland, or the great ports along the Irish coast to become enemy naval bases under a native government or a foreign protectorate. Its position is logical, as is that of the Irish separatists which contradicts it point by point. It takes little intelligence to understand that Gladstone has done Ireland greater damage than Disraeli did, and that the most fervid enemy of the Irish Catholics is the head of English Vaticanism, the Duke of Norfolk.

The second deduction is even more obvious, and it is this: the Irish parliamentary party has gone bankrupt. For twenty-seven years it has talked and agitated. In that time it has collected 35 million francs from its supporters, and the fruit of its agitation is that Irish taxes have gone up 88 million francs and the Irish population has decreased a million. The representatives themselves have improved their own lot, aside from small discomforts like a few months in prison and some lengthy sittings. From the sons of ordinary citizens, pedlars, and lawyers without clients they have become well-paid syndics, directors of factories and commercial houses, newspaper owners, and large landholders. They have given proof of their altruism only in 1891,[1] when they sold their leader, Parnell, to the pharisaical conscience of the English Dissenters without exacting the thirty pieces of silver.

JAMES JOYCE

[1] Actually Parnell's leadership was rejected in December 1890.

39

Ireland at the Bar[1]

1907

Several years ago a sensational trial was held in Ireland. In a lonely place in a western province, called Maamtrasna, a murder was committed.[2] Four or five townsmen, all belonging to the ancient tribe of the Joyces, were arrested. The oldest of them, the seventy year old Myles Joyce, was the prime suspect. Public opinion at the time thought him innocent and today considers him a martyr. Neither the old man nor the others accused knew English. The court had to resort to the services of an interpreter. The questioning, conducted through the interpreter, was at times comic and at times tragic. On one side was the excessively ceremonious interpreter, on the other the patriarch of a miserable tribe unused to civilized customs, who seemed stupefied by all the judicial ceremony. The magistrate said:

'Ask the accused if he saw the lady that night.' The question was referred to him in Irish, and the old man broke out into an involved explanation, gesticulating, appealing to the others accused and to heaven. Then he quieted down, worn out by his effort, and the interpreter turned to the magistrate and said:

'He says no, "your worship".'

'Ask him if he was in that neighbourhood at that hour.' The old man again began to talk, to protest, to shout, almost beside himself with the anguish of being unable to understand or to make

---

[1] Translated from the Italian of 'L'Irlanda alla Sbarra', *Il Piccolo della Sera*, Trieste, September 16, 1907.

[2] On August 17, 1882, a man named Joyce, his wife and three of his four children were murdered in County Galway by a party of men who believed that they were informers. The trial of ten men was held during November and three of them were hanged at Galway on December 16 for the murders. Myles Joyce was generally considered to be an innocent victim of public indignation.

himself understood, weeping in anger and terror. And the interpreter, again, dryly:

'He says no, "your worship".'

When the questioning was over, the guilt of the poor old man was declared proved, and he was remanded to a superior court which condemned him to the noose. On the day the sentence was executed, the square in front of the prison was jammed full of kneeling people shouting prayers in Irish for the repose of Myles Joyce's soul. The story was told that the executioner, unable to make the victim understand him, kicked at the miserable man's head in anger to shove it into the noose.[1]

The figure of this dumbfounded old man, a remnant of a civilization not ours, deaf and dumb before his judge, is a symbol of the Irish nation at the bar of public opinion. Like him, she is unable to appeal to the modern conscience of England and other countries. The English journalists act as interpreters between Ireland and the English electorate, which gives them ear from time to time and ends up being vexed by the endless complaints of the Nationalist representatives who have entered her House, as she believes, to disrupt its order and extort money. Abroad there is no talk of Ireland except when uprisings break out, like those which made the telegraph office hop these last few days.[2] Skimming over the dispatches from London (which, though they lack pungency, have something of the laconic quality of the interpreter mentioned above), the public conceives of the Irish as highwaymen with distorted faces, roaming the night with the object of taking the hide of every Unionist. And by the real sovereign of Ireland, the Pope, such news is received like so many dogs in church. Already weakened by their long journey, the cries are nearly spent when they arrive at the bronze door. The messengers of the people who never in the past have renounced the Holy See, the only Catholic people to whom faith also means the exercise of faith, are rejected in favour of messengers of a monarch, descended from

[1] A description of the hanging by one of the few eyewitnesses is included in Frederick J. Higginbotham, *The Vivid Life* (London, 1934) pp. 40–3.

[2] Joyce is referring to the Belfast riots and several incidents of cattle-raiding which occurred in connection with peasant evictions in August 1907, and remained in the news during September. On August 15 there was an attack on a landlord's house in Galway, and on August 27, a state of disturbance was proclaimed in counties Clare, Galway, Leitrim, Roscommon and King's county. By the end of August, the English Parliament was considering an Evicted Tenants Act to remedy the problem.

apostates, who solemnly apostasized himself on the day of his coronation, declaring in the presence of his nobles and commons that the rites of the Roman Catholic Church are 'superstition and idolatry'.

*　　*　　*　　*

There are twenty million Irishmen scattered all over the world. The Emerald Isle contains only a small part of them. But, reflecting that, while England makes the Irish question the centre of all her internal politics she proceeds with a wealth of good judgment in quickly disposing of the more complex questions of colonial politics, the observer can do no less than ask himself why St. George's Channel makes an abyss deeper than the ocean between Ireland and her proud dominator. In fact, the Irish question is not solved even today, after six centuries of armed occupation and more than a hundred years of English legislation, which has reduced the population of the unhappy island from eight to four million, quadrupled the taxes, and twisted the agrarian problem into many more knots.

In truth there is no problem more snarled than this one. The Irish themselves understand little about it, the English even less. For other people it is a black plague. But on the other hand the Irish know that it is the cause of all their sufferings, and therefore they often adopt violent methods of solution. For example, twenty-eight years ago, seeing themselves reduced to misery by the brutalities of the large landholders, they refused to pay their land rents and obtained from Gladstone remedies and reforms. Today, seeing pastures full of well fed cattle while an eighth of the population lacks means of subsistence, they drive the cattle from the farms. In irritation, the Liberal government arranges to refurbish the coercive tactics of the Conservatives, and for several weeks the London press dedicates innumerable articles to the agrarian crisis, which, it says, is very serious. It publishes alarming news of agrarian revolts, which is then reproduced by journalists abroad.

I do not propose to make an exegesis of the Irish agrarian question nor to relate what goes on behind the scene in the two-faced politics of the government. But I think it useful to make a modest correction of facts. Anyone who has read the telegrams launched from London is sure that Ireland is undergoing a period of unusual crime. An erroneous judgment, very erroneous. There is less crime in Ireland than in any other country in Europe. In Ireland there is no organized underworld. When one of those events which the Parisian journalists, with atrocious irony, call 'red idylls' occurs, the whole country is shaken by it. It is true that in recent months there were two violent deaths in Ireland, but at the hands of British troops in Belfast, where the soldiers fired without warning on an unarmed crowd and killed a man and woman. There were attacks on cattle; but not even these were in Ireland, where the crowd was content to open the stalls and chase the cattle through several miles of streets, but at Great Wyrley in England, where for six years bestial, maddened criminals have ravaged the cattle to such an extent that the English companies will no longer insure them. Five years ago an innocent man, now at liberty, was condemned to forced labour to appease public indignation. But even while he was in prison the crimes continued. And last week two horses were found dead with the usual slashes in their lower abdomen and their bowels scattered in the grass.

JAMES JOYCE

40

Oscar Wilde: The Poet of 'Salomé'[1]

1909

Oscar Fingal O'Flahertie Wills Wilde. These were the high-sounding titles that with youthful haughtiness he had printed on the title-page of his first collection of poems, and in this proud gesture, by which he tried to achieve nobility, are the signs of his vain pretences and the fate which already awaited him. His name symbolizes him: Oscar, nephew of King Fingal and the only son of Ossian in the amorphous Celtic *Odyssey*, who was treacherously killed by the hand of his host as he sat at table. O'Flahertie, a savage Irish tribe whose destiny it was to assail the gates of medieval cities; a name that incited terror in peaceful men, who still recite, among the plagues, the anger of God, and the spirit of fornication, in the ancient litany of the saints: 'from the wild O'Flaherties, libera nos Domine.' Like that other Oscar, he was to meet his public death in the flower of his years as he sat at table, crowned with false vine leaves and discussing Plato. Like that savage tribe, he was to break the lance of his fluent paradoxes against the body of practical conventions, and to hear, as a dishonoured exile, the choir of the just recite his name together with that of the unclean.

Wilde was born in the sleepy Irish capital fifty-five years ago. His father was a ranking scientist, who has been called the father of modern otology. His mother, who took part in the literary-revolutionary movement of '48, wrote for the Nationalist newspaper under the pseudonym 'Speranza', and incited the public, in

[1] Translated from the Italian of 'Oscar Wilde: Il Poeta di "Salome" ', *Il Piccolo della Sera*, Trieste, March 24, 1909. The article was written on the occasion of the performance of Strauss's *Salomé* in Trieste.

her poems and articles, to seize Dublin Castle. There are circumstances regarding the pregnancy of Lady Wilde and the infancy of her son which, in the eyes of some, explain in part the unhappy mania (if it may be called that) which later dragged him to his ruin;[1] and at least it is certain that the child grew up in an atmosphere of insecurity and prodigality.

The public life of Oscar Wilde began at Oxford University, where, at the time of his matriculation, a pompous professor named Ruskin was leading a crowd of Anglo-Saxon adolescents to the promised land of the future society — behind a wheelbarrow.[2] His mother's susceptible temperament revived in the young man, and, beginning with himself, he resolved to put into practice a theory of beauty that was partly original and partly derived from the books of Pater and Ruskin. He provoked the jeers of the public by proclaiming and practising a reform in dress and in the appearance of the home. He made lecture tours in the United States and the English provinces and became the spokesman of the aesthetic school, while around him was forming the fantastic legend of the Apostle of Beauty. His name evoked in the public mind a vague idea of delicate pastels, of life beautified with flowers. The cult of the sunflower, his favourite flower, spread among the leisured class, and the little people heard tell of his famous white ivory walking stick glittering with turquoise stones, and of his Neronian hair-dress.

The subject of this shining picture was more miserable than the bourgeois thought. From time to time his medals, trophies of his academic youth, went to the pawnshop, and at times the young wife of the epigrammatist had to borrow from a neighbour the money for a pair of shoes. Wilde was constrained to accept a position as editor of a very petty newspaper,[3] and only with the presentation of his brilliant comedies did he enter the short last phase of his life — luxury and wealth. *Lady Windermere's Fan* took London by storm. In the tradition of the Irish writers of comedy that runs from the days of Sheridan and Goldsmith to Bernard Shaw, Wilde became, like them, court jester to the English. He became the standard of elegance in the metropolis,

[1] Lady Wilde so badly wanted her second child to be a girl that she talked of the unborn child as a girl and prepared for a daughter. When Oscar Wilde was born she was bitterly disappointed.

[2] Ruskin set his pupils to work making roads in order to improve the country.

[3] *The Woman's World*, a fashion magazine.

and the annual income from his writings reached almost half a million francs. He scattered his gold among a series of unworthy friends. Every morning he bought two expensive flowers, one for himself and one for his coachman; and until the day of his sensational trial, he was driven to the courtroom in a two-horse carriage with its brilliantly outfitted coachman and powdered page.

His fall was greeted by a howl of puritanical joy. At the news of his condemnation, the crowd gathered outside the courtroom began to dance a pavane in the muddy street. Newspaper reporters were admitted to the prison, and through the window of his cell fed on the spectacle of his shame. White bands covered up his name on theatre billboards. His friends abandoned him. His manuscripts were stolen, while he recounted in prison the pain inflicted on him by two years of forced labour. His mother died under a shadow. His wife died. He was declared bankrupt and his goods were sold at auction. His sons were taken from him. When he got out of prison, thugs urged on by the noble Marquis of Queensbury[1] were waiting in ambush for him. He was hunted from house to house as dogs hunt a rabbit. One after another drove him from the door, refusing him food and shelter, and at nightfall he finally ended up under the windows of his brother, weeping and babbling like a child.

The epilogue came rapidly to an end, and it is not worth the effort to follow the unhappy man from the slums of Naples to his poor lodgings in the Latin Quarter where he died from meningitis in the last month of the last year of the nineteenth century.[2] It is not worth the effort to shadow him, like the French spies did. He died a Roman Catholic, adding another facet to his public life by the repudiation of his wild doctrine. After having mocked the idols of the market place, he bent his knees, sad and repentant that he had once been the singer of the divinity of joy, and closed the book of his spirit's rebellion with an act of spiritual dedication.

* * * *

This is not the place to examine the strange problem of the life of Oscar Wilde, nor to determine to what extent heredity and the epileptic tendency of his nervous system can excuse that which has been imputed to him. Whether he was innocent or guilty of

[1] Father of Lord Alfred Douglas.
[2] Actually, on November 30, 1900.

the charges brought against him, he undoubtedly was a scapegoat. His greater crime was that he had caused a scandal in England, and it is well known that the English authorities did everything possible to persuade him to flee before they issued an order for his arrest. An employee of the Ministry of Internal Affairs stated during the trial that, in London alone, there are more than 20,000 persons under police surveillance, but they remain footloose until they provoke a scandal. Wilde's letters to his friends were read in court, and their author was denounced as a degenerate obsessed by exotic perversions: 'Time wars against you; it is jealous of your lilies and your roses','I love to see you wandering through violet-filled valleys, with your honey-coloured hair gleaming'. But the truth is that Wilde, far from being a perverted monster who sprang in some inexplicable way from the civilization of modern England, is the logical and inescapable product of the Anglo-Saxon college and university system, with its secrecy and restrictions.

Wilde's condemnation by the English people arose from many complex causes; but it was not the simple reaction of a pure conscience. Anyone who scrutinizes the graffiti, the loose drawings, the lewd gestures of those people will hesitate to believe them pure at heart. Anyone who follows closely the life and language of men, whether in soldiers' barracks or in the great commercial houses, will hesitate to believe that all those who threw stones at Wilde were themselves spotless. In fact, everyone feels uncomfortable in speaking to others about this subject, afraid that his listener may know more about it than he does. Oscar Wilde's own defence in the *Scots Observer*[1] should remain valid in the judgment of an objective critic. Everyone, he wrote, sees his own sin in Dorian Gray (Wilde's best known novel). What Dorian Gray's sin was no one says and no one knows. Anyone who recognizes it has committed it.

Here we touch the pulse of Wilde's art — sin. He deceived himself into believing that he was the bearer of good news of neo-paganism to an enslaved people. His own distinctive qualities, the qualities, perhaps, of his race — keenness, generosity, and a sexless intellect — he placed at the service of a theory of beauty which, according to him, was to bring back the Golden Age and

[1] 'Mr. Wilde's Rejoinder', *Scots Observer*, v. 4 no. 86 (July 12, 1890) 279, a reply to an unfavourable review of *The Picture of Dorian Gray*. Wilde wrote: 'Each man sees his own sin in Dorian Gray. What Dorian Gray's sins are no one knows. He who finds them has brought them.'

the joy of the world's youth. But if some truth adheres to his subjective interpretations of Aristotle, to his restless thought that proceeds by sophisms rather than syllogisms, to his assimilations of natures as foreign to his as the delinquent is to the humble, at its very base is the truth inherent in the soul of Catholicism: that man cannot reach the divine heart except through that sense of separation and loss called sin.[1]

*   *   *   *

In his last book, *De Profundis*, he kneels before a gnostic Christ, resurrected from the apocryphal pages of *The House of Pomegranates*, and then his true soul, trembling, timid, and saddened, shines through the mantle of Heliogabalus. His fantastic legend, his opera[2] — a polyphonic variation on the rapport of art and nature, but at the same time a revelation of his own psyche — his brilliant books sparkling with epigrams (which made him, in the view of some people, the most penetrating speaker of the past century), these are now divided booty.

A verse from the book of Job is cut on his tombstone in the impoverished cemetery at Bagneux. It praises his facility, 'eloquium suum', — the great legendary mantle which is now divided booty. Perhaps the future will also carve there another verse, less proud but more pious:

> *Partiti sunt sibi vestimenta mea et super*
> *vestem meam miserunt sortis.*[3]

JAMES JOYCE

[1] Compare Aherne in Yeats's *Tables of the Law*, which Joyce knew by heart: 'and in my misery it was revealed to me that man can only come to that Heart through the sense of separation from it which we call sin.'

[2] Salomé.

[3] Psalms 21:19, which reads, '*Diviserunt* sibi . . . miserunt *sortem.*'

41

Bernard Shaw's Battle with the Censor[1]

'THE SHEWING-UP OF BLANCO POSNET'

1909

Dublin, 31 August

There is one gay week every year in the Dublin calendar, the last week of August, in which the famous Horse Show draws to the Irish capital a vari-coloured crowd, of many languages, from its sister island, from the continent, and even from far-off Japan. For a few days the tired and cynical city is dressed like a newly-wed bride. Its gloomy streets swarm with a feverish life, and an unaccustomed uproar breaks its senile slumber.

This year, however, an artistic event has almost eclipsed the importance of the Show, and all over town they are talking about the clash between Bernard Shaw and the Viceroy. As is well known, Shaw's latest play, 'The Shewing-Up of Blanco Posnet', was branded with the mark of infamy by the Lord Chamberlain of England, who banned its performance in the United Kingdom. The censor's decision probably came as no surprise to Shaw, because the same censor did the same thing to two other of his theatrical works, 'Mrs. Warren's Profession' and the very recent 'Press Cuttings'; and Shaw probably considers himself more or less honoured by the arbitrary proclamation which has condemned his comedies, together with Ibsen's 'Ghosts', Tolstoy's 'The Power of Darkness', and Wilde's 'Salomé'.

However, he would not give up, and he found a way to elude the frightened vigilance of the censor. By a strange chance, the

---

[1] Translated from the Italian of 'La Battaglia Fra Bernard Shaw e la Censura. "Blanco Posnet Smascherato" ', *Il Piccolo della Sera*, Trieste, September 5, 1909.

city of Dublin is the only place in all the British territory in which the censor has no power; in fact, the old law contains these words: 'except the city of Dublin.' Shaw, then, offered his play to the company of the Irish National Theatre, which accepted it and announced its performance just as though nothing were out of the ordinary. The censor was apparently rendered powerless. Then the Viceroy of Ireland intervened to uphold the prestige of authority. There was a lively exchange of letters between the representative of the King and the writer of comedy, severe and threatening on the one side, insolent and scoffing on the other,[1] while Dubliners, who care nothing for art but love an argument passionately, rubbed their hands with joy. Shaw held fast, insisting on his rights, and the little theatre was so filled at the first performance that it literally sold out more than seven times over.

A heavy crowd thronged about the Abbey Theatre that evening, and a cordon of giant guards maintained order; but it was evident at once that no hostile demonstration would be made by the select public who jammed every nook of the little *avant garde* theatre. In fact, the report of the evening performance mentioned not even the lightest murmur of protest; and at the curtain fall, a thunderous applause summoned the actors for repeated curtain calls.

Shaw's comedy, which he describes as a sermon in crude melodrama, is, as you know, in a single act. The action unfolds in a wild and woolly city of the Far West, the protagonist is a horse thief, and the play limits itself to his trial. He has stolen a horse which he thought belonged to his brother, to repay himself for a sum taken from him unjustly. But while he is fleeing from the city, he meets a woman with a sick baby. She wants to get back to town in order to save the life of her child, and, moved by her appeal, he gives her the horse. Then he is captured and taken to the city to be tried. The trial is violent and arbitrary. The sheriff acts as prosecutor, shouting at the accused, banging the table, and threat-

---

[1] A typed translation of this article in the Slocum Collection of the Yale University Library bears this handwritten note by Shaw: 'There was no exchange of letters between myself and Dublin Castle. The campaign was conducted by Lady Gregory and W. B. Yeats. I did not interfere. G. Bernard Shaw, 21 July 1949.' Joyce unconscionably attributed the correspondence to Shaw, probably to add colour to the narration. See Lady Gregory, *Our Irish Theatre* (N. Y. and London, 1913) pp. 140–68 and Appendix II, and 'The Blanco Posnet Controversy', *Shaw Bulletin*, no. 7 (January 1955) 1–9 (which includes this translation in a slightly different version).

ening witnesses with revolver in hand. Posnet, the thief, sets forth some primitive theology. The moment of sentimental weakness in which he yielded to the prayers of a poor mother has been the crisis of his life. The finger of God has touched his brain. He no longer has the strength to live the cruel, animal life he had led before this encounter. He breaks out into long, disjointed speeches (and it is here that the pious English censor covered his ears), which are theological insofar as their subject is God, but not very churchly in diction. In the sincerity of his convictions, Posnet resorts to the language of the mining camp; and, among other reflections, when he is trying to say that God works secretly in the hearts of men, to the language of horse thieves.

The play ends happily. The baby which Posnet tried to save dies, and the mother is apprehended. She tells her story to the court and Posnet is acquitted. Nothing more flimsy can be imagined, and the playgoer asks himself in wonder why on earth the play was interdicted by the censor.

Shaw is right; it is a sermon. Shaw is a born preacher. His lively and talkative spirit cannot stand to be subjected to the noble and bare style appropriate to modern playwriting. Indulging himself in wandering prefaces and extravagant rules of drama, he creates a dramatic form which is much like a dialogue novel. He has a sense of situation, rather than of drama logically and ethically led to a conclusion. In this case he has dug up the central incident of his 'Devil's Disciple' and transformed it into a sermon. The transformation is too abrupt to be convincing as a sermon, and the art is too poor to make it convincing as drama.

And may not this play reflect a crisis in the mind of its writer? Earlier, at the end of 'John Bull's Other Island', the crisis was set forth. Shaw, as well as his latest protagonist, has had a profane and unruly past. Fabianism, vegetarianism, prohibitionism, music, painting, drama — all the progressive movements in art and politics — have had him as champion. And now, perhaps, some divine finger has touched his brain, and he, in the guise of Blanco Posnet, is shown up.

JAMES YOYCE [!]

42

The Home Rule Comet[1]

1910

The idea of Irish autonomy has gradually become surrounded
with a pallid and tenuous substantiality, and just a few weeks
ago, when a royal decree dissolved the English parliament, something pale and wavering was seen dawning in the East. It was the
Home Rule comet, vague, distant, but as punctual as ever. The
sovereign Word which in an instant made twilight fall on the
demi-gods at Westminster had called from the darkness and the
void the obedient and unknowing star.

This time, however, it could be made out very poorly because
the skies were cloudy. The fog which usually covers the British
shores grew so thick that it cloaked them in a fixed and impene-
trable cloud bank, behind which could be heard the orchestral
music of the electoral elements in discord — the fiddles of the
nobles agitated and hysterical, the raucous horns of the people,
and, from time to time, a passing phrase on the Irish flutes.

The uncertainty of the political situation in England is evident
from the fact that their agencies hurl forth from morning to night
enigmatic dispatches which contradict themselves. In fact, the
tenor of the debates held recently in the United Kingdom makes
an impartial examination of the situation very difficult. Aside
from the three party heads, Asquith, Balfour, and Redmond, who
always know how to maintain a certain dignified bearing not unbecoming to fatuous leaders, the electoral campaign which has
just ended indicates a significant lowering of the tone of English
public life. Has such a speech ever been heard from the lips of the
Chancellor of the Exchequer?[2] the Conservatives are asked. But

---

[1] Translated from the Italian of 'La Cometa dell' "Home Rule," ' *Il Piccolo
della Sera*, Trieste, December 22, 1910.

[2] Lloyd George.

the jibes of the warlike Welsh minister pale before the vulgar vituperations of Conservatives like representative Smith,[1] and the well known lawyer Carson[2] and the director of the 'National Review',[3] while the two Irish factions, forgetting their common enemy, have waged underground war in an attempt to exhaust the gamut of coarse language.

Another cause of confusion is that the English parties no longer answer to their names. It is the Radicals who want to continue the present political tariff policy of free trade, while the Conservatives champion tariff reform at the top of their voices. It is the Conservatives who want to take away the legislative power from Parliament and give it instead to the nation as a whole by means of the plebiscite. Finally, it is the clerical and intransigent Irish party which comprises the majority of an anticlerical and Liberal government.

This paradoxical situation is accurately reflected in the characters of the party heads. Not to speak of Chamberlain or Rosebery, who have gone, respectively, from extreme Radicalism and Gladstonian Liberalism to the ranks of Imperialism (while the young minister Churchill[4] has made his ideal voyage in the opposite direction). we find the causes of Anglican Protestantism and of conciliatory Nationalism led by a religious renegade and a converted Fenian.

Balfour,[5] in fact, a worthy disciple of the Scottish school, is a sceptic rather than a politician, who, urged more by the instinct for nepotism innate in the Cecil family than by individual choice, assumed the leadership of the Conservative party after the death of his uncle, the lamented Marquis of Salisbury. Not a day passes that the reporters fail to point out his distracted and quibbling attitude. His tricks make his own followers laugh. And even if the orthodox army has met with three consecutive clashes under his vacillating flag, each more serious than the last, his biographer (who perhaps will be another member of the Cecil family) will be able to say of him that in his philosophical essays he dissected and laid bare with great art the intimate fibres of the religious and psychological principles whose champion he became by a turn of

---

[1] Frederick Edwin Smith, Earl of Birkenhead (1872–1930).
[2] Sir Edward Carson (1854–1935), the Ulster Unionist leader.
[3] Leopold James Maxse (1864–1932).
[4] Winston Churchill.
[5] Arthur James Balfour (1838–1930).

the parliamentary wheel. O'Brien,[1] the 'leader' of the Irish dissi-
dents, who calls his band of 10 representatives the 'All for Ireland'
party, has become what every good fanatic becomes when his
fanaticism dies before he does. Now he fights in league with the
Unionist magistrates who would probably have issued a warrant
for his arrest twenty years ago; and nothing remains of his fiery
youth except those violent outbursts which make him seem
epileptic.

In the midst of such confusions it is easy to understand how the
dispatches contradict themselves, and announce that Home Rule
is at the door, and write its obituary six hours later. The un-
initiated cannot be too sure in the case of comets, but at any rate
the passage of the celestial body so long awaited has been com-
municated to us by the official observatory.

*   *   *   *

Last week, the Irish leader Redmond[2] proclaimed the happy
news to a crowd of fishermen. English democracy, he said, has
broken the power of the Lords once and for all,[3] and within a few
weeks, perhaps, Ireland will have her independence. Now, it is
necessary to be a voracious nationalist to be able to swallow such
a mouthful. As soon as it is seated on the ministerial benches, the
Liberal cabinet will be confronted by a conglomeration of troubles,
among which the foremost is the double balance.[4] When this
matter is settled for good or for bad, peers and commoners will
declare a treaty of peace in honour of the coronation of George V.
So far the way is clear, but only prophets can tell us where a
government as heterogeneous as the present one will end. To
remain in power, will it try to appease the Welsh and the Scots
with ecclesiastical and agrarian measures? If the Irish exact
autonomy as the price for the support of their votes, will the
cabinet hasten to blow the dust off one of their many Home Rule
bills and present it to the House again?

[1] William O'Brien (1852–1928).
[2] John Redmond (1856–1918).
[3] The results of the election of December 1910 assured the passage of the
Parliament Act (in August 1911), which ended the veto power of the House of
Lords, and paved the way for passage of the Home Rule Act.
[4] Since the Liberals and the Unionists emerged from the elections of December
1910 with 272 seats apiece, the balance of power rested in the two minor parties,
the Labour party, with 47 votes, and the Irish party, with 84 votes.

The history of Anglo-Saxon liberalism teaches us the answer to these and similarly ingenuous questions very clearly. The Liberal ministers are scrupulous men, and once again the Irish problem will cause symptomatic rifts in the body of the cabinet, in the face of which it will plainly appear that the English electorate really did not authorize the government to legislate in its favour. And, following the Liberal strategy (which aims to wear down the separatist sentiment slowly and secretly, while creating a new, eager social class, dependent, and free from dangerous enthusiasms, by means of partial concessions), if the government introduces a reform bill, or the semblance of one, which Ireland will haughtily refuse, will not that be the propitious moment for the intervention of the Conservative party? Faithful to its cynical tradition of bad faith, will it not take this occasion to declare the Irish dictatorship intolerable, and start a campaign to reduce the number of Irish members from 80 to 40 on the basis of the depopulation, more unique than rare in a civilized country, which was and still is the bitter fruit of misgovernment?

The connection, then, between the abolition of the Lords' veto and the granting of autonomy to the Irish is not as immediate as some would have us believe. In the final count, that is the business of the English themselves, and admitting that the English people no longer have the worship for their spiritual and temporal fathers that they once had, it is still probable that they will proceed with the reform of the upper house as slowly and cautiously as they are proceeding with the reform of their medieval laws, with the reform of their pompous and hypocritical literature, with the reform of their monstrous judicial system. And in anticipation of these reforms, it will matter very little to the credulous ploughman in Ireland whether Lord Lansdowne or Sir Edward Grey rules the lot of the Ministry of Foreign Affairs.

*　　*　　*　　*

The fact that Ireland now wishes to make common cause with British democracy should neither surprise nor persuade anyone. For seven centuries she has never been a faithful subject of England. Neither, on the other hand, has she been faithful to herself. She has entered the British domain without forming an integral part of it. She has abandoned her own language almost entirely and accepted the language of the conqueror without being able to assimilate the culture or adapt herself to the mentality of which this language is the vehicle. She has betrayed her heroes, always in the hour of need and always without gaining recompense. She has hounded her spiritual creators into exile only to boast about them. She has served only one master well, the Roman Catholic Church, which, however, is accustomed to pay its faithful in long term drafts.

What long term alliance can exist between this strange people and the new Anglo-Saxon democracy? The phrase-makers who speak so warmly about it today will soon see (if they do not see it already) that between the English nobles and the English workers there is a mysterious communion of blood; and that the highly praised Marquis of Salisbury, a refined gentleman, spoke not only for his caste but for his race when he said: 'Let the Irish stew in their own juice.'

JAMES JOYCE

43

[William Blake][1]

1912

In 1911 Joyce was again invited to participate in the evening lecture series at the Università Popolare Triestina. Four years before he had spoken there on Irish subjects, but this time he announced that he would deal with 'Verismo ed idealismo nella letteratura inglese (Daniele De Foe — William Blake).' He delivered the two lectures early in March 1912; of the first only a fragment, though an important one, is now available,[2] of the second almost the whole.

Joyce's resemblance to Defoe is clear enough, and he is closer to Blake than may at first appear.[3] While he took pride in grounding his art on brute, honest fact, he insisted also on the mind's supremacy over all it surveyed. Beyond these general resemblances, his lectures suggest two specific affinities. Defoe and Blake, in their different ways, were working with the conception of an archetypal man. Robinson Crusoe summarizes a people and a time as Bloom does. Blake's Albion, the universal man who symbolizes eternity, is related to that other giant form, Finnegan, in whose life, death and awakening Joyce finds all human enterprise and aspiration.

[1] Translated from the Italian of an untitled, incomplete holograph manuscript of twenty-two pages, numbered 11 to 30 plus two unnumbered correction sheets, in the Slocum Collection of the Yale University Library.

[2] A single typed page in the Joyce papers at the Cornell University Library bears the heading, in Stanislaus Joyce's hand: 'Lecture on Defoe', and the notation '–33– –34– –35– –36–'. This is probably Stanislaus Joyce's copy of pages 33–36 of Joyce's holograph manuscript which John Slocum bought from him in 1950 and presented to Sylvia Beach, who owned (and still owns) the bulk of the Italian lecture on Defoe. Because of a prior arrangement by the James Joyce Estate, the lecture on Defoe has had to be omitted here.

[3] On the resemblances between Joyce and these authors see: Harry Levin, *James Joyce* (Norfolk, Conn., 1941), pp. 18–19; Northrop Frye, 'Blake and Joyce', *James Joyce Review*, v. 1 no. 1 (Feb. 1957) 39–47; Richard Ellmann, 'The Backgrounds of *Ulysses*', *Kenyon Review*, v. 16 (Summer 1954) 371–7.

[*The manuscript begins here.*] of an ethical and practical interpretation, are not moral aphorisms. Looking at St. Paul's cathedral, Blake heard with the ear of the soul the cry of the little chimney sweep, who symbolizes oppressed innocence in his strange literary language. Looking at Buckingham Palace, he sees with the eye of the mind the sigh of the hapless soldier running down the palace wall in the form of a drop of blood.[1] While he was still young and vigorous, remaking himself with these visions, he had the power to etch their image in a hammered verse or a sheet of copper, and these verbal or mental etchings often comprise an entire sociological system. The prison, he writes, is built with stones of law; the brothel with bricks of religion.[2] But the continual strain of these voyages into the unknown and the abrupt return to natural life slowly but inexorably corrode his artistic power. The visions, multiplying, blind the sight; and toward the end of his mortal life, the unknown for which he yearned covered him with the shadows of vast wings, and the angels with whom he conversed as an immortal with immortals hid him in the silence of their garments.

If I have evoked from the shades with bitter words and violent verses the figure of a weak, second or third rank politician, I have given you the wrong idea of Blake's personality. As a young man he belonged to the literary-revolutionary school that included Miss Wollstonecraft, and the famous, perhaps I should say the notorious, author of the *Rights of Man*, Thomas Paine. Even among the members of this circle, Blake was the only one with the courage to wear in the street the red cap, emblem of the new era. He soon took it off, though, never to wear it again, after the massacres in the Paris prisons that occurred in September 1792. His spiritual rebellion against the powers of this world was not made of the kind of gunpowder, soluble in water, to which we are more or less accustomed. In 1799, he was offered the position of drawing master to the royal family. Afraid that in the artificial atmosphere of the court his art might die of inanition, he refused it; but at the same time, in order not to offend the king, he gave up all the other lower-class students that formed his major source

[1] *How the Chimney-sweeper's cry*
Every black'ning Church appalls;
And the hapless Soldier's sigh
Runs in blood down Palace walls.
Blake, 'London'.

[2] From 'Proverbs of Hell' in 'The Marriage of Heaven and Hell'.

of income. After his death, Princess Sophia sent his widow a private gift of a hundred pounds sterling. Mrs. Blake sent it back, thanking her politely, saying that she was able to get along on little, and that she didn't want to accept the gift because, if it were used for another purpose, the money might help to restore the life and hopes of someone less fortunate than her.

There was evidently a distinct difference between that undisciplined and visionary heresiarch and those most orthodox church philosophers, Francesco Suarez, *Europae atque orbis universi magister et oculus populi Christiani*,[1] and Don Giovanni Mariana di Talavera,[2] who had written for the stupefaction of posterity a logical and sinister defence of tyrannicide in the preceding century. The same idealism that possessed and sustained Blake when he hurled his lightning against human evil and misery prevented him from being cruel to the body even of a sinner, the frail curtain of flesh, as he calls it in the mystical book of *Thel*, that lies on the bed of our desire.[3] The episodes that show the primitive goodness of his heart are numerous in the story of his life. Although he had difficulty making a living and spent only half a guinea a week to maintain the little house where he lived, he gave forty pounds to a needy friend. Having seen a poor, phthisic art student pass his window each morning with a portfolio under his arm, he took pity on him and invited him into the house, where he fed him and tried to cheer his sad and dwindling life. His relations with his younger brother Robert recall the story of David and Jonathan. Blake loved him, supported him, and took care of him. During his long sickness, he spoke to him of the eternal world and comforted him. For many days before his death, he watched over his sickbed without interruption, and at the supreme moment he saw the beloved soul break loose from the lifeless body and rise toward heaven clapping its hands for joy. Then, serene and exhausted, he lay down in a deep sleep and slept for seventy-two hours in a row.

[1] Francisco Suárez (1548–1617). 'Jesus, too, seems to have treated his mother with scant courtesy in public but Suarez, a jesuit theologian and Spanish gentleman, has apologized for him.' *Portrait*, p. 513 (276).

[2] Mariano de Talavera y Garcés (1771–1861), a Venezuelan priest and politician. See the *Portrait*, p. 517 (280): 'Apply to the jesuit theologian Juan Mariana de Talavera who will explain to you in what circumstances you may lawfully kill your king and whether you had better hand him poison in a goblet or smear it for him upon his robe or saddlebow.'

[3] 'Why a little curtain of flesh on the bed of our desire?'

I have already referred to Mrs. Blake two or three times, and perhaps I should say something about the poet's married life. Blake fell in love when he was twenty years old. The girl, who was rather foolish it seems, was named Polly Woods. The influence of this youthful love shines through Blake's first works, the *Poetical Sketches* and *Songs of Innocence*, but the incident ended suddenly and brusquely. She thought him crazy, or little better, and he thought her a flirt, or something worse. This girl's face appears in certain drawings in the prophetic book of *Vala*, a soft and smiling face, symbol of the sweet cruelty of woman, and of the illusion of the senses. To recuperate from this defeat, Blake left London and went to live in the cottage of a gardener named Bouchier.[1] This gardener had a daughter, Catherine, about twenty-four, whose heart was filled with compassion at hearing of the young man's misfortune in love. The affection born from this pity and its recognition finally united them. The lines from *Othello*:

> *She loved me for the dangers I had passed,*
> *And I loved her that she did pity them.*[2]

come to mind when we read this chapter of Blake's life.

Like many other men of great genius, Blake was not attracted to cultured and refined women. Either he preferred to drawing-room graces and an easy and broad culture (if you will allow me to borrow a commonplace from theatrical jargon) the simple woman, of hazy and sensual mentality, or, in his unlimited egoism, he wanted the soul of his beloved to be entirely a slow and painful creation of his own,[3] freeing and purifying daily under his very eyes, the demon (as he says) hidden in the cloud. Whichever is true, the fact is that Mrs. Blake was neither very pretty nor very intelligent. In fact, she was illiterate, and the poet took pains to teach her to read and write. He succeeded so well that within a

---

[1] Actually, Boucher. Joyce is following Edwin Ellis's error in *The Real Blake* (London, 1907), which seems to be the major source of his knowledge of Blake's life in this lecture.

[2] Joyce's translation:

> *Ella m'amava per le mie sventure*
> *Ed io l'amavo per la Sua pietà.*

[3] In Act II of *Exiles* Robert Hand says to Richard Rowan; 'You love this woman. I remember all you told me long ago. She is yours, your work,' and 'You have made her all that she is.' Joyce's alliance to Nora Barnacle bears a vague resemblance to that which he attributes to Blake and Catherine Boucher.

few years his wife was helping him in his engraving work, retouching his drawings, and was cultivating in herself the visionary faculty.

Elemental beings and spirits of dead great men often came to the poet's room at night to speak with him about art and the imagination. Then Blake would leap out of bed, and, seizing his pencil, remain long hours in the cold London night drawing the limbs and lineaments of the visions, while his wife, curled up beside his easy chair, held his hand lovingly and kept quiet so as not to disturb the visionary ecstasy of the seer. When the vision had gone, about daybreak his wife would get back into bed, and Blake, radiant with joy and benevolence, would quickly begin to light the fire and get breakfast for the both of them. We are amazed that the symbolic beings Los and Urizen and Vala and Tiriel and Enitharmon and the shades of Milton and Homer came from their ideal world to a poor London room, and no other incense greeted their coming than the smell of East Indian tea and eggs fried in lard. Isn't this perhaps the first time in the history of the world that the Eternal spoke through the mouth of the humble?

So the mortal life of William Blake unfolded. The bark of his married life that had weighed anchor under the auspices of pity and gratitude sailed among the usual rocks for almost half a century. There were no children. In the early years of their life together there were discords, misunderstandings easy to understand if we keep in mind the great difference in culture and temperament that separated the young couple. It is even true, as I said before, that Blake almost followed Abraham's example of giving to Hagar what Sarah refused.[1] The vestal simplicity of his wife ill accorded with the temperament of Blake, for whom until the last days of his life exuberance was the only beauty. In a scene of tears and accusations that occurred between them, his wife fell in a faint, and injured herself in such a way that she was unable to have children.[2] It is a sad irony to think that this poet of childish innocence, the only writer who has written songs for children with the soul of a child, and who has illuminated the phenomenon of gestation with a light so tender and mystical in his

---

[1] 'He claimed the right of Abraham to give to Hagar what Sarah refused.' Ellis, p. 90.

[2] Joyce takes this dubious information from Ellis, p. 91.

strange poem *The Chrystal Cabinet*, was destined never to see the sight of a real human child at his fireside. To him who had such great pity for everything that lives and suffers and rejoices in the illusions of the vegetable world, for the fly, the hare, the little chimney sweep, the robin, even for the flea, was denied any other fatherhood than the spiritual fatherhood, intensely natural though it is, that still lives in the lines of *Proverbs*:[1]

> *He who mocks the Infant's Faith*
> *Shall be mock'd in Age & Death.*
> *He who shall teach the Child to Doubt*
> *The rotting Grave shall ne'er get out.*
> *He who respects the Infant's faith*
> *Triumphs over Hell & Death.*

Over Blake's fearless and immortal spirit, the rotting grave and the king of terrors had no power. In his old age, surrounded at last by friends and disciples and admirers, he began, like Cato the Elder, to study a foreign language. That language was the same in which tonight I try, by your leave, in so far as I can, to recall his spirit from the twilight of the universal mind,[2] to detain it for a minute and question it. He began to study Italian in order to read the *Divina Commedia* in the original and to illustrate Dante's vision with mystical drawings. Gaunt and weakened by the afflictions of illness, he would prop himself up on several pillows and spread a large drawing-book on his knees, forcing himself to trace the lines of his last vision on the white pages. It is the attitude in which he lives for us in Phillips' drawing in the National Gallery in London. His brain did not weaken; his hand did not lose its old mastery. Death came to him in the form of a glacial cold, like the tremors of cholera, which possessed his limbs and put out the light of his intelligence in a moment, as the cold darkness that we call space covers and extinguishes the light of a star. He died singing in a strong, resounding voice that made the rafters ring. He was

---

[1] Actually, from 'Auguries of Innocence'. Joyce's translation:

> *Chiunque si beffa della fede del bambino*
> *Sarà beffato nella vecchiaja e nella morte,*
> *Chiunque insegna al bambino il dubbio*
> *Non escirà mai dalla putrida fossa,*
> *Chiunque rispetta la fede del bambino*
> *Trionferà sull'inferno e sulla morte.*

[2] The 'anima mundi'; see footnote 5, p. 83 above.

singing, as always, of the ideal world, of truth, the intellect and the divinity of the imagination. 'My beloved, the songs that I sing are not mine,' he said to his wife, 'no, no, I tell you they are not mine.'

A full study of Blake's personality should logically be divided into three phases — the pathological, the theosophical, and the artistic. The first, I believe, we can dismiss without many qualms. Saying that a great genius is mad, while at the same time recognizing his artistic worth, is like saying that he had rheumatism or suffered from diabetes. Madness, in fact, is a medical term that can claim no more notice from the objective critic than he grants the charge of heresy raised by the theologian, or the charge of immorality raised by the police. If we must accuse of madness every great genius who does not believe in the hurried materialism now in vogue with the happy fatuousness of a recent college graduate in the exact sciences, little remains for art and universal philosophy. Such a slaughter of the innocents would take in a large part of the peripatetic system, all of medieval metaphysics, a whole branch of the immense symmetrical edifice constructed by the Angelic Doctor, St. Thomas Aquinas, Berkeley's idealism, and (what a combination) the scepticism that ends with Hume. With regard to art, then, those very useful figures, the photographer and court stenographer, would get by all the more easily. The presentation of such an art and such a philosophy, flowering in the more or less distant future in the union of the two social forces felt more strongly in the market-place every day — women and the proletariat — will reconcile, if nothing else, every artist and philosopher to the shortness of life on earth.

To determine what position Blake must be assigned in the hierarchy of occidental mystics goes beyond the scope of this lecture. It seems to me that Blake is not a great mystic. The orient is the paternal home of mysticism, and now that linguistic studies have put us in the position to understand oriental thought (if that ideational energy that created the vast cycles of spiritual activity and passivity of which the *Upanishads* speak can be called thought) the mystical books of the occident shine, if at all, with a reflected light. Blake is probably less inspired by Indian mysticism than Paracelsus, Jacob Behmen,[1] or Swedenborg; at any rate, he

---

[1] The English name for Boehme.

is less objectionable. In him, the visionary faculty is directly connected with the artistic faculty. One must be, in the first place, well-disposed to mysticism, and in the second place, endowed with the patience of a saint in order to get an idea of what Paracelsus and Behmen mean by their cosmic exposition of the involution and evolution of mercury, salt, sulphur, body, soul and spirit. Blake naturally belongs to another category, that of the artists, and in this category he occupies, in my opinion, a unique position, because he unites keenness of intellect with mystical feeling. This first quality is almost completely lacking in mystical art. St. John of the Cross, for example, one of the few idealist artists worthy to stand with Blake, never reveals either an innate sense of form or a coordinating force of the intellect in his book *The Dark Night of the Soul*, that cries and faints with such an ecstatic passion.

The explanation lies in the fact that Blake had two spiritual masters, very different from each other, yet alike in their formal precision — Michelangelo Buonarotti and Emanuel Swedenborg. The first of Blake's mystical drawings that we have, *Joseph of Arimathea among the Rocks of Albion*, has in one corner the words: *Michelangelo pinxit*. It is modelled after a sketch made by Michelangelo for his *Last Judgment*, and symbolizes the poetic imagination in the power of the sensual philosophy. Beneath the drawing Blake has written: 'This is one of the Gothic Artists who built the cathedrals in what we call the Dark Ages, wandering about in sheepskins and goatskins, of whom the world was not worthy.' Michelangelo's influence is felt in all of Blake's work, and especially in some passages of prose collected in the fragments, in which he always insists on the importance of the pure, clean line that evokes and creates the figure on the background of the uncreated void.

The influence of Swedenborg, who died in exile in London when Blake was beginning to write and draw, is seen in the glorified humanity with which all of Blake's work is stamped. Swedenborg, who frequented all of the invisible worlds for several years, sees in the image of man heaven itself and Michael, Raphael, and Gabriel, who, according to him, are not three angels, but three angelic choirs. Eternity, which had appeared to the beloved disciple and to St. Augustine as a heavenly city, and to Alighieri as a heavenly rose, appeared to the Swedish mystic in the likeness of a heavenly man, animated in all his limbs by a fluid angelic life that forever leaves and re-enters, systole and diastole of love and wisdom. From this vision he developed that immense system of what he called correspondences which runs through his masterpiece *Arcana Coelestia*, the new Gospel which, according to him, will be the apparition in the heavens of the Son of Man foretold by St. Matthew.

Armed with this two-edged sword, the art of Michelangelo and the revelations of Swedenborg, Blake killed the dragon of experience and natural wisdom, and, by minimizing space and time and denying the existence of memory and the senses, he tried to paint his works on the void of the divine bosom. To him, each moment shorter than a pulse-beat was equivalent in its duration to six thousand years,[1] because in such an infinitely short instant the work of the poet is conceived and born. To him, all space larger than a red globule of human blood was visionary, created by the hammer of Los, while in a space smaller than a globule of blood we approach eternity, of which our vegetable world is but a shadow. Not *with* the eye, then, but *beyond* the eye, the soul and the supreme love must look, because the eye, which was born in the night while the soul was sleeping in rays of light, will also die in the night. Dionysius the pseudo-Areopagite, in his book *De Divinis Nominibus*, arrives at the throne of God by denying and overcoming every moral and metaphysical attribute, and falling into ecstasy and prostrating himself before the divine obscurity, before that unutterable immensity which precedes and encompasses the supreme knowledge in the eternal order. The mental process by which Blake arrives at the threshold of the infinite is a similar process. Flying from the infinitely small to the infinitely large, from a drop of blood to the universe of stars, his soul is consumed by the rapidity of flight, and finds itself renewed and winged and immortal on the edge of the dark ocean of God. And although he based his art on such idealist premises, convinced that eternity was in love with the products of time, the sons of God with the sons of [*The manuscript ends here.*]

[1] Repeated from 'James Clarence Mangan', p. 81 above.

44

The Shade of Parnell[1]

1912

B_y passing the bill for parliamentary autonomy on its second reading,[2] the House of Commons has resolved the Irish question, which, like the hen of Mugello, looks newborn, though it is a hundred years old. The century which began with the transaction of buying and selling the Dublin parliament[3] is now closing with a triangular pact between England, Ireland, and the United States. It was graced with six Irish revolutionary movements which, by the use of dynamite, rhetoric, the boycott, obstructionism, armed revolt, and political assassination, have succeeded in keeping awake the slow and senile conscience of English Liberalism.

The present law was conceived, in the full maturity of time, under the double pressure of the Nationalist party at Westminster which has been jumbling up the workings of the British legislative body for half a century, and the Irish party across the Atlantic, which is blocking the greatly desired Anglo-American alliance.[4] Conceived and moulded with masterful cunning and art, the law forms a worthy capstone to the tradition handed down to posterity by that pluterperfect[5] Liberal statesman, William Gladstone. It suffices to say that, while it reduces the strong phalanx of 103 Irish members actually represented at Westminster to a band of 40 representatives, it pushes these into the arms of the little

---

[1] Translated from the Italian of 'L'Ombra di Parnell', *Il Piccolo della Sera*, Trieste, May 16, 1912.

[2] The third Home Rule Bill, passed on May 9, 1912.

[3] The Act of Union of 1800; see footnote 3, p. 162 above.

[4] The English liberals had for some time been trying to arrange an arbitration treaty with the United States. This is one arm of the 'triangular pact' that Joyce conceives of above; the other was the Home Rule Bill.

[5] 'Sopraperfetto', translated here by Mr. Deasy's word in *Ulysses*, p. 34 (30).

Labour party; and from this incestuous embrace there will probably be born a coalition which will operate from the left, that is to say from the Liberal party's point of operations in its campaign against Conservatism to the extreme left.

Into its tangle of financial qualifications, there is no chance of penetrating. At any rate, the Irish government about to be born will have to cover a deficit ably created by the British treasury, either by manipulation of local and imperial taxes, or by a reduction of its administrative expenses, or by an increase in direct taxes, in any case provoking the disillusioned hostility of the middle and lower classes. The Irish separatist party would like to reject this Greek gift, which makes the Chancellor of the Exchequer in Dublin a titular minister fully responsible to the taxpayers and at the same time dependent on the British cabinet, one who has the power to tax without being able to control the collections of his department — a transmitter which cannot work unless the dynamo at London sends a current of the necessary voltage.

It doesn't matter — there is an appearance of autonomy. At the recent national assembly held at Dublin, the recriminations and protests of the Nationalists who belong to the bitterly sceptical school of John Mitchel did not disturb the popular rejoicing very much. The representatives, grown old in the constitutional struggle and weakened by so many years of deluded hopes, hailed in their speeches the end of a long era of misunderstanding. A young orator, Gladstone's nephew, invoked the name of his uncle amid the frenzied acclamation of the crowd, and hailed the prosperity of the new nation. Within two years at the most, with or without the consent of the House of Lords, the doors of the old Irish parliament will be reopened; and Ireland, released from its century-old prison, will walk forth toward the palace like a new bride, escorted by musicians and ritual bridal torches. A grandnephew of Gladstone, if there is one, will scatter flowers beneath the feet of the sovereign; but there will be a ghost at the banquet — the shade of Charles Parnell.

*　　*　　*　　*

His most recent critic has tried to minimize the greatness of this strange spirit by pointing out the different sources of his agile parliamentary tactics. But even if we grant the historical critic that obstructionism was invented by Biggar and Ronayne, that the doctrine of the independence of the Irish party was launched by Gavan Duffy, that the Agrarian League was the creation of Michael Davitt, these concessions only make more conspicuous the extraordinary personality of a leader who, without forensic gifts or any original political talent, forced the greatest English politicians to carry out his orders; and, like another Moses, led a turbulent and unstable people from the house of shame to the verge of the Promised Land.[1]

The influence exerted on the Irish people by Parnell defies critical analysis. He had a speech defect and a delicate physique; he was ignorant of the history of his native land; his short and fragmentary speeches lacked eloquence, poetry, and humour; his cold and formal bearing separated him from his own colleagues; he was a Protestant, a descendant of an aristocratic family, and, as a crowning disgrace, he spoke with a distinct English accent. He would often come to meetings an hour or an hour and a half late without apologizing. He would neglect his correspondence for weeks on end. The applause and anger of the crowd, the abuse and praise of the press, the denunciations and defence of the British ministers never disturbed the melancholy serenity of his character. It is even said that he did not know by sight many of those who sat with him on the Irish benches. When the Irish people presented him with a national gratuity of 40,000 pounds sterling in 1887, he put the cheque into his billfold, and in the speech which he delivered to the immense gathering made not the slightest reference to the gift which he had received.

When he was shown the copy of *The Times* containing the famous autograph letter which would have proved his implication in the barbarous assassination in Phoenix Park, he put his finger on one letter in the handwriting and said simply, 'I have not made an 's' that way since '78.' Later, when the inquiries of the Royal Commission revealed the conspiracy which had been formed against him and the perjurer and forger Pigott blew out his brains in a Madrid hotel, the House of Commons, without regard to party, greeted Parnell's entrance with an ovation that remains without precedent in the annals of the British Parliament. Is it necessary to say that Parnell made no response to the ovation

[1] Joyce plays on this image of Moses and the Promised Land in the 'Aeolus' episode of *Ulysses*.

with a smile or a bow or a gesture, but merely passed to his place beyond the aisle and sat down? Gladstone was probably thinking of this incident when he called the Irish leader an intellectual phenomenon.

Nothing more unusual can be imagined than the appearance of this intellectual phenomenon in the midst of the moral suffocation of Westminster. Now, looking back at the scene of the drama and hearing again the speeches that shook the minds of his listeners, it is useless to deny that all the eloquence and all those triumphs of strategy begin to smell stale. But time is kinder to the 'uncrowned king' than to the jester and the phrase-maker. The light of his sovereign bearing, mild and proud, silent and disconsolate, makes Disraeli look like a diplomatic opportunist who dines when he can at rich men's houses, and Gladstone like an imposing major domo who has gone to night school. How lightly Disraeli's wit and Gladstone's culture weigh in the balance today. Today how flimsy seem the studied gibes, the greasy locks, and the stupid novels of Disraeli; and the high-sounding periods, the Homeric studies, the speeches on Artemis and on marmalade of Gladstone.

Although Parnell's strategy was to make use of any English party, Liberal or Conservative, at his pleasure, a nexus of circumstances involved him in the Liberal movement. Gladstonian liberalism was an inconstant algebraic symbol whose coefficient was the movement's political pressure and whose index was his personal profit. While he temporized in internal politics, contradicting and justifying himself in turn, he always maintained (as much as he was capable of it) a sincere admiration for liberty in the house of others. It is necessary to keep in mind this elastic quality of Gladstone's liberalism in order to understand the nature and magnitude of Parnell's task.

To put it in few words, Gladstone was a self-seeking politician. He raged at the restless iniquity of O'Connell in 1835,[1] but he was the English legislator who proclaimed the moral and economic necessity for Irish autonomy. He thundered against the admission of Jews to public office, but he was the minister who, for the first time in English history, raised a Jew to the peerage. He spoke fiercely against the Boers who rebelled in 1881, but after the defeat of Majuba he concluded a treaty with Transvaal which the English themselves called a cowardly surrender. In his first

[1] Daniel O'Connell was pressing for repeal of the Union, among other reforms.

parliamentary speech he warmly defended against Earl Grey's accusation of cruelty his own father, a rich slave owner in Demerara who had made two million francs from the sale of human flesh, while in his last letter to another 'childhood friend', the Duke of Westminster, he invoked all the lightning available on the head of the great assassin of Constantinople.[1]

Parnell, convinced that such liberalism would yield only to force, united behind him every element of Irish life and began to march, treading on the verge of insurrection. Just six years after his entrance into Westminster he held in his hands the fate of the government. He was imprisoned, but in his cell at Kilmainham he concluded a pact with the ministers who had imprisoned him.[2] When the attempt at blackmail failed with Pigott's confession and suicide, the Liberal government offered him a portfolio. Parnell not only refused it, he ordered all his followers as well to refuse ministerial duties, and forbade the municipalities and public corporations in Ireland to receive officially any member of the British royal house until the English government should restore autonomy to Ireland. The Liberals had to accept these humiliating conditions, and in 1886 Gladstone read the first Home Rule Bill at Westminster.

Parnell's fall came in the midst of these events like lightning from a clear sky. He fell hopelessly in love with a married woman, and when her husband, Captain O'Shea, asked for a divorce, the ministers Gladstone and Morley openly refused to legislate in favour of Ireland if the sinner remained as head of the Nationalist Party. Parnell did not appear at the hearings to defend himself. He denied the right of a minister to exercise a veto over the political affairs of Ireland, and refused to resign.

He was deposed in obedience to Gladstone's orders. Of his 83 representatives only 8 remained faithful to him.[3] The high and low clergy entered the lists to finish him off. The Irish press emptied on him and the woman he loved the vials of their envy. The citizens of Castlecomer threw quicklime in his eyes. He went from county to county, from city to city, 'like a hunted deer', a

[1] Abdul Hamid II, Sultan of Turkey, who was denounced as inhuman in Gladstone's letter of March 13, 1897, later published as a pamphlet, *Letter to the Duke of Westminster*, regarding the Greco-Turkish war.

[2] The so-called Kilmainham Treaty of April 1882.

[3] The vote in Committee Room no. 15 was 44 against and 26 for the retention of Parnell as leader.

spectral figure with the signs of death on his forehead. Within a year he died of a broken heart at the age of 45.

The ghost of the 'uncrowned king' will weigh on the hearts of those who remember him when the new Ireland in the near future enters into the palace 'fimbriis aureis circumamicta varietatibus';[1] but it will not be a vindictive ghost. The melancholy which invaded his mind was perhaps the profound conviction that, in his hour of need, one of the disciples who dipped his hand in the same bowl with him would betray him. That he fought to the very end with this desolate certainty in mind is his greatest claim to nobility.

In his final desperate appeal to his countrymen, he begged them not to throw him as a sop to the English wolves howling around them.[2] It redounds to their honour that they did not fail this appeal. They did not throw him to the English wolves; they tore him to pieces themselves.

JAMES JOYCE

[1] Psalms 44:14–15 in the Vulgate translation. These Latin words (meaning 'girded with golden fringes, in varied colours') are used in the 'office of the Virgin', the 'little office' mentioned in the *Portrait*, p. 355–6 (118): 'On Saturday mornings when the sodality met in the chapel to recite the little office . . . the imagery of the psalms of prophecy soothed his barren pride.'

[2] 'Do not flingamejig to the twolves!' *Finnegans Wake*, p. 479.

45

The City of the Tribes

ITALIAN ECHOES IN AN IRISH PORT.[1]

1912

Galway, August.

The lazy Dubliner, who travels little and knows his own country only by hearsay, believes that the inhabitants of Galway are descendants of Spanish stock, and that you can't go four steps in the dark streets of the City of the Tribes without meeting the true Spanish type, with olive complexion and raven hair. The Dubliner is both right and wrong. Today in Galway the black eyes are scarce enough, and the raven hair, too, since a Titian red predominates for the most part. The old Spanish houses are falling to ruins, and clumps of weeds grow in the protruding bay windows. Outside the city walls rise the suburbs — new, gay, and heedless of the past, but you have only to close your eyes to this bothersome modernity for a moment to see in the twilight of history the 'Spanish city'. It lies scattered among innumerable little islands, cut by rivulets, cataracts, conduits, and canals, at the lower end of a vast gulf of the Atlantic Ocean in which the entire British navy could anchor. At the mouth of the gulf, the three Aran islands, lying on the grey waters like a sleeping whale,[2] form a natural breakwater and take the force of the Atlantic waves. The little lighthouse of the southern island casts a weak ray of light toward the west, the last greeting of the old world to the new, and

---

[1] Translated from the Italian of 'La Città delle Tribù; Ricordi Italiani in un Porto Irlandese', *Il Piccolo della Sera*, Trieste, August 11, 1912.

[2] 'They halted, looking towards the blunt cape of Bray Head that lay on the water like the snout of a sleeping whale.' *Ulysses*, p. 9 (5–6). Joyce also uses this phrase in 'The Mirage of the Fisherman of Aran' (p. 234 below).

calls stubbornly but in vain to the foreign merchant, who, for many years, has not come near these parts.

* * * *

And yet, in the Middle Ages these waters were cut by thousands of foreign ships. The signs at the corners of the narrow streets record the city's connection with Latin Europe — Madeira Street, Merchant Street, Spaniards Walk, Madeira Island, Lombard Street, Velasquez de Palmeira Boulevard. Oliver Cromwell's correspondence shows that the port of Galway was the second most important harbour in the United Kingdom, and the prime market in the entire Kingdom for the Spanish and Italian trade. In the first decade of the fourteenth century, a Florentine merchant, Andrea Gerardo, was tax collector of the government, and on the list of officials of the seventeenth century we find the name of Giovanni Fante. The city itself has as guardian Saint Nicholas of Bari, patron of sailors and babies, and the so-called 'seal of the college' bears his likeness. The papal envoy, Cardinal Rinuccini, came to Galway during the trial of the martyr king, and placed the city under the papal flag.[1] The clergy and religious orders refused to recognize his authority, so the fiery Cardinal broke the bell in the Church of the Carmelites, and posted two priests of his own following at the church door to prevent the entrance of the faithful. The parish house of Saint Nicholas still preserves a record of another Italian prelate of the Middle Ages[2] — an autograph letter of the notorious Borgia.[3] In the same place there is a curious document, left by an Italian traveller of the sixteenth century, in which the writer says that, although he had travelled throughout the world, he had never seen in a single glance what he saw in Galway — a priest elevating the Host, a pack chasing a deer, a ship entering the harbour under full sail, and a salmon being killed with a spear.

Almost all the wine imported into the United Kingdom from Spain, Portugal, the Canary Islands, and Italy passed through this port, the annual import amounting to 1500 'tuns', that is to say, almost two million litres.[4] This trade was so important that

---

[1] Giovanni Battista Rinuccini (1592–1653), the papal nuncio, came to Ireland with money and arms to support the Catholic uprising during the reign of Charles I, the 'martyr king'.

[2] 'The plump shadowed face and sullen oval jowl recalled a prelate, patron of arts in the middle ages.' *Ulysses*, p. 5 (1).

[3] Pope Alexander VI (Roderigo Lanzol Borgia).

[4] In the 'Cyclops' chapter of *Ulysses* (p. 322 [312]), the Citizen says: 'We had our

the government of Holland proposed to buy a large tract of land near the city and pay for it by covering the ground with pieces of silver. Afraid of the foreign competition, the Galway merchants had their envoy reply that they would accept if the silver pieces would be placed end-up on the ground. The answer of the Dutch to this most kind counter-offer has not yet arrived.

*   *   *   *

For many centuries, the entire municipal and church adminis-tration was in the hands of the descendants of the fourteen tribes, whose names are recorded in four limping verses. The strangest and most interesting historical document in the city archives is the map of the city made for the Duke of Lorraine in the seventeenth century, when His Highness wished to be assured of the city's greatness on the occasion of a loan requested of him by his English confrère, the happy monarch.[1] The map, full of symbolic expres-sions and engravings, was the work of Henry Joyce,[2] Dean of the Canons of the city. All the margins of the parchment are heavy with the heraldic arms of the tribes, and the map itself is little more than a topographic symphony on the theme of the number of the tribes. Thus, the map maker enumerates and depicts four-teen bastions, fourteen towers on the wall, fourteen principal streets, fourteen narrow streets, and then, sliding down into a minor mode, six gardens, six altars for the procession of Corpus Domini, six markets, and six other wonders. Among these last, in fact, the last of the last, the worthy Dean enumerates 'the old pigeon house located in the southern part of the city'.

*   *   *   *

Of all the tribes, the most famous was that of the Lynches. During the century and a half that runs from the founding of the city to the devastating invasions of the Cromwellian soldiery, a member of this family filled the post of chief magistrate a good eighty-three times. The most tragic event in the city's history was the expiation of a crime committed in 1493 by the young Walter

---

trade with Spain and the French and with the Flemings before those mongrels were pupped, Spanish ale in Galway, the winebark on the winedark waterway.'

[1] Charles II.

[2] Joyce always paid special attention to the appearance of his patronymic.

Lynch, the only son of the chief magistrate James Lynch Fitz-Stephen.[1] The magistrate, a rich wine merchant, took a voyage that year to Spain, where he was the guest of a Spanish friend of his, a certain Gomez. This man's son, listening every night to the tales of the traveller, was very much attracted to far-away Ireland, and asked his father's permission to accompany their guest when he returned to his native land. The father hesitated. Times were dangerous, and travellers were accustomed to make out their wills before setting out for shores known or unknown. But the magistrate Lynch guaranteed the safety of the youth, and they left together.

When they arrived in Galway, the young Spaniard became the friend of the magistrate's son, Walter, a wayward young man of impetuous nature, who was paying court to Agnes Blake, the daughter of another nobleman of the city. Very soon, love arose between Agnes and the foreigner, and one night when Gomez was leaving the Blake house, Walter Lynch, who was waiting in ambush, stuck a knife in his back, and then, in a blind rage, dragged the body along the street and threw it into a ditch.

The crime was discovered and young Walter was arrested and tried. His father, chief magistrate of the city, was the judge. Deaf to the call of blood, and mindful only of the honour of the city and of his own pledged word, he condemned the assassin to death. In vain his friends tried to dissuade him. The people, full of pity for the unhappy youth, besieged the judge's home, the dark and gloomy castle that still shadows the main street. But the magistrate was inexorable, even when the hangman refused to execute the sentence. Father and son spent the night before the execution together in the prison cell, praying until dawn. When the hour of execution arrived, father and son appeared at a window of the house. They kissed and bade each other farewell, then the father himself hanged his son from the window beam before the eyes of the horrified crowd.

The old Spanish houses are falling to ruin. The castles of the tribes are demolished. Clumps of weeds grow in the windows and the open courtyards. Over the gateways, the noble coats of arms, cut in the darkened rock, are fading — the wolf of the Campi-

---

[1] Joyce gave his friend Vincent Cosgrave the fictional name of 'Lynch' in the *Portrait* and *Ulysses* with this history of the family in mind.

doglio with the two twins,[1] the two-headed eagle of the Haps-burgs,[2] the black bull of the Darcys, descendants of Charlemagne. In the city of Galway, writes an old chronicler, reign the passions of pride and lust.

* * * *

The evening is quiet and grey. From the distance, beyond the waterfall, comes a murmur. It sounds like the hum of bees around a hive. It comes closer. Six young men appear, playing bagpipes, at the head of a band of people. They pass, proud and warlike, with heads uncovered, playing a vague and strange music. In the uncertain light you can hardly distinguish the green plaids hang-ing from the right shoulder and the saffron-coloured kilts. They enter the street of the Convent of Offerings, and, as the vague music spreads in the twilight, at the windows of the convent appear, one by one, the white veils of the nuns.

JAMES JOYCE

[1] The Capitoline Wolf, emblem of the city of Rome.
[2] The national coat of arms of Austria.

46

The Mirage of the Fisherman of Aran

ENGLAND'S SAFETY VALVE IN CASE OF WAR.[1]

1912

Galway, 2 September

The little ship carrying a small load of travellers moves away from the quay under the watchful eyes of the Scottish agent absorbed in a private fantasy of calculation. It leaves the little port of Galway and enters open water, leaving behind on its right the village of Claddagh, a cluster of huts outside the walls of the city. A cluster of huts, and yet a kingdom. Up until a few years ago the village elected its own king, had its own mode of dress, passed its own laws, and lived to itself. The wedding rings of the inhabitants are still decorated with the king's crest: two joined hands supporting a crowned heart.

We set out for Aranmor, the holy island that sleeps like a great shark on the grey waters of the Atlantic Ocean,[2] which the islanders call the Old Sea. Beneath the waters of this bay and along its coast lie the wrecks of a squadron of the unfortunate Spanish Armada. After their defeat in the English Channel, the ships set sail for the North, where the storms and the waves scattered them. The citizens of Galway, remembering the long friendship between Spain and Ireland, hid the fugitives from the vengeance of the English garrison and gave the shipwrecked a decent burial, wrapping their bodies in white linen cloth.

The waters have repented. Every year on the day before the

[1] Translated from the Italian of 'Il Miraggio del Pescatore di Aran. La Valvola dell'Inghilterra in Caso di Guerra', *Il Piccolo della Sera*, Trieste, September 5, 1912.

[2] Repeated with a slight variation from 'The City of the Tribes'; see footnote 2, p. 229 above.

Feast of the Assumption, when the herring fishing begins, the waters of the bay are blessed. A flotilla of fishing boats departs from Claddagh preceded by a flagship, on whose deck stands a Dominican friar. When they reach an appropriate place the flotilla stops, the fishermen kneel down and uncover themselves, and the friar, muttering prayers of exorcism, shakes his aspergill on the sea, and divides the dark air in the form of a cross.

A border of white sand on the right indicates the place where the new transatlantic port is, perhaps, destined to rise. My companion spreads out a large map on which the projected lines curve, ramify, and cross each other from Galway to the great Canadian ports. The voyage from Europe to America will take less than three days, according to the figures. From Galway, the last port in Europe, to Saint John, Newfoundland, a steamship will take two days and sixteen hours, and from Galway to Halifax, the first port in Canada, three days and ten hours. The text of the booklet attached to the map bristles with figures, estimates of cost, and oceanographic pictures. The writer makes a warm appeal to the British admiralty, to the railway societies, to the Chambers of Commerce, to the Irish population. The new port would be a safety valve for England in case of war. From Canada, the granary and warehouse of the United Kingdom, great cargos of grain would enter the Irish port, thus avoiding the dangers of navigation in Saint George's Channel and the enemy fleets. In time of peace, the new line would be the shortest way between one continent and the other. A large part of the goods and passengers which are now landed at Liverpool would in the future land at Galway, proceeding directly to London, via Dublin and Holyhead. The old decadent city would rise again. From the new world, wealth and vital energy would run through this new artery of an Ireland drained of blood. Again, after about ten centuries, the mirage which blinded the poor fisherman of Aran, follower and emulator of St. Brendan, appears in the distance, vague and tremulous on the mirror of the ocean.

Christopher Columbus, as everyone knows, is honoured by posterity because he was the last to discover America. A thousand years before the Genoese navigator was derided at Salamanca, Saint Brendan weighed anchor for the unknown world from the bare shore which our ship is approaching; and, after crossing the ocean, landed on the coast of Florida. The island at that time was wooded and fertile. At the edge of the woods he found the hermitage of Irish monks which had been established in the fourth century after Christ by Enda, a saint of royal blood. From this hermitage came Finnian, later Bishop of Lucca. Here lived and dreamed the visionary Saint Fursa, described in the hagiographic calendar of Ireland as the precursor of Dante Alighieri. A medieval copy of the Visions of Fursa depicts the voyage of the saint from hell to heaven, from the gloomy valley of the four fires among the bands of devils up through the universe to the divine light reflected from innumerable angels' wings. This vision would have served as a model for the poet of the *Divine Comedy*, who, like Columbus, is honoured by posterity because he was the last to visit and describe the three regions of the soul.

* * * *

On the shore of the bay fragile little boats of stretched canvas are drawn up to dry. Four islanders come nimbly down to the sea over rocks covered with purple and rust-coloured seaweed, like that seen in the shops of herb-sellers in Galway. The fisherman of Aran has sure feet. He wears a rough sandal of untanned cowhide, without heels, open at the arch, and tied with rawhide laces.[1] He dresses in wool as thick as felt and wears a big black hat with a wide brim.

We stop in one of the steep little streets, uncertain. An islander, who speaks an English all his own, says good morning, adding that it has been a horrible summer, praise be to God. The phrase, which at first seems one of the usual Irish blunders, rather comes from the innermost depths of human resignation. The man who said it bears a princely name, that of the O'Flaherties, a name which the young Oscar Wilde proudly had printed on the title page of his first book. But time and the wind have razed to the ground the bygone civilization to which he belongs — the sacred druids of his island, the territory ruled by his ancestors, the language, and perhaps even the name, of that hermit of Aran who was called the dove of the church.[2] Around the stunted shrubs which grow on the hills of the island his imagination has woven legends and tales which reveal the depths of his psyche. And under his apparent simplicity he retains a slight trace of scep-

---

[1] Pampooties. 'The tramper Synge is looking for you.... He's out in pampooties to murder you.' *Ulysses*, p. 197 (188).
[2] St. Columkill.

ticism, and of humour. He looks away when he has spoken and lets
the eager enthusiast jot down in his notebook the astounding fact
that yonder hawthorn tree was the little tree from which Joseph
of Arimathea cut his walking stick.

An old lady comes toward us and invites us to enter her house.
She places on the table an enormous tea pot, a small loaf of bread,
and some salted butter. The islander, who is her son, sits near the
fireplace and answers the questions of my companion in an embar-
rassed and humble manner. He doesn't know how old he is, but
he says that he will soon be old. He doesn't know why he hasn't
taken a wife, perhaps because there are no women for him. My
companion goes on to ask why there are no women for him, and
the islander, removing his hat from his head, sinks his face in the
soft wool, confused and smiling. Aran, it is said, is the strangest
place in the world. A poor place, but no matter how poor it is,
when my companion tries to pay, the old lady rejects the money
almost angrily and asks us if we are trying to dishonour her house.

* * * *

A fine and steady drizzle falls from the grey clouds. The rainy
mist comes in from the West, while the little ship calls desperately
for the laggards. The island disappears little by little, wrapped in
a smoky veil. Three Danish sailors sitting stationary on the ridge of
the slope also·disappear. They were out in the ocean for the summer
fishing and made a stop at Aran. Silent and melancholy, they
seem to be thinking of the Danish hordes who burned the city of
Galway in the eighth century, of the Irish lands which are included
in the dowries of the girls of Denmark, according to legend, and
which they dream of reconquering. On the islands and on the sea
falls the rain. It rains as it can rain only in Ireland. Under the
forecastle, where a girl is noisily making love to one of the crew,
holding him on her knees, we again open the map. In the twilight
the names of the ports cannot be distinguished, but the line that
leaves Galway and ramifies and spreads out recalls the motto
placed near the crest of his native city by a mystic and perhaps
even prophetic head of a monastery:

> *Quasi lilium germinans germinabit,*
> *et quasi terebinthus extendans ramos suos.*[1]

JAMES JOYCE

[1] 'It will grow like a sprouting lily, stretching out its branches like the terebinth
tree.'

47

Politics and Cattle Disease

1912

When Joyce was preparing to leave Trieste for a visit to Dublin in July, 1912, his friend Henry N. Blackwood Price, an Ulsterman, asked him to find out the address of William Field, M.P. Price was much concerned over the foot and mouth disease in Ireland, and wanted Field, who as a Blackrock butcher was also involved, to know of a purported cure that had been developed in Austria. Joyce sent the address, Price wrote to Field, and Field had the letter published in the Evening Telegraph *for August 19, 1912. Joyce parodied the letter in* Ulysses, *where he attributes it to Mr. Deasy and makes Blackwood Price Deasy's cousin.[1] But he became quite interested in the problem, and, according to a letter of his brother Charles dated September 6, 1912, wrote a sub-editorial for the* Freeman's Journal *about it.[2] This article, which appeared as a sub-editorial in the* Freeman's Journal *on September 10, 1912, shows how completely and quickly Joyce could work up a subject that interested him, and throws some light on the sympathy for cattle which he displays in* Ulysses.

Though the country has not been deceived by the pitiable endeavours of Unionists and factionists to make political capital out of the national calamity involved in the outbreak of the foot

[1] A comparison of Price's actual letter with Joyce's parody is made in Richard Ellmann, 'The Backgrounds of *Ulysses*', *Kenyon Review*, v. 16 (Summer 1954) 354–6.

[2] The letter from Charles Joyce to Stanislaus Joyce is in the Cornell University Library. Although this article is unsigned, it is the only editorial on the hoof and mouth disease that appears in the *Freeman's Journal* after September 6. That Joyce was on familiar terms with the editor is apparent in a short article that follows immediately after 'Politics and Cattle Disease' announcing the publication

and mouth disease in a few Irish districts, Mr. Dillon[1] renders a valuable service by pointing out the injury done by the dishonest clamour in which the mischief-makers have indulged. They have, he points out, played into the hands of English Protectionists like Mr. Henry Chaplin[2] and Mr. Bathurst,[3] whose object is not the security of English herds, but the prolonged exclusion of Irish cattle from the English markets. By enabling such enemies of the Irish farmer to raise the cry that any relaxation of the restrictions that may be proposed is due, not to Mr. Runciman's[4] unbiased opinion that the conditions justify the relaxation, but to 'Irish dictation', they have simply raised fresh obstructions to the fair treatment of the Irish stock-owners and traders' claims. All these stupid threats and calls upon the Irish Party to 'turn out the Government' have been ammunition to the English exclusionists. We have seen how the *Globe* has turned them to account. It will have been noticed, too, that none of these Unionist fire-eaters have appealed to their own Party for assistance in the matter. According to the London correspondent of the *Irish Times*, 'Irish members of all shades of opinion are asking for the removal of restrictions, but without success.' This will be news to most people. Hitherto Irish members of the Unionist shade of opinion have been only remarkable for their silence on the matter. Not one of the Irish Unionist Party attended the deputation to Mr. Runciman. Mr. Chaplin and Mr. Bathurst have been allowed to rampage without a word of protest from an Irish Unionist member. Yet the Unionist landlords, land agents, and eleven-months' men, and the defeated factionist candidates who have been joining in their cry, have not addressed a word of protest or appeal to the Irish Unionist leaders to put a snaffle on Mr. Chaplin. The simple

---

of an article by 'Mr. James Joyce, an Irish-Italian journalist' on the Galway Harbour scheme in the *Piccolo della Sera*, and summarizing part of the article. Since 'The Mirage of the Fisherman of Aran' h:⸱⸱ ⸱⸱een published in Italian only five days before in Trieste, this information mu ⸱t have reached the editor through Joyce.

[1] John Dillon (1851–1927), son of John Blake Dillon, and one of the three leaders of the Irish Party.

[2] Later first Viscount Chaplin (1840–1923), a prominent English conservative spokesman for agricultural interests in parliament.

[3] Charles Bathurst, first Viscount Bledisloe (who is still alive), an English member of parliament and cattle-breeder, prominent in agricultural affairs.

[4] Walter Runciman, later first Baron Runciman (1847–1937), an English ship-owner, whose interests in this case were directly opposed to those of Chaplin and Bathurst.

fact is sufficient to explain the motives and purpose of all the Unionist talk upon the matter.

Mr. Dillon points out what would be the certain consequence of action of the kind recommended to the Irish Party. Not only would it involve the sacrifice of the Home Rule Bill and the Home Rule movement, but it would defeat the very object alleged by these advisers. After such an incident no British Minister dare open the English ports for months, because his motives would be instantly challenged. Equally bad and dangerous has been the talk about the unimportance of the disease, and the advice given by some foolish people to the farmers to conceal it. Fortunately the Irish farmers have not listened to the advice. They have proved their commonsense by reporting every suspicious case. Their anxiety to assist the public authorities has been proved by the fact that a majority of the cases so reported have proved to be cases of some other ailment. It is obvious that only by such action can the confidence of the trading public be so restored that the English Minister will be free to act upon the facts disclosed. The talk that the disease is only 'like measles in children and that all the cattle should be allowed to get it', like the foolish advice to farmers to conceal cases of the disease, is probably the explanation of the extraordinary official suggestion that the healthy areas should be denied their rights 'until the situation disclose itself further'. The situation is fully disclosed, because the Irish stock-owners have been perfectly above-board in the matter. They ought not to be held responsible for the stupidities of irresponsible speakers like those whom we have quoted. But a moment's reflection will convince the stock-owners that stupid people of the kind are worth as much as ten outbreaks of the disease to persons like the Right Hon. Henry Chaplin and Mr. Charles Bathurst.

We do not mean to urge that the Irish farmers and traders should relax their efforts or cease their agitation. Quite the contrary. The situation is critical, and they have sound and solid reasons for demanding the reopening of the ports to healthy Irish stock. These sound and solid reasons are only weakened by menaces that defeat themselves, and by declarations that allow slanderers to say that the disease is being concealed in Ireland. The stock-owners can point to the fact that since the original outbreak, when the existence of the disease could scarcely have been suspected, not a single prosecution for concealment has taken place, though the Constabulary and the officials of the Department are actively watching for symptoms of the disease all over the country. A fact of that kind is the most complete justification of the demand for equality of treatment with the English healthy areas, which the Irish stock-owners and traders are pressing. In putting forward that demand they have the full and hearty co-operation of the Irish Party and its Leader. The influence of the Party will be exercised no less strongly, because it is being used in a legitimate and reasonable way, and in a manner that will leave the exclusionists with no ground for slander. The Irish Department is, we have the strongest grounds for believing, no less active. Mr. Russell[1] has not concealed his endorsement of the claim of the Irish stock-owners. On the contrary, he has taken the strong step of publicly proclaiming his agreement. His statement is the best justification for a vigorous agitation against the unreasonable prolongation of the embargo. It is essential to maintain that agitation, but it is no less essential to discountenance the use of silly and mischievous language, which is the only justification the intimidators of Mr. Runciman can plead for their attitude.

[1] George Russell, editor of the agricultural newspaper the *Irish Homestead*, who was involved in agricultural affairs all his life.

48

Gas from a Burner

1912

In September 1909, *Joyce, then on a visit to Dublin, signed a contract with the Dublin firm of Maunsel and Co. to publish* Dubliners. *But George Roberts, the manager of the firm, began to find reasons first for delaying and then for censoring the manuscript. Negotiations dragged along for three years, until finally Joyce returned to Dublin in July* 1912, *and brought the matter to a head. Both Joyce and Roberts consulted solicitors; Roberts was advised that the use of actual names for public houses and the like was libellous, and began to demand so many changes that there was no possibility of agreement. At length he decided to accept Joyce's offer to purchase the sheets for the book, which John Falconer, a Dublin printer, had finished. But Falconer, hearing of the dispute, decided he wanted nothing to do with so unpleasant a book, and guillotined the sheets. Joyce left Dublin full of bitterness, which he vented by writing this broadside on the back of his contract with Maunsel and Co. for the publication of* Dubliners, *while he was on the train between Flushing and Salzburg.*

Ladies and gents, you are here assembled
To hear why earth and heaven trembled
Because of the black and sinister arts
Of an Irish writer in foreign parts.
He sent me a book ten years ago.[1]
I read it a hundred times or so,
Backwards and forwards, down and up,
Through both ends of a telescope.
I printed it all to the very last word

[1] George Roberts is the speaker.

But by the mercy of the Lord
The darkness of my mind was rent
And I saw the writer's foul intent.
But I owe a duty to Ireland:
I hold her honour in my hand,
This lovely land that always sent
Her writers and artists to banishment
And in a spirit of Irish fun
Betrayed her own leaders, one by one.
'Twas Irish humour, wet and dry,
Flung quicklime into Parnell's eye;[1]
'Tis Irish brains that save from doom
The leaky barge of the Bishop of Rome
For everyone knows the Pope can't belch
Without the consent of Billy Walsh.[2]
O Ireland my first and only love
Where Christ and Caesar are hand and glove!
O lovely land where the shamrock grows!
(Allow me, ladies, to blow my nose)
To show you for strictures I don't care a button
I printed the poems of Mountainy Mutton[3]
And a play he wrote (you've read it I'm sure)
Where they talk of 'bastard', 'bugger' and 'whore'[4]
And a play on the Word and Holy Paul
And some woman's legs that I can't recall
Written by Moore, a genuine gent
That lives on his property's ten per cent:[5]
I printed mystical books in dozens:

[1] This incident, which Joyce also mentions in 'The Shade of Parnell' (p. 227 above) occurred at Castlecomer in the summer of 1891, according to Parnell's biographer and friend, R. Barry O'Brien.

[2] His Grace the Most Reverend William J. Walsh, D.D., Archbishop of Dublin.

[3] Joseph Campbell, author of *The Mountainy Singer*, published by Maunsel in 1909.

[4] Campbell's *Judgment: a Play in Two Acts*, published by Maunsel in 1912, contains on p. 25 the words 'bastard' and 'whore'.

[5] *The Apostle*, published by Maunsel in 1911. Moore's play, in which Christ (the Word) and Paul meet after Christ's death, includes a dialogue between Christ and Mary in which Mary laments her lost beauty. In a long preface Moore surveys the Bible for evidence of sensuality and remarks (p. 9) 'In Samuel we read how David was captured by the sweetness of Bathsheba's legs while bathing . . .', and (p. 26) 'It may be doubted whether Paul always succeeded in subduing these infirmities of the flesh, but we would not love him less, even if we knew that he had loved St. Eunice not wisely but too well.'

I printed the table-book of Cousins[1]
Though (asking your pardon) as for the verse
'Twould give you a heartburn on your arse:[2]
I printed folklore from North and South
By Gregory of the Golden Mouth:[3]
I printed poets, sad, silly and solemn:
I printed Patrick What-do-you-Colm:[4]
I printed the great John Milicent Synge
Who soars above on an angel's wing
In the playboy shift[5] that he pinched as swag
From Maunsel's manager's travelling-bag.[6]
But I draw the line at that bloody fellow,
That was over here dressed in Austrian yellow,
Spouting Italian by the hour
To O'Leary Curtis[7] and John Wyse Power[8]
And writing of Dublin, dirty and dear,
In a manner no blackamoor printer could bear.
Shite and onions![9] Do you think I'll print
The name of the Wellington Monument,
Sydney Parade and Sandymount tram,
Downes's cakeshop and Williams's jam?
I'm damned if I do — I'm damned to blazes!
Talk about *Irish Names of Places*![10]
It's a wonder to me, upon my soul,
He forgot to mention Curly's Hole.[11]
No, ladies, my press shall have no share in

---

[1] James Cousins, a Dublin Theosophist and poet. The 'table-book' is probably his *Etain the Beloved and Other Poems*, published by Maunsel in 1912.

[2] An expression of Joyce's father; see *Ulysses*, p. 122 (115).

[3] Maunsel published Lady Gregory's *Kiltartan History Book* in 1909 and *The Kiltartan Wonder Book* in 1910.

[4] Padraic Colum.

[5] The word 'shift', spoken by a character in Synge's *Playboy of the Western World* caused a riot at the Abbey Theatre in 1907; Maunsel published the play in the same year.

[6] Roberts was a traveller in ladies' underwear.

[7] A Dublin journalist.

[8] An official in the Royal Irish Constabulary in Dublin Castle, and a man of considerable cultivation. He figures largely in *Ulysses* in the characters of Jack Power and John Wyse Nolan.

[9] An expression of Joyce's father; see *Ulysses*, p. 125 (117).

[10] *The Origin and History of Irish Names of Places*, by Patrick Weston Joyce, no relation to James.

[11] A bathing pool at Dollymount, Clontarf.

So gross a libel on Stepmother Erin.[1]
I pity the poor — that's why I took
A red-headed Scotchman[2] to keep my book.
Poor sister Scotland! Her doom is fell;
She cannot find any more Stuarts to sell.
My conscience is fine as Chinese silk:
My heart is as soft as buttermilk.
Colm can tell you I made a rebate
Of one hundred pounds on the estimate
I gave him for his Irish Review.[3]
I love my country — by herrings I do!
I wish you could see what tears I weep
When I think of the emigrant train and ship.
That's why I publish far and wide
My quite illegible railway guide.
In the porch of my printing institute
The poor and deserving prostitute
Plays every night at catch-as-catch-can
With her tight-breeched British artilleryman
And the foreigner learns the gift of the gab
From the drunken draggletail Dublin drab.
Who was it said: Resist not evil?[4]
I'll burn that book, so help me devil.
I'll sing a psalm as I watch it burn
And the ashes I'll keep in a one-handled urn.
I'll penance do with farts and groans
Kneeling upon my marrowbones.
This very next lent I will unbare
My penitent buttocks to the air
And sobbing beside my printing press
My awful sin I will confess.
My Irish foreman from Bannockburn[5]
Shall dip his right hand in the urn
And sign crisscross with reverent thumb
Memento homo[6] upon my bum.

[1] As Dr. Oliver Gogarty remarks, in *Mourning Becomes Mrs. Spendlove* (N.Y., 1948) p. 61, Roberts was an Ulster Scot, so Erin is only his stepmother.
[2] Roberts himself.
[3] The *Irish Review* was edited by Colum from March 1912–July 1913.
[4] Christ, in the Sermon on the Mount.   [5] In Scotland.
[6] 'Memento, homo, quia pulvis es', the words of the priest on Ash Wednesday as he marks the cross of ashes on the communicant's forehead.

49

Dooleysprudence[1]

1916

During the First World War Joyce was, from the point of view of British consular authorities in Switzerland, offensively neutral. He had remained in Austrian Trieste until the end of June 1915, when, to avoid internment, he went to Switzerland. He gave his word to the Austrian officials that he would take no part in the war, and had no difficulty in keeping it. 'Dooleysprudence' reflects his pacifist irritation with both sides; its defence of the isolated exile recalls 'The Holy Office', but here as in Ulysses *the artist is the common man, not the heroic stag.*

Who is the man when all the gallant nations run to war
Goes home to have his dinner by the very first cablecar
And as he eats his canteloup contorts himself in mirth
To read the blatant bulletins of the rulers of the earth?
    It's Mr Dooley,[2]
    Mr Dooley,
    The coolest chap our country ever knew
    'They are out to collar
    The dime and dollar'
    Says Mr Dooley-ooley-ooley-oo.

Who is the funny fellow who declines to go to church
Since pope and priest and parson left the poor man in the lurch

---

[1] A typed copy of this poem is in the Slocum Collection of the Yale University Library. As the title playfully implies, Joyce is substituting private good sense for the folly of society's legal codes.
[2] The popular song 'Mr. Dooley' was written by Billy Jerome, in 1901, with reference to Finley Peter Dunne's character.

And taught their flocks the only way to save all human souls
Was piercing human bodies through with dumdum bulletholes?
>It's Mr Dooley,
>Mr Dooley,
>The mildest man our country ever knew
>'Who will release us
>From Jingo Jesus'
>Prays Mr Dooley-ooley-ooley-oo.

Who is the meek philosopher who doesn't care a damn
About the yellow peril or the problem of Siam
And disbelieves that British Tar is water from life's fount
And will not gulp the gospel of the German on the Mount?
>It's Mr Dooley,
>Mr Dooley,
>The broadest brain our country ever knew
>'The curse of Moses
>On both your houses'
>Cries Mr Dooley-ooley-ooley-oo.

Who is the cheerful imbecile who lights his long chibouk
With pages of the pandect, penal code and Doomsday Book
And wonders why bald justices are bound by law to wear
A toga and a wig made out of someone else's hair?
>It's Mr Dooley,
>Mr Dooley,
>The finest fool our country ever knew
>'They took that toilette
>From Pontius Pilate'
>Thinks Mr Dooley-ooley-ooley-oo.

Who is the man who says he'll go the whole and perfect hog
Before he pays the income tax or licence for a dog
And when he licks a postage stamp regards with smiling scorn
The face of king or emperor or snout of unicorn?
>It's Mr Dooley,
>Mr Dooley,
>The wildest wag our country ever knew
>'O my poor tummy
>His backside's gummy!'
>Moans Mr Dooley-ooley-ooley-oo.

Who is the tranquil gentleman who won't salute the State
Or serve Nabuchodonesor or proletariat
But thinks that every son of man has quite enough to do
To paddle down the stream of life his personal canoe?
        It's Mr Dooley,
        Mr Dooley,
        The wisest wight our country ever knew
        'Poor Europe ambles
        Like sheep to shambles'
        Sighs Mr Dooley-ooley-ooley-oo.

50

Programme Notes for the
English Players

1918/19

In the spring of 1918 Joyce and an English actor named Claud Sykes formed a troupe which they called the English Players, and began to give plays in Zurich and other Swiss cities. Joyce had a large share in the choice of the repertory, which was predominantly Irish, the first production being Wilde's Importance of Being Earnest. *In June 1918, the Players presented their first triple bill, and Joyce wrote the programme notes. He took Barrie on sufferance, but was specially interested in the plays of Synge and Shaw. He had known Synge in Paris in 1902, and Synge had shown him the manuscript of* Riders to the Sea. *Joyce objected to the way in which the catastrophe was brought about, and his programme note indicates he still suspected that the play contained Aristotelian flaws. His note to* The Dark Lady of the Sonnets *suggests a different view of Shakespeare from Shaw's, such as in fact he developed in the 'Scylla and Charybdis' episode of* Ulysses. *The last sentence of the note seems to refer to death, but is probably a cryptic reference to Joyce's theory that Shakespeare's life was clouded by Anne Hathaway's infidelity.*

Joyce persuaded the Players to produce another play by an Irishman, Edward Martyn's The Heather Field, *in March 1919. Martyn was a founder of the Irish Literary Theatre, and this play was one of the two which the theatre presented in May 1899, the other being Yeats's* Countess Cathleen. *Martyn was closer to the tradition of Ibsen than the other Irish dramatists, and on the basis of* The Heather Field *Joyce, like many others, had built up high hopes which Martyn's later work dispelled.*

THE TWELVE POUND LOOK
By J. M. Barrie

One Sims is about to be knighted: possibly, as the name would suggest, for having patented a hairgrower. He is discovered rehearsing his part with his wife whose portrait we see on the wall, painted by a Royal Academician, also knighted, presumably for having painted the label for the hairgrower. A typist is announced. This typist is his runaway wife of some fourteen years before. From their conversation we learn that she left him not for another man but to work out her salvation by typewriting. She had saved twelve pounds and bought a typewriter. The twelve pound look,[1] she says, is that look of independence in a wife's eye which every husband should beware of. The new knight's new wife, 'noted for her wit' — chary of it, too — seems likely to acquire the look if given time. Typewriters, however, are rather scarce at present.

RIDERS TO THE SEA
By John M. Synge

Synge's first play, written in Paris in 1902 out of his memories of Aran. The play shows a mother and her dead son, her last, the *anagke*[2] being the inexorable sea which claims all her sons, Seumas and Patch and Stephen and Shaun. Whether a brief tragedy be possible or not (a point on which Aristotle had some doubts) the ear and the heart mislead one gravely if this brief scene from 'poor Aran' be not the work of a tragic poet.

THE DARK LADY OF THE SONNETS
By G. B. Shaw

Mr. Shaw here presents three orthodox figures — a virgin queen, a Shakespeare sober at midnight and a free giver of gold and the dark-haired maid of honour, Mary Fitton, discovered in the eighties by Thomas Tyler and Mr. Harris.[3] Shakespeare comes to Whitehall to meet her and learns from a well-languaged beef-

---

[1] 'The divileen ... with her cygncygn leckle and her twelve pound lach.' *Finnegans Wake*, p. 511.

[2] Greek *Destiny*.

[3] Mary Fitton was first identified with the dark lady by Thomas Tyler in his introduction to the facsimile first quarto of the *Sonnets*. Frank Harris enlarged upon the theory in his book *The Man Shakespeare* (1909), one of the sources of Stephen's account of Shakespeare's life in the 'Scylla and Charybdis' chapter of *Ulysses*.

eater that Mr. W. H. has forestalled him. The poet vents his spleen on the first woman who passes. It is the queen and she seems not loth to be accosted. She orders the maid of honour out of the way. When Shakespeare, however, begs her to endow his theatre she refers him with fine cruelty to her lord treasurer and leaves him. The most regicide of playwrights prays God to save her and goes home weighing against a lightened purse, love's treason, an old queen's leer and the evil eye of a government official, a horror still to come.

THE HEATHER FIELD
By Edward Martyn

Edward Martyn, the author of the 'Heather Field', has in company with W. B. Yeats inaugurated the Irish National Theatre. He is an accomplished musician and man of letters. As a dramatist he follows the school of Ibsen and therefore occupies a unique position in Ireland, as the dramatists writing for the National Theatre have chiefly devoted their energies to peasant drama. The plot of the 'Heather Field', the best known of Martyn's plays, is as follows:

Carden Tyrrell has made an unhappy marriage early in his youth and is now living on bad terms with his wife, Grace. He is an idealist who has never cared for the ordinary routine of life. Forced to settle down on his estate and finding most of his neighbours uncongenial, he has idealized farming and is engaged at the opening of the play in trying to bring into cultivation a vast tract of heather land. To carry on this work he has had to borrow large sums of money. His friend Barry Ussher and his brother Miles warn him of the danger he is running, but in vain. They urge that he is likely to get little profit from his work, for Ussher knows that it is very hard to reclaim lands on which heather grows, for the wild heather may break out upon them soon again. Grace learns that Carden intends borrowing further large sums of money and fears that he will ruin himself. Carden has admitted to his brother Miles that he hears mysterious voices in the air and that every day life is becoming more and more unreal to him. Convinced that he has lost his reason, Grace confides to her friend, Lady Shrule, that she has arranged for two doctors to come and see Carden; she hopes to have him certified as a lunatic and put under restraint. Lady Shrule sympathizes, but neither she nor her husband will do

anything to help. The doctors come on an excuse of examining
Kit, Carden's son, but the plan is defeated by Barry Ussher who
warns them of the danger they are running by falling in with Grace's
scheme. However matters go from bad to worse; Carden quarrels
with his tenants, thus losing further money and having to have
police protection. He is unable to pay the interest on the sums he
has borrowed and is threatened with financial ruin. At this crisis
Kit comes back from a ride and shows his father some wild heather
buds which he has found in the heather field. Carden loses his
reason and memory; his mind goes back to happy days before his
marriage. As Grace tried to domesticate him, so he has tried to
domesticate the heather field, and in each case the old wild nature
avenges itself.

51

Letter on Pound[1]

1925

Ezra Pound was more responsible than any other person for the recognition that Joyce received from 1913 to 1922. Pound brought his work to the attention of Dora Marsden, editor of the Egoist, *which published* A Portrait of the Artist as a Young Man *in instalments from 1914 to 1915. He talked about Joyce's book, reviewed it, forced his friends to read it, persuaded other friends to obtain grants for Joyce from the Royal Literary Fund and the British Treasury Fund, brought Joyce into touch with other writers, encouraged him with* Ulysses, *and in 1920, when they first met, persuaded him to leave Trieste and go to Paris. He did not have much interest in* Finnegans Wake, *and said so to Joyce's annoyance, but they remained friends. For his part Joyce did not read much of Pound's work, and when Ernest Walsh, the editor of* This Quarter, *asked him for an encomium, he restricted his praise to Pound's personal kindness.*

8 Avenue Charles Picquet
Paris, France
March 13, 1925

Dear Mr. Walsh:

I am glad to hear that the first number of your review will shortly appear. It was a very good thought of yours in dedicating this number to Mr. Ezra Pound and I am very happy indeed that you allow me to add my acknowledgment of thanks to him to the others you are publishing. I owe a great deal to his friendly help, encouragement and generous interest in everything that I

[1] Published in *This Quarter*, Paris, v. 1 no. 1 (Spring 1925) 219.

have written, as you know there are many others who are under a similar debt of gratitude to him. He helped me in every possible way in the face of very great difficulties for seven years before I met him, and since then he has always been ready to give me advice and appreciation which I esteem very highly as coming from a mind of such brilliance and discernment.

I hope that your review, setting out under so good a name, will have the success which it deserves

Sincerely yours,

JAMES JOYCE

52

Letter on Hardy[1]

1928

Cher Monsieur,

La demande que vous venez de me faire au sujet d'une contribution éventuelle de ma part à votre numéro spécial dédié à la mémoire de Thomas Hardy me touche profondément. Je crains malheureusement de manquer des titres nécessaires pour donner une opinion qui ait une valeur quelconque sur l'oeuvre de Hardy, dont j'ai lu les romans il y a tant d'années que je préfère ne pas en faire le compte; et en ce qui concerne son oeuvre poétique, je dois vous avouer que je l'ignore complètement. Il y aurait donc de ma part une singulière audace à émettre le moindre jugement sur la figure vénérable qui vient de disparaître: il vaut mieux que je laisse ce soin aux critiques de son pays.

Mais quelque diversité de jugement qui pourrait exister sur cette oeuvre (s'il en existe), il paraît par contre évident à tous que Hardy offrait dans son attitude de poète vis-à-vis du public, un honorable exemple de probité et d'amour-propre dont nous autres clercs avons toujours un peu besoin, spécialement à une époque ou le lecteur semble se contenter de moins en moins de la pauvre parole écrite et où, par conséquent, l'écrivain tend à s'occuper de plus en plus des grandes questions qui, du reste, se règlent très bien sans son aide.

JAMES JOYCE

Paris, 10 février 1928.

[1] Published in *Revue Nouvelle*, Paris, v. 4 nos. 38–9 (Jan.–Feb. 1928) 61. This issue was a special Hardy number. Joyce had serious reservations about Hardy's work when he read him as a young man, but he avoids mentioning them here.

53

Letter on Svevo[1]

1929

Ettore Schmitz ('Italo Svevo') was a Triestine industrialist who came to Joyce to study English in 1907. Joyce soon recognized that his pupil was a man of unusual literary sensitivity, and told him of his own writings. Schmitz then confessed that he had himself written and published two novels some years before, and he left them with Joyce. Joyce was curious to see what kind of work Schmitz had written, and was impressed by the subtle irony he discovered in the novels. He told him at their next lesson, as Stanislaus Joyce recalls, that there were pages of Senilità *that could not have been written better by the greatest French master, and quoted long passages by heart. Schmitz, whose work had been unnoticed or, when noticed, scorned, was deeply moved by this praise. He in turn commented on the* Portrait *as Joyce wrote it.*

Schmitz continued to write but did not obtain any recognition until the 1920's. Then Joyce brought his work to the attention of Valéry Larbaud and Benjamin Crémieux, who praised it highly in Le Navire d'Argent, and gradually the novels of 'Svevo' came to be accepted as outstanding in Italy too. Schmitz died in an automobile accident in 1928, and the review Solario *devoted a section to his work. Joyce was asked to contribute, and, as in his letter about Pound, refrained from commenting on his work and confined himself to his character.*

D̲ear Colleague:

I thank you very much for the kindness of including me in Solario's tribute to the memory of my old friend Italo Svevo.

Translated from the Italian of the original letter, published in *Solaria*, Florence, v. 4 nos. 3–4 (Mar.–Avr. 1929) 47, in a section entitled 'Omaggio a Svevo'.

And I willingly consent, although I believe that now his literary fate should be entrusted entirely to his books, and that passing judgment on them should be the concern especially of the critics of his own country.

The thought will always please me that chance gave me an opportunity to have a part, no matter how small, in the recognition that his own country and an international public accorded Svevo in the last years of his life. I retain the memory of a lovable person, and an admiration of long standing that matures, rather than weakens, with the years.

Paris, 31–V–1929

JAMES JOYCE

54

From a Banned Writer to a Banned Singer[1]

1932

From 1929 to 1934 Joyce spent a good deal of time seeking to promote the fortunes of John Sullivan, an Irish-French tenor with an extraordinary voice. Sullivan's family had come from Cork, and ultimately from Kerry, and Joyce, who came to know the singer in Paris, took up his cause with a fellow-countryman's zeal, and a fellow-tenor's understanding. He was convinced that Sullivan had not received anything like his deserts from critics and impresarios, and devoted himself to securing new engagements for him. On Sullivan's behalf he got in touch with Otto Kahn, Sir Thomas Beecham, Lady Cunard, and dozens of other people. That his campaign was not altogether successful was due mostly to the fact that Sullivan's voice was in decline. It remained powerful but had lost something of its timbre; Sullivan knew this but Joyce loyally refused to believe it.

As part of his advocacy Joyce wrote 'From a Banned Writer to a Banned Singer' and published it in the New Statesman and Nation *and* Hound and Horn *in 1932. It is the most benign of any of his writings about contemporaries, and perhaps his most charming minor work. In the style of* Finnegans Wake, *but with much less compli-*

[1] Published in *The New Statesman and Nation*, London, n.s., v. 3 no. 53 (Feb. 27, 1932) 260–1. The Gorman papers in the collection of Dr. H. K. Croessmann contain a number of incomplete typed parts of this work, which was originally entitled 'Sullivan'. We wish to acknowledge the important help of Walter B. Scott, Jr., and the information supplied by Edmund Epstein, Helen Joyce, John V. Kelleher, Robert Mayo, W. M. Merchant, Vivian Mercier, T. W. Pugh, Louis Rossi, Fritz Senn, Jr., Claude Simpson, Gerald Slevin, Stuart Small, Norman Spector, Ruth von Phul, Lola Urbach, Daniel Weiss, and Ottocaro Weiss in preparing the notes to this work.

*cation, he reviews Sullivan's principal roles and compares him with
other tenors of the time.*

He[1] strides, booted with anger, along the spurs of Monte
Rossini, accompanied solely by Fidelion,[2] his mastiff's voice.[3] They
quarrel consonantly about the vocality of the wind, calling each
and its other clamant names.[4]

* * * *

Just out of kerryosity[5] howlike is a Sullivan? It has the forte-
faccia[6] of a Markus Brutas,[7] the wingthud of a spread-eagle,[8] the
body uniformed of a metropoliceman[9] with the brass feet of a
collared grand.[10] It cresces up in Aquilone[11] but diminuends
austrowards.[12] It was last seen and heard of by some macgillic-
cuddies above a lonely valley of their reeks,[13] duskening the grey-
light as it flew, its cry echechohoing among the anfractuosities:
pour la dernière fois![14] The blackbulled ones,[15] stampeding, drew

[1] John Sullivan, singing the role of Arnold in Rossini's *William Tell*, his finest
role.

[2] A pun on Fido, and Beethoven's *Fidelio*, but centrally 'Fide-lion' — trust in
the lion (the emblem of Zurich), the super-patriot William Tell.

[3] A pun on 'His Master's Voice', the name of the English branch of Victor
recordings, and the company's motto, which pictures a dog listening to a gramo-
phone speaker. Tell, as the leader and motivator of the Swiss patriots, is Arnold's
master, and 'his mastiff's voice' because he is a basso.

[4] This refers to the duet in the second act, in which Tell questions Arnold's
loyalty when he finds that he is in love with the daughter of the Austrian tyrant.

[5] 'Curiosity' and 'Kerry', the county from which Sullivan's family came.

[6] 'Bold face', *i.e.*, 'cheek'. Joyce mentions Sullivan's bullying in his letter to
Harriet Weaver of March 18, 1930.

[7] Brutus is the latinized form of the Celtic name Brito. Sullivan is the noblest
Roman-Irishman of them all.

[8] He has broad shoulders.

[9] A pun on 'Metropolitan' Opera and on 'Dublin Metropolitan Police', who
were chosen for size.

[10] Sullivan had feet like a Collard grand piano.

[11] The north wind, with a pun on 'aquiline' and 'aquila' — eagle; a reference
to Sullivan's nose.

[12] Southward (Auster, the south wind). Joyce is also commenting on the range
of Sullivan's vocal dynamics, and on the progress of his family, from Mt. Eagle
(Aquilone) in the extreme west of Kerry southward and əastward (austrowards) to
Cork, and later, in Sullivan's own career, to Paris and Italy (towards Austria).

[13] Macgillicuddy's Reeks, mountains in Kerry. Sullivan had left Ireland as a
child, but he had returned there recently to sing.

[14] Arnold's aria at the opening of Act IV of *William Tell*, as he visits his paternal home 'for the last time'. This was Sullivan's last visit to Ireland.

[15] The Irish, dominated by the black-clad clergy and papal bulls, also the
Kerry cows, a small black breed.

in their horns,[1] all appailed and much upset, which explaints the guttermilk on their overcoats.

* * * *

A pugilant gang theirs, per Bantry![2] Don Philip,[3] Jay Hell,[4] Big O'Barry of the Bornstorms,[5] Arthur,[6] siruraganist who loosed that chor. Damnen.[7] And tramp, tramp, tramp.[8] And T. Deum sullivamus.[9]

Faust of all, of curse, damnation.[10] But given Parigot's[11] Trocadéro[12] for his drawingroom with Ballaclavier[13] in charge at the pianone[14] the voice becomes suburban, sweethearted and subdued.[15] The heat today was really too much of a hot thing and even Impressario[16] is glad to walk his garden in the cool of the

[1] A reference to the Irish folksaw, 'Kerry cows have long horns'; Sullivan stampeded his Irish critics, who drew in their horns when he sang in Ireland.

[2] A bay in Cork. 'Per Bantry!' is like 'Parbleu!'; also a reference to the Bantry gang, an anti-Parnellite Irish parliamentary group.

[3] Philip O'Sullivan Beare (c. 1590–1660), who served heroically in the Spanish army.

[4] John L. Sullivan, American prize fighter.

[5] The reference is, first, to Donall O'Sullivan Beare (c. 1560–1618), lord of Beare and Bantry (now in counties Kerry and Cork) who bore the storming of Dunboy Castle, in Bantry Bay, and a terrible retreat of 170 miles in the winter of 1603 that reduced his following from 1,000 to 35; second, to Barry Sullivan (1821–91), an Irish actor from Cork, who was noted for his majesty and power, and spent most of his life as a strolling player, barnstorming Scotland, England, Australia, and the United States, as well as Ireland. Barry Sullivan was noted for his temper fits (borrán, Irish *anger*, storms) and his violent quarrels with managers.

[6] Sir Arthur Sullivan (1842–1900), who was organist for the Royal Opera, Covent Garden, and composer of 'The Lost Chord', with a play on Irish *cor*, knot.

[7] The 'great big D——' that the gallant captain in Gilbert and Sullivan's *Pinafore* could never bring himself to utter.

[8] Timothy Daniel Sullivan (1827–1914), who wrote 'God Save Ireland', to the tune of 'Tramp, Tramp, Tramp'. Compare *Finnegans Wake*, p. 93: 'I am the Sullivan that trumpeting tramp.'

[9] A reference to all three musical Sullivans: Timothy Daniel; Sir Arthur, who wrote a 'Te Deum' on the recovery of the Prince of Wales in 1872; and the singer John, implied in the phrase 'Te deum laudamus' that lies behind Joyce's phrase.

[10] Berlioz' *The Damnation of Faust*.

[11] 'Parigot' is a term for Parisian popular speech; here probably just Paris.

[12] The old concert hall in Paris, now replaced by a new Trocadéro. It was much smaller than the Opera.

[13] Balaclava, and 'The Charge of the Light Brigade', with a play on German *Klavier*, 'piano'.

[14] Comic Italian for 'big piano'. The accompanist played loud.

[15] Faust's voice, the tenor role which Sullivan sang.

[16] Mephistopheles, the impresario who calls up the fiddlers of hell to aid him in the seduction of Marguerite, and who impresses his will on Faust. Frank Budgen

evening,[1] fanning his furnaceface with his sweltertails. *Merci, doux crépuscule!*[2]

* * * *

Who is this that advances in maresblood caftan,[3] like Hiesous in Finisterre,[4] his eyeholes phyllistained,[5] his jewbones[6] of a cross-backed?[7] A little child shall lead him.[8] Why, it's Strongman Simpson, Timothy Nathan,[9] now of Simpson's on the Grill![10] Say, Tim Nat,[11] bald[12] winepresser,[13] hast not one air left? But yeth he hath. Regard! Auscult![14] He upbraces for supremacy to the potence of Mosthigh and calls upon his baiters[15] and their templum: You daggones,[16] be flat![17]

* * * *

remarks: 'I asked Joyce why his friend Sullivan, the Paris-Kerry tenor, was so loth to sing in an opera that has become the standby of the Académie Nationale, and he replied: "That Samson from the land of Dan has told me that what bothers him is not so much the damnation of Faust as the domination of Mephistopheles." ' *James Joyce and the Making of Ulysses* (London, 1937) p. 16.

[1] *Genesis* 3:8, 'And they heard the voice of the Lord God walking in the garden in the cool of the day.' Joyce changes God into the Devil, and even the Devil can't stand the heat.

[2] Faust's aria in Part III of the opera.

[3] Isaiah 63:1–2, 'Who is this that cometh . . . with dyed garments from Bozrah? . . . Wherefore art thou red in thy apparel, and thy garments like him that treadeth in the winevat?'

[4] Jesus in Spain (Finisterre), or Brittany (Finistère) where Renan wrote his un-Christian *Vie de Jésus*. As strange a sight as the Irish Sullivan in the role of the Hebrew Samson in Saint-Saëns' *Samson et Dalila*. Also Christ on the Day of Judgment (Latin *finis*, end, and *terra*, world).

[5] 'Blinded by the Philistines' and 'shamed by a woman' (Samson's Phyllis was Dalila).

[6] Samson the Israelite had slain a horde of Philistines with the jawbone of an ass.

[7] Samson bore the cross of blindness.

[8] Isaiah 11:6. At the beginning of the last scene of the opera Samson is led in by a child, who later conducts him to the central pillars of the temple.

[9] The Irish Hebrew, John Sullivan as Samson.

[10] Samson, formerly a strong man, now turns the mill of the Philistines. There is a pun on Simpson's in the Strand, a London restaurant.

[11] Samson took his first wife from the city of Timnath.

[12] Samson was shorn of his locks.

[13] Samson, about to become the instrument of God's revenge, as Isaiah in Isaiah 63:3–4, 'I have trodden the winepress alone; and of the people there was none with me: for I will tread them in mine anger.' Also a reference to Samson's work at the mill, and to Sullivan's bibulousness.

[14] Listen! (Latin).

[15] Irish pronunciation of 'beaters', the Philistines, who are baiting him.

[16] The Philistines, worshippers of Dagon, with a play on 'dog-gone'. Perhaps also 'Dagoes', the Italian ring which had refused to acknowledge Sullivan's talent.

[17] Samson's last note in the opera is a B-flat, and he has just flattened the Philistines. Also a play on 'Lie down, you dogs!'

What was in that long long note he just delivered? For the laib[1] of me I cannot tell. More twopenny tosh[2] and luxus languor[3] about I singabob you? No such thing, O son of an envelope.[4] Dr to J. S.[5] Just a pennyplain loafletter from Braun and Brotmann[6] and it will take no rebutter.[7] You may bark Mrs Liebfraumich[8] as long as you love but you must not burk the baker. Pay us disday our daily bread. And oblige.

* * * *

On his native heath.[9] Speech! Speech! cry the godlets.[10] We are in land of Dan.[11] But their words of Muskerry[12] are harsh after that song of Othello.[13] *Orateur ne peut, charlatan ne daigne, Sullivan est.*[14]

* * * *

11.59 p.m.[15] *Durch diese hohle Gasse muss er kommen.*[16] Guillaume's shot telled, sure enough. But will that labour member for Melckthal[17] be able to bring off his coo[18] for the odd and twentieth

[1] German *Laib*, 'loaf', and *Leib*, 'body'; also 'for the life of me'.

[2] 'Nonsense' (British).

[3] *Lapsus linguae*, but also sweet nothings.

[4] Joyce is playing on Sullivan's 'delivery' of a 'note'.

[5] Debit to John Sullivan.

[6] Joyce implies that Sullivan's singing of the final lines in *Samson* is not prettified but simply a wonderful display of his power, based on an appetite for bread (*Brot*) and meat (*Braun*).

[7] An answer to a reply to a legal rejoinder.

[8] Liebfraumilch is a wine; Joyce is saying that a singer may drink as much as he like, but he must also eat.

[9] Sullivan sang in Dublin on April 27, 1930, and was called upon to make a speech after singing Verdi's *Otello*.

[10] The audience sitting in the 'gods', or balcony.

[11] The land of Daniel O'Connell, a land of oratory, also the birthplace of Samson, see footnote 16, p. 260–1 above; O'Connell was a Kerryman.

[12] The name of two baronies in County Cork.

[13] 'The words of Mercury are harsh after the songs of Apollo' (last line, *Love's Labour's Lost*). Sullivan gave a mediocre speech.

[14] Compare Otello's words near the end of the opera: 'Otello fu' ('Othello was'). Joyce is playing on the motto of the Rohans, a prominent noble family of France: 'Roy ne puys, Duc ne daygne, Rohan suys.' The whole sentence means: 'He cannot be an orator, would not deign to be a charlatan, for he is Sullivan.'

[15] It is near the end of Rossini's *William Tell*.

[16] 'He will have to come through this narrow pass' — the opening line of Act IV, Scene 3, in Schiller's *Wilhelm Tell*, and a German catch-phrase.

[17] A valley in the canton of Unterwalden, Switzerland. Melcthal is the father of Arnold, the tenor role sung by Sullivan. Joyce presents Arnold, the rebel, as a left-wing M.P.

[18] 'Coup', and 'song', with particular reference to the high C's, at which Sullivan was adept.

supererogatory time? *Wartemal!*[1] That stagesquall has passed
over like water off a Helvetian's back. And there they are, yodel-
ling yokels, none the worse for their ducking and *gewittermassen*[2]
as free as you fancy to quit their homeseek *heimat* and leave the
ritzprinz[3] of their chyberschwitzerhoofs[4] all over the worlds,
cisalpic and transatlantine. And how confederate[5] of gay old
Gioacchino[6] to have composed this finale so that Kamerad
Wagner might be saved the annoyance of finding flauts for his
Feuerzauber![7] *Pass auf!*[8] Only four bars more![9] He draws the
breathbow: that arrownote's coming.[10] Aim well, Arnold, and
mind puur blind Jemmy in the stalls![11] But, great Scott, whas is
thas for a larm![12] Half a ton of brass in the band, ten thousand
throats from Thalwyl:[13] Libertay.[14] libertay lauded over the land
(Tay!) And pap goes the Calville![15]

* * * *

Saving[16] is believing but can thus be? Is this our model vicar of
Saint Wartburgh's,[17] the reverend Mr Townhouser, Mus.Bac.,

[1] 'Let's see!' (German).

[2] German, *gewissermassen*, 'in a certain way', plus *Gewitter*, 'storm' — a reference to the storm music in the opera.

[3] The Swiss César Ritz (1850–1918), prince of *hôteliers*, founded Ritz hotels all
over the world.

[4] The Swiss dialect word *chaibe*, 'low-class', plus Khyber, the famous mountain
pass, plus German *Schweizerhof*, 'a Swiss-type hotel'. Joyce is saying that the
Swiss have abused their hard-won freedom by emigrating to become first and
third class hostelers in cities and mountain resorts all over the world.

[5] The Swiss form of government is a Confederation.

[6] Gioacchino Antonio Rossini.

[7] The magic fire music in *Die Walküre*. Joyce is saying that Rossini anticipated
some of the effects of Wagner's fire-music in this finale.

[8] 'Pay attention!' (German).

[9] The thunderous close of *William Tell*.

[10] Sullivan, as Arnold, prepares to join in the closing chorus with the same
intensity as that of Tell, preparing to shoot the apple from his son Jemmy's head,
earlier in the opera.

[11] Purblind (partly blind) James Joyce in the audience.

[12] German 'Was ist das für ein Lärm?' ('What kind of noise is this?')

[13] Thalwil is a Swiss commune, and suggests 'Tell-ville.'

[14] The opera ends on these words: 'Liberté redescends des cieux!'

[15] A queening apple; Sullivan's arrownote has hit the mark. Also a play on
'Pop Goes the Weasel'.

[16] *Tannhäuser*, Act I; Joyce playfully assumes that Tannhäuser has set out to
reform Venus.

[17] Castle Wartburgh, where Tannhäuser had been a chivalrous Knight before
coming under the influence of Venus; also the castle Wartburg, Luther's refuge
after the Diet of Worms, and St. Werburgh's, a Dublin Protestant church.

discovered flagrant in a *montagne de passe?*[1] She is obvious and is on her threelegged sofa in a half yard of casheselks,[2] Madame de la Pierreuse.[3] How duetonically[4] she hands him his harp that once,[5] bitting[6] him, whom caught is willing:[7] do blease to, fickar![8] She's as only roman as any *puttana maddonna*[9] but the trouble is that the reverend T is reformed.[10] She, *simplicissima*, wants her little present from the reverend since she was wirk worklike[11] never so nice with him. But he harps along about Salve Regina Terrace[12] and Liza, mine Liza,[13] and sweet Marie.[14] Till she cries: bilk![15] And he calls: blak![16] O.u.t. spells out![17]

* * * *

Since we are bound for a change of supper, was that really in faith the reverend Townhouser for he seemed so verdamnably like? *Ecco trovato!*[18] Father Lucullus[19] Ballytheacker,[20] the parish priest of Tarbert.[21] He was a songful soul at the keyboard and

---

[1] The Venusberg, a play on *maison de passe* (brothel).

[2] French *cachesexe*, 'G-string.' Venus' is silk.

[3] French *Pierreuse*, 'street-walker'. Venus is intended.

[4] They sing a duet, accompanied by the harp, a diatonic instrument.

[5] Thomas Moore's 'The Harp that Once Thro' Tara's Hall'. Venus asks Tannhäuser to play for her on the harp.

[6] 'Bidding', plus German *bitten*, 'to ask'.

[7] German, *um Gottes willen*.

[8] 'Vicar', plus German *ficken*, 'to have intercourse'.

[9] 'God's bitch of a Mother', a vulgar Triestine curse, which also appears in *Ulysses*, p. 605 (583).

[10] 'Roman . . . reformed' — Holy Roman Catholic, and Protestant.

[11] A play on German *wirken*, 'to work on something', and *wirklich*, 'really'.

[12] *Salve Regina*, the antiphon to the Blessed Virgin Mary, with a play on St. Mary's Terrace; the name of two streets in Dublin.

[13] Elizabeth, Tannhäuser's pure love at Castle Wartburgh. Compare Joyce's use of the phrase 'Mild und leise' from *Tristan and Isolde* as 'Mildew Lisa' in *Finnegans Wake*, p. 40.

[14] Tannhäuser's last words in Act I are: 'My hope rests in Mary!'

[15] 'Cheat.'

[16] 'Unchaste.'

[17] Tannhäuser deserts Venus.

[18] 'There he is revealed.' Joyce is suggesting that Sullivan's Irishness appears in his singing the role of Tannhäuser, too.

[19] Lucius Licinius Lucullus (*c.* 110–56 B.C.), a Roman general noted for his extravagant living.

[20] Bally-the-acker; Irish *baile*, 'town', and German *Acker*, 'field': town of the fields, to suggest his rustic nature. Also 'belly-the-acre', to suggest the proportions of a gourmet, the belly aches.

[21] A village in Kerry.

could achieve his Château Kirwan[1] with cigar thuriferant,[2] without ministrance from platform or pulpit, chase or church. Nor used he to deny his Mary[3] neither. *Nullo modo.*[4] Up to maughty[5] London came a muftimummed[6] P.P.[7] Censored.[8]

* * * *

Have you got your knife handy? asks the bellman Saint Andy.[9] Here he is and brandnew, answers Bartholomew.[10] Get ready, get ready, scream the bells of Our Lady.[11] And make sure they're quite killed,[12] adds the gentle Clotilde.[13] Your attention, sirs, please, bawls big Brother Supplice.[14] *Pour la foi! Pour la foi!* booms the great Auxerrois.[15]

* * * *

Grand spectacular exposition of gorge cutting, mortarfiring and general martyrification, bigleighted[16] up with erst classed instrumental music. *Pardie!*[17] There's more sang in that Sceine[18] than

[1] In this context, a poor Irish imitation of French wine; see *Ulysses*, p. 162 (153): 'sprawling suburbs, jerrybuilt, Kerwan's mushroom houses, built of breeze.'

[2] Carried like a thurible or censer.

[3] The Virgin Mary, and women in general; he does not deny women as Peter denied Christ. Having detailed Tannhäuser's worldly leanings in song and wine, Joyce adds women.

[4] 'By no means.'

[5] Mighty naughty, from the song 'It's a Long Way to Tipperary': 'Up to mighty London came an Irishman one day.'

[6] Disguised in civilian dress.

[7] Parish Priest.

[8] Sullivan's off-duty diversions, like those of the Parish Priest, need not be detailed.

[9] The church of St. André. Joyce uses the rhythms of the nursery rhyme 'Oranges and lemons, say the bells of St. Clement's', about the bells of London. Here the bells of Paris converse before the Massacre of St. Bartholomew's Day, in Meyerbeer's *Huguenots*. Joyce begins to run down the alphabet of churches.

[10] The church of St. Barthelémy.

[11] The Cathedral of Notre Dame.

[12] Charles IX is said to have remarked to his mother, Catherine de' Medici, when he was finally persuaded by her to authorize the massacre: 'Eh bien, qu'on les tue, qu'on les tue tous!'

[13] The church of St. Clotilde.

[14] 'Torture'; also the church of St. Sulpice.

[15] The bells of St. Germain l'Auxerrois ring to signal the beginning of the massacre.

[16] German *begleiten*, 'to accompany'. Meyerbeer's *Huguenots* is on.

[17] By God! Here, as in *Pour la fois* of the preceding section, Joyce is commenting on the irony of the Catholics' claim that it is God's will that the Huguenot should die.

[18] 'Song in that scene'; also 'blood in the Seine'. In Act III Raoul de Nangis, sung by Sullivan, sings: 'Look! The Seine is full of blood and bodies.'

mayer's beer[1] at the Guildhall. Is he a beleaper[2] in Irisk luck? Can he swhipstake[3] his valentine[4] off to Dublin and weave her a frock of true blue[5] poplin[6] to be neat for the time Hugenut Cromwell comes over, gentlest lovejesus as ever slit weasand?[7] Their cause is well sainted[8] and they are centain to won.[9] Still I'll pointe[10] half my crown on Raoul de Nangis, doublet mauve and cuffs of buff.[11] Attagirl![12] *Ah ah ah ah ah ah viens!*[13] Piffpaff,[14] but he's done it, the bully mastiff[15] again. And woops with him through the window[16] tallyhoed by those friers[17] pecheurs[18] who are self-barked.[19] Dominie's canes.[20] Can you beat that, you papish yelpers? To howl with the pups![21]

[1] Joyce undoubtedly knew that Meyerbeer's name was originally Meyer-Beer.

[2] Raoul, a believer, escapes by leaping out of a window in Act IV.

[3] Irish sweepstake.

[4] Valentine, the Catholic love of the Huguenot de Nangis.

[5] Extreme Toryism, associated with Orangeism in Ireland.

[6] From the French *popeline*, 'papal', since poplin was originally woven at the papal city of Avignon. The Huguenots who came to Dublin in the seventeenth century were mostly weavers, who introduced the manufacture of poplin, since then one of the most important Irish textiles.

[7] The windpipe. Raoul de Nangis wants to escape with Valentine, and Joyce suggests that he take her to Dublin to be ready for the comparable massacre of the Catholics by the Cromwellian Huguenots.

[8] St. Bris, in Act III, sings: *Pour cette cause sainte*
   J'obéirai sans crainte.

Joyce apparently knew an Italian libretto that contained the chorus 'La causa è santa'. See Bloom's reflections in *Ulysses*, p. 166 (156–7): 'bloodhued poplin: lustrous blood. The huguenots brought that here. *La causa è santa!* Tara tara. Great chorus that. Tara. Must be washed in rainwater. Meyerbeer. Tara: bom bom bom.'

[9] 'Certain to win', and 'a hundred to one'.

[10] 'Punt' (bet), from French *ponter*.

[11] Raoul lacks the white scarf that the Catholics wore as a sign of recognition. Valentine chooses the Huguenot Raoul over her Catholic wooers.

[12] Joyce approves of the decision.

[13] Valentine brings a white scarf to enable Raoul to escape through the Catholic lines, so that they may be married.

[14] The title of an aria, expressing hatred for all Catholics, sung by Marcel early in the opera. Here he makes Raoul determine not to wear the Catholic scarf.

[15] Marcel is Raoul's faithful retainer, and is a basso.

[16] Raoul leaves Valentine and leaps through the window to fight with the Huguenots.

[17] Friars, bent on frying the Huguenots.

[18] 'Fishers' of souls, out to make converts by the sword; and 'sinners'. The Dominicans were known as 'frères prêcheurs', The Order of Friar Preachers.

[19] Self-castrated.

[20] Dominicans, known in the middle ages as 'Domini canes', 'hounds of the Lord'.

[21] 'To hell with the Pope!' and with the Catholics who instigated the massacre.

*   *   *   *

Enrico,[1] Giacomo[2] and Giovanni,[3] three dulcetest of our songsters,[4] in liontamers overcoats,[5] holy communion ties and cliqueclaquehats,[6] are met them at a gaslamp. It is kaputt and throws no light at all on the trio's tussletusculums.[7] Rico is for carousel[8] and Giaco[9] for luring volupy but Nino,[10] the sweetly dulcetest, tuningfork among tenors, for the best of all; after hunger and sex comes dear old *somnium*, brought on by prayer. Their lays, blent of feastings, June roses and ether,[11] link languidly in the unlit air. Arrives a type[12] in readymade, dicky and bowler hat, manufactured by Common Sense and Co. Ltd., carrying a bag of tools. Preludingly he conspews a portugaese[13] into the gutter, recitativing: now then, gents, by your leave! And, to his job. Who is this hardworking guy? No one but Geoge,[14] Geoge who shifts the garbage can, Geoge who stokes in the engine room, Geoge who has something to say to the gas[15] (*tes gueules!*)[16] and mills the wheel go right go round and makes the world grow lighter. *Lux!* The aforesung Henry.[17] James and John[18] stand mouthshut. Wot did I say? Hats off, *primi assoluti!*[19] Send him

---

[1] Enrico Caruso.

[2] Giacomo Lauri Volpi.

[3] Giovanni Martinelli.

[4] All three were tenors.

[5] Joyce's father described one of his son's Triestine colleagues who came to Dublin in 1909 to set up the Volta Cinema as 'a hairy mechanic in a lion-tamer's coat.' Here Joyce seems to mean a very formal costume.

[6] A 'claque' is an opera hat; also a faction paid to applaud their patron's arias with special enthusiasm.

[7] Vocal struggle.

[8] A pun on 'Caruso', who, Joyce says, excels in animated parts (carousel).

[9] Giacomo Lauri Volpi ('luring volupy') is best for love songs.

[10] Giovanni Martinelli, best for lullabies.

[11] Caruso, Volpi, and Martinelli.

[12] French, 'guy'. Sullivan is meant.

[13] French *portugais*, a kind of oyster. Compare *Ulysses*, p. 325 (316), 'gob, he spat a Red bank oyster out of him right in the corner.'

[14] The name is meant to suggest a common man.

[15] French, *gars*, 'guys'.

[16] 'Shut your traps!' (French). Sullivan takes over from the three inferior tenors. They are in darkness, but he brings light.

[17] Caruso.

[18] Volpi and Martinelli.

[19] 'Star performers!' (Italian). It is not enough for them to stand 'mouth-shut'; they must also take off their hats to Sullivan.

canorious, long to lung over us, high topseasoarious! Guard safe
our Geoge![1]

[1] The three tenors hail Sullivan's kingship by singing 'God Save the King':

> *Send him victorious,*
> *Happy and glorious,*
> *Long to reign over us,*
> *God save the King!*

55

Ad-Writer[1]

1932

After Italo Svevo's death Joyce wrote his widow, Signora Livia Veneziani Svevo, that he would be glad to do anything he could for Svevo's memory. But when asked to write a preface to the English translation of Senilità (As a Man Grows Older) *Joyce became extremely reluctant, feeling probably that he was not going to play the man of letters after avoiding the role all his life. The publisher was insistent; Joyce suggested other names; finally Stanislaus Joyce was invited to write the preface and devote it chiefly to his brother's enthusiasm for Svevo. Joyce was asked to comment on the preface and wrote 'Ad-Writer' with humorous evasiveness.*

2, Avenue Saint-Philibert, Passy,
PARIS.

Dear Mr. Huntington,[2]
I do not think I can usefully add anything to what my learned friend, the professor of English at the University of Trieste[3] (see titlepage) has written in his preface to *Senilita, (As) A man grows older.*

With regard to the other book by the author of *Senilita* the only things I can suggest as likely to attract the British reading public are a preface by Sir J. M. Barrie, author of *My Lady Nicotine*, opinions of the book (to be printed on the back of its jacket) from two deservedly popular personalities of the present day, such as the rector of Stiffkey and the Princess of Wales and

---

[1] Published in *A James Joyce Yearbook*, ed. by Maria Jolas (Paris, 1949) p. 170, from an unsigned letter found in Paul Leon's papers.
[2] Constant Huntington, Chairman of G. Putnam's Sons Ltd.
[3] Joyce's brother, Stanislaus.

269

(on the front of the jacket) a coloured picture by a Royal Academician representing two young ladies, one fair and the other dark
but both distinctly nice-looking, seated in a graceful though of
course not unbecoming posture at a table on which a book stands
upright, with title visible, and underneath the picture three lines
of simple dialogue, for example:

Ethel: Does Cyril spend too much on cigarettes?

Doris: Far too much.

Ethel: So did Percy (points) — till I gave him ZENO.[1]

Sincerely yours,
JAMES JOYCE

22-5-1932

[1] Svevo's novel *The Confessions of Zeno* deals with a hero who is desperately
and absurdly trying to give up smoking.

56

Epilogue to Ibsen's 'Ghosts'[1]

1934

While Joyce never abandoned his devotion to Ibsen as a dramatist, there is evidence, in his last pronouncement about him, that he thought some of Ibsen's techniques rather funny. So, in writing an epilogue to Ghosts *in April 1934, after seeing the play performed, he out-Ibsens Ibsen by following up two devices, Spreading the Guilt and the Horrible Hint. Captain Alving points out that he is assumed to have fathered two children, one out of wedlock and one in, the first (Regina) healthy, the second (Oswald) congenitally sick. Pursuing the trail of guilt with the zeal of the ghost in* Hamlet, *and profiting from suggestions in* Ghosts *that Parson Manders and Mrs. Alving were once in love, the captain wickedly implies that Manders was Oswald's begetter. He declares with equal effrontery that his own sins supplied incomparable material for a dramatic masterpiece. Joyce's interest in the profligate father, compounded of Shakespeare's dead king and Ibsen's dead rogue, is in the temper of* Finnegans Wake.

Dear quick, whose conscience buried deep
The grim old grouser[2] has been salving,
Permit one spectre more to peep.
I am the ghost of Captain Alving.

Silenced and smothered by my past
Like the lewd knight in dirty linen[3]
I struggle forth to swell the cast
And air a long-suppressed opinion.

---

[1] Printed in Gorman, pp. 226–7 (224–5).
[2] Ibsen.
[3] Falstaff in the *Merry Wives of Windsor*.

For muddling weddings into wakes
No fool could vie with Parson Manders.
I, though a dab at ducks and drakes,
Let gooseys serve or sauce their ganders.[1]

My spouse bore me a blighted boy,
Our slavey pupped a bouncing bitch.
Paternity, thy name is joy
When the wise sire knows which is which.

Both swear I am that self-same man
By whom their infants were begotten.
Explain, fate, if you care and can
Why one is sound and one is rotten.

Olaf[2] may plod his stony path
And live as chastely as Susanna
Yet pick up in some Turkish bath
His *quantum est* of *Pox Romana*.

While Haakon hikes up primrose way,
Spreeing and gleeing while he goes,
To smirk upon his latter day
Without a pimple on his nose.

I gave it up I am afraid
But if I loafed and found it fun
Remember how a coyclad maid
Knows how to take it out of one.

The more I dither on and drink
My midnight bowl of spirit punch
The firmlier I feel and think
Friend Manders came too oft to lunch.

Since scuttling ship Vikings like me
Reck not to whom the blame is laid,

---

[1] That is, the Captain does not prescribe rules of sexual conduct.
[2] Olaf and Haakon are opposite types, like Shaun and Shem in *Finnegan's Wake*.

Y.M.C.A., V.D., T.B.
Or Harbourmaster of Port-Said.

Blame all and none[1] and take to task
The harlot's lure, the swain's desire.
Heal by all means but hardly ask
Did this man sin or did his sire.

The shack's ablaze. That canting scamp,
The carpenter, has dished the parson.[2]
Now had they kept their powder damp[3]
Like me there would have been no arson.

Nay more, were I not all I was,
Weak, wanton, waster out and out,
There would have been no world's applause
And damn all to write home about.

[1] As Ibsen also implies, everyone is to blame.
[2] Engstrand, the carpenter, sets the orphanage afire toward the end of the play, but for purposes of blackmail makes Parson Manders feel responsible.
[3] By excessive drinking.

57

Communication de M. James Joyce sur le Droit Moral des Écrivains[1]

1937

M. James Joyce (Irlande). — Il me paraît intéressant et curieux de signaler un point particulier de l'histoire de la publication d'*Ulysse* aux Etats-Unis qui précise un aspect de droit de l'auteur sur son oeuvre qui n'avait pas été jusqu'ici mis en lumière. L'importation d'*Ulysse* aux Etats-Unis fut interdite dès 1922 et cette interdiction ne fut levée qu'en 1934. Dans ces conditions, impossible de prendre un copyright pour les Etats-Unis. Or en 1925, un éditeur américain sans scrupules mit en circulation une édition tronquée d'*Ulysse*, dont l'auteur n'etait pas maître, n'ayant pu prendre le copyright. Une protestation internationale signée par 167 écrivains fut publiée et des poursuites engagées. Le résultat de ces poursuites fut l'arrêt rendu par une Chambre de la Cour Suprême de New-York le 27 décembre 1928, arrêt qui interdisait aux défenseurs (les éditeurs) 'd'utiliser le nom du demandeur (Joyce) 1°, dans aucune revue, périodique ou autre publication publiée par eux; 2°, au sujet d'aucun livre, écrit, manuscrit, y compris l'ouvrage intitulé *Ulysse*.' (Joyce contre Two Worlds Monthly and Samuel Ross, II Dep. Supreme Court New York, 27 dec. 1928).

Il est, je crois, possible de tirer une conclusion juridique de cet arrêt dans le sens que, sans être protégée par la loi écrite du copyright et même si elle est interdite, une oeuvre appartient à son

<hr>

[1] An address that Joyce delivered to the 15th International P.E.N. Congress, held in Paris, June 20–7, 1937; published in *XVᵉ Congrès International de la Fédération P.E.N.*, (Paris, 1937) p. 24.

auteur en vertu d'un droit naturel et qu'ainsi les tribunaux peuvent protéger un auteur contre la mutilation et la publication de son ouvrage comme il est protégé contre le mauvais usage qu'on pourrait faire de son nom. (*Vifs applaudissements.*)

Index

277